T0296676

Nursing the Nation

Critical Issues in Health and Medicine

Edited by Rima D. Apple, University of Wisconsin–Madison and
Janet Golden, Rutgers University–Camden

Growing criticism of the U.S. health-care system is coming from consumers, politicians,
the media, activists, and health-care professionals. Critical Issues in Health and Medicine is a collection of books that explores these contemporary dilemmas from a variety of perspectives, among them political, legal, historical, sociological, and comparative,
and with attention to crucial dimensions such as race, gender, ethnicity, sexuality, and
culture.

For a list of titles in the series, see the last page of the book.

Nursing the Nation

Building the Nurse Labor Force

Jean C. Whelan

Rutgers University Press

New Brunswick, Camden, and Newark, New Jersey, and London

Library of Congress Cataloging-in-Publication Data

Names: Whelan, Jean C. (Jean Catherine), author.
Title: Nursing the nation: building the nurse labor force / Jean C. Whelan.
Description: New Brunswick: Rutgers University Press, 2021. | Series: Critical issues
    in health and medicine | Includes bibliographical references and index.
Identifiers: LCCN 2020019377 | ISBN 9780813585987 (paperback) |
    ISBN 9781978821781 (cloth) | ISBN 9780813585994 (epub) | ISBN 9780813586007 (pdf) |
    ISBN 9781978814288 (mobi)
Subjects: MESH: Nursing Staff—supply & distribution | History of Nursing | Health
    Workforce—history | History, 20th Century | History, 21st Century | United States
Classification: LCC RT86.75.U65 | NLM WY 11 AA1 | DDC 331.12/91362173—dc23
LC record available at https://lccn.loc.gov/2020019377

A British Cataloging-in-Publication record for this book is available from the British Library.

⊖ The paper used in this publication meets the requirements of the American National
Standard for Information Sciences—Permanence of Paper for Printed Library Materials,
ANSI Z39.48-1992.

www.rutgersuniversitypress.org

Manufactured in the United States of America

For Mark and Paul

Contents

Illustrations

Abbreviations

AGNMB	Association of Graduate Nurses of Manhattan and Bronx
AHA	American Hospital Association
AJN	*American Journal of Nursing*
AMA	American Medical Association
ANA	American Nurses Association
ASSTSN	American Society of Superintendents of Training Schools of Nursing
CGNS	Committee on the Grading of Nursing Schools
CNC	Cadet Nurse Corps
CPP	College of Physicians of Philadelphia
HEW	Department of Health, Education and Welfare
INAP	Illinois Nurses Association Papers
IOM	Institute of Medicine
ISNA	Illinois State Nurses' Association
ITSN	Illinois Training School for Nurses
JAMA	*Journal of the American Medical Association*
LPN	Licensed Practical Nurse
NAA	Nurses Associated Alumnae of the United States
NACGN	National Association of Colored Graduate Nurses
NACLI	Nurses' Association of the Counties of Long Island
NB14	Nursing Bureau of District 14, of the New York State Nurses' Association
NBMB	Nursing Bureau of Manhattan and Bronx
NCND	Nursing Council on National Defense
NLNE	National League for Nursing Education
NOPHN	National Organization for Public Health Nursing
NPR	Chicago Nurses Professional Registry
NYCR	New York Central Registry
NYCRNA	New York Counties Registered Nurses' Association
NYSNA	New York State Nurses Association
PAGN	Protective Association of Graduate Nurses of New York State
PCJN	*Pacific Coast Journal of Nursing*
TNHR	Trained Nurse and Hospital Review
VNA	Visiting Nurse Association

Nursing the Nation

Introduction

Modern health care cannot exist without professional nurses. Throughout the twentieth century, there was seldom a sustained period when the supply of nurses was equal to demand. Whether the complaint was too many or too few, there has been little satisfaction with the number of nurses working at any point of time since the inception of American professional nursing. This book offers a historical analysis of the relationship between the development of nurse employment arrangements with patients and institutions and the appearance of nurse shortages from 1890 to 1950. During this time, pervasive structural problems arose within the nurse labor market and led to differences between the supply of and demand for nurses. The response to nursing supply and demand problems by health-care institutions and policy-making organizations failed to address nurse workforce issues adequately, and this failure resulted in nurse shortages, which were at times profound and lengthy.

Woven throughout this book is attention to two historical realities of the nursing profession. The first is the racial composition and segregated nature of the early twentieth-century nursing workforce. Until the mid-twentieth century, nursing existed as two separate occupations, one occupied by white women, another by black women. The existence of a segregated nurse educational system, a system that paradoxically enabled distinct and unequal educational experiences at that same time it provided a haven for African American nurses to learn and practice, existed for over eighty years. African American nurses were for the most part educated and employed in the approximately eighty-eight black hospital-based schools of nursing operating in the United States. As late as the mid-1960s historically black hospital-based schools of nursing were responsible for educating and distributing to the public the vast majority of African American nurses.[1]

Working patterns differed for African American nurses. Historians have traditionally viewed African American nurses as favoring the public health field, which imposed less restrictive employment practices based on race and offered the chance of promotional opportunities not present in hospitals.[2] Evidence that African American nurses did work as private duty nurses appear in reports of at least two registries operating in New York City in the 1920s along lines similar to white professional private duty registries.[3] Yet few records have survived fully documenting the working lives of black private duty nurses. This book, as a history of the American nurse workforce, recognizes the importance of including the experience of all nurses and does so by blending the stories of African American nurses into the whole.

The second historical reality is the gendered nature of the nursing profession. Gender represents a major driving force in considering any labor market. The extreme gendering of nursing as an occupation in which women predominate historically led to assumptions regarding adequate compensation rates, resolution of nurse supply problems, and the value attributed to nursing as an occupation. Nurse leaders and hospital administrators, as well as health-care analysts, typically approached the nurse labor market with very conventional ideas regarding the permanence of its predominantly women's workforce in the labor market. The assumption that nurses remained in the labor force for only short periods of time before leaving to raise families re-enforced the view that replenishment of the supply of nurses via increases in the number of new student recruits was a necessary expedient to resolve nurse supply problems. Such assumptions also promoted an acceptance of the nurse workforce as composed predominantly of temporary workers for whom attractive working conditions were an unnecessary luxury. Yet, many nurses did not fit the mold of full-time workers and disregarded the exhortations of professional leaders to make nursing their prime activity, choosing instead to incorporate work into a mosaic of life activities. Nursing offered women a fluid occupation in which to enter and leave the workforce as familial responsibilities required.

Establishing professional nursing as a women's occupation was a conscious decision on the part of early nurse leaders who viewed presumed feminine characteristics of caring and helpfulness as ideal for those who nursed. As a women's profession, nursing offered women workers opportunities for jobs and professional advancement that were closed to women in other fields. At the same time, there existed—and still exists—no logical reason why men cannot nurse, as they did. Men historically nursed and established strong careers in the field, although in very small numbers. Private duty nurses who were men often exerted a monopoly over jobs caring for men patients and also enjoyed wage rates higher than those of women nurses. However, due to the limited nature of the men's private duty labor market and a dearth of sources on the subject, this book concentrates on the work of women private duty nurses as the main subject of interest.

The members of the nursing workforce established the conventions of their employment conditions and created an infrastructure of distribution to the public; this infrastructure sometimes succeeded, but more often failed, in supplying sufficient nurses for an increasingly technologically driven health-care system growing more and more dependent on nurses for efficient operation. The roots of twentieth-century nurse shortages reflected the peculiarities of a system developed in the late nineteenth century, which attempted to deliver nursing care to a new patient population at minimal cost. By examining the origins and development of nurses' work this book illuminates the complicated nature of the nurse labor market, identifies its numerous problems and dysfunctions, situates the underpinnings of the appearance of nurse shortages, and scrutinizes solutions implemented to address them.

The ways in which earlier generations of nurses were employed, utilized, and compensated caused misdistribution of nurse resources and long-term problems in ensuring an adequate supply of nurses to the sick public. A decades-long reliance on student nurse workers, for instance, who delivered the majority of patient care, artificially reduced the financial cost of nurse services and lulled hospitals into assuming nursing care was obtained through cost-cutting measures.

The job market for nursing school graduates revolved around the private hiring of nurses by a small number of patients who could afford private care, reducing job opportunities and chances for steady employment. Intense competition from nonprofessional nurse workers stymied nurses' efforts at controlling the labor market and required significant time and effort from nurses as they fought intrusions into their practices. Poor employment conditions within hospitals failed to attract a stable nursing workforce, while the itinerant nature of the workforce led to repeated disruptions in reliable care delivery.

Attempts at developing strategies to resolve shortages on the part of nurses themselves, medical experts, and government officials resulted in tactics that were neither effective nor safe for patient care. The result was that for the first half of the twentieth century, hospitals grappled with a nurse workforce insufficient to meet patient care demand, nurses struggled with poor working conditions, physicians grumbled that they needed more nurses, and patients worried about who would take care of them.

A shortage of nurses is not a new phenomenon and stemmed from core problems in work design and management. Over the past thirty years, contemporary researchers have observed the cyclical nature of nursing shortages.[4] Historians and economists taking a longer view identify significant nurse shortages dating from the post–World War II era.[5] Some suggest nurse shortages have an even earlier origin, having persisted throughout most of the twentieth century.[6]

Unresolved workforce issues increase the difficulties in retaining qualified staff and threaten the provision of care. An acceleration in attrition rates of actively employed registered nurses, significant job dissatisfaction among nurses, and increased incidence of nurse alienation and burnout point to large problems existing within nurses' workplace environment.[7] In response to these issues, the Institute of Medicine (now called the National Academy of Medicine) released a landmark report, *The Future of Nursing: Leading Change, Advancing Health* (2010). The report noted the need for a fundamental transformation of the nursing profession to deal adequately with a health-care system undergoing complex and rapid changes to maintain adequate delivery of nurse services in the years ahead.[8]

Although historians have identified the rigorous circumstances under which earlier generations of nurses worked, few have concentrated on the actual employment situation that characterized nurses' professional life.[9] There has been less study of the role professional associations and groups had in the supply and demand for nurses. Knowledge of the nurses' labor market is critical for providing fuller comprehension of similar problems in today's rapidly changing workforce. This book provides that knowledge by offering the first extensive examination of how nurses arranged their working conditions and by synthesizing the historical context of the complex factors creating nurse distribution problems.

Background

American professional nursing traces its roots to the late nineteenth century, when the phenomenal growth of hospitals, attributed to changing patterns of work and living arrangements, required more skilled caregivers. Improvements in medical therapeutics, newer conceptions of disease and illness, and the growing power of physicians removed sick care from a home setting and established hospitalization as routine for ill individuals. Necessary for the acceptance of hospitals by the public was the presence of an educated group of nurse workers who could carry out the more complicated and technologically driven treatment regimens required by the tremendous growth of scientific medicine. Installing a corps of reliable, respectable nurses provided a cadre of caregivers conversant with the demands of modern medical practice and assured the growing number of middle-class patients that hospitals were safe.[10] Unlike hospital attendants, who traditionally delivered care in mid-nineteenth-century hospitals and whom professional nurses rapidly replaced, nurses were able to able to read and write, use math to calculate dosages and solutions, observe and record patient parameters such as pulses and other vital functions, including responses to treatment, and consult with physicians. These new health-care workers revolutionized the delivery of sick care and created a new occupational field welcoming to women workers.

By 1900, approximately six hundred hospital-based schools of nursing operated in the United States using an apprenticeship-based form of pedagogy.[11] Students worked in the hospital learning whatever nursing procedures the particular institutions provided for their patients and, in return for their education and a small stipend, delivered the majority of patient care.[12] As most schools were bereft of formal teaching staffs, the students used a method of learning that was self-taught and experimental. By using student labor, hospitals came to rely on an inexpensive but transitory workforce. Upon completion of the educational program, students received a diploma and were sent out to find employment.

As early modern hospitals tended not to hire their graduates, the majority of nurses sought work in the private duty sector, where they had direct employment from a sick patient. Patients or their families hired a nurse either upon the advice of the attending physician or when the family's ability to care for ill members was lacking. Late nineteenth-century private duty nurses, typically employed for the duration of an illness, provided home-based care twenty-four hours a day, seven days a week. When middle-class patients began seeking hospital care, private duty nurses followed them into the hospital. Although the setting changed, the work arrangement remained the same, with patients hiring nurses to provide full-service care.[13] Those unable to afford private nursing received their care through the student training system in the hospitals; if patients were at home and medically indigent, they might meet the eligibility requirements for the services of a visiting nurse.

Two characteristics of private duty nursing highlight the differences between the private employment of nurses and our current institution-based nurse work arrangements. First, private duty nursing reflected an entrepreneurial approach in which nurses assumed responsibility for generating their income and a steady supply of patients. Moreover, while hospitals imposed restrictions on private nurses regarding patient charges and other working conditions, nurses relied on their ingenuity to obtain employment and controlled their work schedules as independent contractors. The second key characteristic was that private duty nurses provided care that mirrored familial traditions, in which family members, usually women, were the main providers of care throughout the course of illness. This structure remained a significant part of private duty nursing with minor variations throughout the first half of the twentieth century. The patient-nurse relationship became the model of modern nursing practice; this model has been replicated and reinvented throughout the twentieth century and the present day.[14]

For private duty nurses, the unique circumstances of caring for one patient who was also their employer created a situation plagued with dysfunction. Beginning in the 1920s, issues surrounding acceptable rates of patient charges, hours of work, the means through which nurses obtained patient cases, negotiations over working conditions, and competition with other less-trained nurse workers consumed the working lives of private duty nurses. By then, a steady increase in the number of new nurses entering the labor market, graduates of a growing number of nursing schools—as well as the presence of a large group of nontrained nurse workers who, in an unregulated labor market, competed equally with professional nurses for patients—considerably lessened the number of job opportunities. Calls for nurses to leave private duty and seek institutional employment increased.

The onset of the Great Depression contributed to further cracks in the system by reducing demand for private duty services. Middle-class patients, unable to afford private duty nurses, expected hospitals to provide personalized care. Private and semiprivate rooms replaced multiple-bed wards, creating a need for more nurses. Hospitals began to understand that hiring graduate nurses was a more efficient and rational use of nursing resources, as technological changes and therapeutics created complex care requirements necessitating practitioners more expert than student nurses. This book argues that hospitals and nurses faced with financial pressures did not suddenly come together as employers and employees in the span of the Great Depression years; rather, a longer, highly contentious, volatile period ensued that ultimately led to the modern staff nurse model.

Despite these difficulties, the private duty system served as the template for nurse employment, setting the patterns for how nurses procured work as well as determining typical and acceptable hours of work, compensatory rates and arrangements, and the ways in which nurses engaged employers in negotiating working conditions. For better or worse, the private duty market was the principal, and in some cases only, job market for nurses. In 1923, estimates indicated that 80 percent of all professional nurses worked in private duty.[15] Moreover, while the percentage of nurses employed in private duty dropped to 55 percent in 1930, 21 percent in 1949, and 13 percent in 1962, throughout the sixty-year period between 1900 and 1960 the private duty field maintained its ranking as one of the largest professional areas of nursing.[16]

By the late 1930s, the idea that the private duty market had hit rock bottom appeared increasingly more evident. A string of circumstances revived for a period the faltering system. Hospital admission rates increased significantly in the closing decades of the 1930s, the result of the growing number of individuals obtaining health insurance policies. Technological demands of patient care continued to intensify rapidly, creating a greater need for experienced nurses. Further, a movement to reduce nurses' daily working hours from twelve to eight resulted in the need for more nurses to cover twenty-four-hour shifts. The overall result was a much higher demand for fully educated hospital nurses. In fact, reports of a national nursing shortage began circulating throughout the health-care system as early as 1936.[17]

Hospitals found they could maintain a nursing service that hired a minimal number of full-time employed nurses supplemented as patient care requirements demanded with per diem nurses, most of whom were private duty nurses temporarily without patient assignments. Nurses also displayed restraint in entering into full-time employment situations. Accustomed to their status as independent contractors, private duty nurses often preferred the self-regulating private market, in which they had control over their work schedules. This system met hospitals' need for registered nurse services while lessening the financial commitment of hiring full-time employees.

The onset of World War II hastened changes in the nurse labor market. With approximately 25 percent of registered nurses serving in the military, there was again a demand for student workers. To deal with the situation, Congress passed the Nurse Training Act of 1943 to create the Cadet Nurse Corps program. The program provided more than $160 million to schools of nursing to increase the number of student nurses, who in turn would free up fully educated nurses for military and other national defense roles.[18] The Cadet Nurse Corps program also continued the student nurse–led system of hospital care delivery and once more hospitals relied on cheap student labor, compliments of the federal government.

As the war abroad ended, a battle between hospitals and nurses percolated at home. Hospital utilization continued to climb, the result of improved treatment modalities; federal programs such as the Hill-Burton Act, which supported building new, more complex health-care institutions; and a larger number of Americans able to access hospital services through health insurance plans provided by employers. A critical element in assuring the success of the post–World War II modern medical care system was nurses. By this time, hospitals, understanding the benefits of a permanently employed nursing staff, demonstrated greater interest in hiring nurses as regular employees and looked forward to employing them as they returned from military service. Expectations were high that nurses would respond by seeking out positions as staff nurses.

The complex characteristics of the post–World War II nurse labor market worked together to limit the number of nurses seeking employment.[19] Perhaps the most glaring and puzzling factor that discouraged nurses from re-entering the workforce were the poor working conditions found in hospital employment. Hospitals, while eager to hire nurses, wanted to do so on their terms; nurses found these terms incompatible with a satisfying career and adequate compensatory arrangements.[20] The first significant nursing shortage occurred in the late 1930s; shortages continued throughout the war years and endured into the postwar era, becoming a national crisis by the 1960s.

Private duty nurses continued to function, but in an increasingly marginalized role. Hospitals, eager to hire nurses in large numbers, discouraged private duty nurses through a variety of tactics that restricted their practice and placed burdensome working rules on them. During the 1940s, younger graduates of nursing programs, particularly those who participated in the Cadet Nurse Corps and completed the required six-month hospital employment period, became accustomed to full-time employment as staff nurses and shunned private duty. As nurses accepted hospital employment as normative, problems remained. Hospitals were unable to maintain a nurse workforce sufficient to meeting patient care needs. Nurses continued to view hospital employment as a temporary situation until marriage or children intervened. Physicians demanded warm bodies to care for their patients. Moreover, it was not clear to patients whether the health worker walking into their rooms to deliver care was a registered nurse, a student nurse, a licensed practical nurse, or a nurses' aide.

Understanding nurse supply and distribution, whether discussing shortages or excesses, requires a critical analysis of the historical structure and organization of nurses' work. The conventions established in the initial decades of the twentieth century became the foundation on which modern-day professional nurses sought employment and carried out their work. Many of the problems experienced in supplying nurses to patients, as well as some of the successes, originated in the early labor market. An examination of the nursing labor market enables greater understanding of similar issues currently plaguing our health-care system today.

We face a growing elderly population with a multitude of nursing care needs. Some of these older people can afford private care, and others rely on various home care services, which has spiked an interest in private nursing services.[21] Also, contemporary hospitals often rely on short-term nurses from agencies; this recalls the private duty per diem system found in the earlier part of the twentieth century. Further, some physicians offer private care services via "boutique" or "concierge" practices, which resemble in many respects private duty nursing, albeit with greater financial rewards.[22] This book analyzes the benefits and burdens of privately financed care, and how it informs current debates over how to deliver essential nursing and health care. It also highlights how a stable, reliable professional nurse workforce remains to be established.

Chapter Overview

Chapter 1 scrutinizes the development of modern professional nursing educational programs in the mid-nineteenth century and the work options available to graduates of such programs. This chapter also details the demographic characteristics of nurse labor market participants prior to World War II.

Chapter 2 examines private duty registries, which were agencies that connected patients with nurses. This chapter also looks at nurses' professional associations, such as the National League for Nursing Education (NLNE) and the American Nurses Association (ANA), and their role in building the framework of nurses' work.

Chapter 3 looks at the New York Central Registry, which was set up and administered specifically by and for nurses. This registry highlights the workings of the private duty nurse market and the challenges nurses encountered as they attempted to monopolize the nursing labor market in the state.

Chapter 4 analyzes the national nurse labor market and the dysfunctions that arose as private duty nursing emerged as the primary occupational role in the nursing profession. The chapter also examines national studies carried out on the experiences of African American nurses, revealing the similarities and dissimilarities between black and white nurses as they sought work.

Chapter 5 covers the end of World War I to the beginning of the Great Depression and describes a "golden age" for private duty registries. This was a time when significant professional registries solidified their status as major distributors of nurses and worked to improve employment conditions and resolve the day-to-day problems involved in distributing nurses to the public.

Chapters 6 and 7 focus on the tumultuous decades of 1930–1950, when the dismantlement of the private duty labor market occurred, leading to significant nurse shortages, which threatened the functionality of hospitals. This period also ushered in the standardized eight-hour day for nurses, which created more opportunities and demand. This era, often referred to as nursing's "great transformation," is traditionally seen as the time when nurses left the private duty field to work as permanent employees in staff nursing positions.[23] It is also a period in which hospitals introduced licensed practical nurses (LPNs) to address nursing shortages. The emergence of LPNs led to tensions between nursing leaders and private duty nurses, who viewed LPNs as a threat to their livelihood. As the market for private duty nurses declined in the 1950s in the push to favor staff nursing positions, the business of the registries dropped off. No longer seen as major players in the nurse labor market, registries' ability to supply and support nurses faded.

The Conclusion provides a contextual understanding of the state of the nurse labor market and connects the current state of nurses' work and the supply of nurses to its historical legacy. This historical analysis of nurses' work places in perspective recent changes in care delivery and broadens our understanding of nurses' issues as we develop strategies for meeting our future health-care needs.

This book confronts one of the most enduring problems faced by the American health-care system. How do we obtain the right number of nurses for patients in need of care at a price society can afford? Ensuring an adequate supply of nurses is a critical function of a modern society, particularly for a country such as the United States, which has built up and depends on a complex, highly technological health-care system. Professional nurses work in a large variety of health-care settings, not only providing services to those in the acute and chronic stages of illness, but also overseeing a wide spectrum of services designed to encourage, maintain, and support a healthy population. The range of services offered by professional nurses means there are few Americans able to go through their lives without contact with a nurse at some point. Their universal presence as a major health-care provider goes unchallenged and when they are in short supply the nation as a whole suffers.

By the late twentieth century the nurse labor market was marked by cyclical shifts in supply and demand exacerbated by fluctuations in workplace settings and employment conditions. The allocation of nursing care services remains a tenacious problem that the American health-care system has failed to address and solve sufficiently. Identifying why this situation exists and the solutions earlier generations used to resolve their nurse distribution problems provides perspective to current nurse supply issues that nurses and policy makers can build upon as they provide care for our nation's citizens. By exploring the genesis of employment patterns in the nurse labor market, this book illuminates the complex foundations from which nurse shortages developed and will provide answers to the question that perennially perplexes the American healthcare system: Why does the United States never seem to have enough nurses?

Chapter 1

Have Cap Will Travel

How and Why Nurses Became Professionals

Educational programs preparing individuals for private nursing work existed from the beginning of the republic. Valentine Seaman, a physician affiliated with the New York Hospital, offered a course of lectures on childbirth care for women wishing to secure work as nurses as early as 1798.[1] In 1839, Philadelphia physician Joseph Warrington initiated a more organized approach to nurse education with the establishment of the Nurse Charity of Philadelphia, designed to prepare nurses to care for individuals during childbirth and the postpartum period. Warrington offered the students a planned program of study, supervised clinical experience, and a certificate upon completion of the program testifying to their abilities as nurses.[2] By 1853, the Nurse Charity took on the characteristics of a school, acquiring living quarters for students, a library, and an organized curriculum.[3] The opening of a hospital and a renaming of the enterprise to the Philadelphia Lying-In Charity Hospital and School of Nursing in 1881 completed the transition of the Nurse Charity to an official school of nursing, which continued operations until 1918.[4] A second Philadelphia institution, the Woman's Hospital, often cited as the first chartered school for nurses in the United States, opened a school for nurses that was incorporated in 1861, although the first students did not arrive until 1864.[5] The two Philadelphia schools also operated registries that placed graduates of their programs with patients requiring private duty care.

The professional schools of nursing established in the nineteenth century aimed not only to reform hospital-based nursing care through the presence of a disciplined and educated corps of student nurse workers but also to establish nursing as a legitimate, respectable, and attractive occupational field for young women.[6] The field most nursing school graduates entered was private duty. The origin of private duty nursing follows traditional patterns of illness care in which families hired outside individuals to care for their sick members. Before the twentieth century, when most sick care took place within the home, family members who fell ill received care directly from unaffected relatives. For common or minor illnesses, the knowledge required for delivery of health care resided within the family domain with its women members. Some diseases required care outside of the home, such as when conditions stretched family resources or when special skills not possessed by the general population were required, or simply when a family had the financial means to employ caregivers, which demanded outside assistance.

Until the late nineteenth century, individuals of varying abilities delivered most hired private nursing care. Many nurses, sometimes referred to as "experienced nurses," acquired competence in nursing simply by doing it; they relied on their experiences with the sick to claim nursing status. Some received nursing knowledge through work with physicians or by employment in existing hospitals. The historical record is not silent on working nurses before the late nineteenth century and the emergence of training schools for nurses; several researchers have uncovered examples of organized, competent delivery of nursing to institutionalized patients.[7] However, the story of how the earliest private nurses worked in patients' homes lacks the documentation found in hospital records dated later.

As evidenced by the increasing number of individuals listed as nurses in the U.S. Census beginning in 1870, private nurses were available to the general population, representing a growing occupational field, particularly for women. Historian Susan Reverby has carefully recorded the life course of "professed nurses," those women who sought paid employment as private nurses minus formal training.[8] The growing popularity of the trade with both patients and physicians made such nurses a fixture within the nursing marketplace. The tradition of hiring outsiders for private nursing care existed well before the advent of professional nurse educational programs and outside their scope; it continued even as those programs spread around the country.

Graduates of the growing number of late nineteenth-century nurse training programs saw the private nursing market as the best possible field for employment. Although some graduates of nursing programs were hired by hospitals, mainly in supervisory or other leadership positions, most health care during this time period occurred in the home. Close study of the private nurse market provides an instrumental glimpse into the evolution of modern health care.

Chloe Cudsworth Littlefield: Portrait of a Private Duty Nurse

In January 1883, Chloe Cudsworth Littlefield, writing to her mother Elizabeth, reported on a significant rite of passage she had recently undergone. "I am wearing my caps have filled out my paper & signed the agreemnt [sic] to remain two years."[9] Littlefield had completed her initial months at the nurse training school of the Woman's Hospital in Philadelphia and by wearing a cap she was noting a tradition that would later become enshrined in nurse education over the next century as the symbol of an educated nurse. Littlefield's prolific and richly detailed family letters and diary offer a fascinating and compelling look at the life and career of a late nineteenth-century private duty nurse. Her story validates historical knowledge about early nurses' work and offers a more nuanced look at nursing practice, suggesting reconsideration of many of the typical portrayals of such nurses.

Chloe Cudsworth Littlefield was born in 1850, the youngest of nine children, to a farming family in upstate New York. As she grew into adulthood, Littlefield, like many women of the era, found it necessary to seek paid employment outside the home. At first she sought jobs with the various manufacturing concerns that dotted the northeast region, serving as a major employment sector for women workers in the late nineteenth century.[10] However, economic security in such jobs eluded Littlefield and in 1881, after she sustained a series of layoffs, she journeyed to Philadelphia to enter the nurse training program of the Woman's Hospital. She was thirty-one.

Nursing was a known occupation to Littlefield, who had already earned a reputation by skillfully caring for sick relatives, including her older brother during his terminal illness. She had also observed firsthand the practice of a trained nurse when Littlefield's sister, Ellen Hubbard, hired one to attend during and after childbirth. Yet, Littlefield's attraction to nursing most likely lay in the more practical and remunerative aspects of the occupation, the expected earnings a nursing career would provide; these earnings promised more stability than those of jobs in the manufacturing sector. Nearing her 1883 graduation from Woman's Hospital, Littlefield confided to Ellen her anticipation that her decision to become a nurse would literally pay off: "Only hope I get a diploma I shall think I have earned it if I do & if I do not I shall not regret the exsperiense [sic] I have you know I will have a better means of support than at one time I was likely ever to have."[11]

The Woman's Hospital program, typical of nurse education programs of the time, was two years in length and consisted of lectures and work in the hospital's wards. After a period of months during which Littlefield acquired basic nursing skills learned by working in the hospital's wards, the school sent her out to deliver private duty care to patients in their homes. This practice provided students with hands-on experience caring for private patients and prepared them for life as a private nurse. At the same time, schools earned income from the monies paid by patients for the student care.

In late 1883 Littlefield graduated and returned to her parents' home in Grafton, New York, and later to Hubbard's house in Springfield, Massachusetts. She settled in Springfield over the next several decades, using it as a base of operations for her work. Initially, Littlefield did not seek out patients; instead, she used her time assisting her parents and sister with household and farm duties, visiting relatives, preparing her wardrobe for eventual work, and caring for relatives who came down with illness—not an uncommon occurrence. In April 1884, she traveled to New York City to attend her niece during childbirth, her first real case as a trained nurse. Sadly, the baby died one day after his birth. Littlefield returned to Springfield shortly afterward and began her career in earnest.

Once embarked on her practice, Littlefield experienced minimal difficulty in obtaining cases and enjoyed a thriving practice. Her reputation among physicians in the area was excellent; many of them engaged her to care for their own ill friends and family members. Littlefield voiced pride in her work, making special note in her diary and letters when she received compliments. In August 1884, she nursed the seriously ill sister of a local physician until the patient succumbed to what was determined upon autopsy to be a cancerous gall bladder. Despite the poor outcome, the attending physician told Littlefield that she was the first nurse he had seen in a long time who knew how to care for a patient.[12] In another instance, Littlefield wrote her mother, "I heard Mrs. Taylor say yesterday that Dr. Stebbins said I was the best nurse in the City."[13] Littlefield's evident delight in physician praise represented not just pride that her work was well received but recognition that a nurse's practice, and consequently her income, was tied to the number of patients who engaged her and was mediated mainly through physicians who admired her skills. A nurse who built up a good standing in the community and was acknowledged as a competent practitioner could look forward to steady work. Littlefield's early success in impressing local physicians with her skills boded well for the future.

In 1884, the private duty nurse market was in its infancy, with few work conventions set. Springfield, although a thriving industrial center, had no systematic method through which trained nurses could obtain work or connect with patients. Springfield's first training school for nurses did not open until 1892; until then trained nurses utilized their own devices in seeking jobs.[14]

Littlefield employed tactics typical of trained nurses of the time and began her job search by visiting some physicians in the area, letting them know she was available for care and using her contacts with other trained nurses to advertise her services. One opportunity that offered promising results occurred when the daughter of Littlefield's sister Ellen (Marion) became seriously ill with croup. Littlefield, involved in her niece's care, thought her interactions with the attending physician would prove helpful. Writing to her father about Marion's illness, Littlefield noted, "Dr. Hooper was here this morning for the fourth and last time. I think his acquaintance may prove beneficial to me in my practice. I haven't taken a case yet but I hope to be ready some time this week if one presents."[15] In early June Littlefield noted in her diary further efforts to obtain work: "I call on Dr. Sprague this evening. She thinks she will have a case for me in 2 or 3 days."[16] Three weeks later, Littlefield received a call to a care for a patient who had experienced a complicated stillborn birth.

Littlefield's use of the term *case* to indicate patients for whom she cared was both conventional and noteworthy, carrying inferences about the autonomy of private duty nurses. As opposed to hospital nurses, who were assigned to patients or specific tasks, private duty nurses, much like physicians, took cases. Taking a case indicated ownership of patient care on the part of the nurse and reinforced the independent nature of private nursing practice. Private duty nurses assumed the entire care of the patient, seeing the patient from the time care was requested until the nurse was no longer needed—either when the patient recovered or died.

Littlefield settled easily into the rhythm of work typical of private duty nurses, with most of her cases lasting anywhere from a few weeks to a couple of months. Once engaged on a case, she moved into the patient's house, fitting into the household routine as the situation demanded. Littlefield's concern for the well-being of her patients often extended to the entire household and she became known for her ability to "take over," restoring order on several different levels at times of crisis when illness struck. For example, in January 1885, Littlefield embarked on a difficult case caring for a patient diagnosed with "consumption of the bowels." The attending physician predicted the patient "would last a few days at most."[17] Yet, Littlefield's treatments swiftly returned the patient to health. Upon recovery, the patient testified that without Littlefield's care, "she would been in her grave."[18]

Littlefield's care encompassed more than the usual bedside attention, which typically ended once the patient was well. For instance, she once delayed her departure from a patient's house until assured the patient's daughter would "take all necessary care of her now." Even then, Littlefield waited a bit longer before leaving, giving up two other cases, until the family hired a replacement "kitchen girl," the original one having left shortly before. Littlefield wrote her mother, telling her, "but of course would not leave them without a girl in the kitchen."[19] On another case, Littlefield felt little compunction in agreeing to carry out work not strictly within the duties of a professional nurse. The patient, a new mother, remarked to Littlefield that she thought the Boston Training School, which eventually became the Massachusetts General Hospital Training School, taught its nurses to do more than those who graduated from Hartford Hospital but noted that nurses from Hartford would wash babies' didees (diapers). Littlefield, no doubt thinking this was a gentle hint that she wash the baby's diapers, replied that while her school did not have her wash diapers, she would do it if the patient wished. However, there was already someone in the household who took on this job, sparing Littlefield the task.[20]

Littlefield's firsthand account highlights both the pressures and mundanity of the twenty-four-hour nature of private duty care, where even rest time depended on how well or poorly the patient fared. Her diary makes frequent note of when she could and could not obtain time for herself: "After 2 P.M. I am sitting down a few minutes for the first time today. I have been busy all morning as I have been most every moment nearly since I have been here."[21] In another case, which required her to travel from her parents' home in New York back to Springfield, she arrived late and was tired but the doctor insisted she go directly to the patient, who happened to be the doctor's brother. Littlefield complied.[22] Other cases presented opportunities for more relaxation. For instance, Littlefield had many patients that were women undergoing childbirth, which allowed her to take walks or naps—assuming a normal birth without health complications. Because many of her cases were in Springfield and close to home, she often used her rest periods to visit her sister and replenish her wardrobe or pick up other needed supplies.

Littlefield's working life was not always this idyllic and often required her to pay consistent attention to the business of nursing. In March 1887, Littlefield made a serious mistake that threatened her professional reputation and livelihood when she mistakenly promised to take two cases at the same time. Both cases, which happened to involve Littlefield relatives, were to attend patients during childbirth, cases which typically consumed up to four weeks of a nurse's time. Littlefield, while on the first case, was alerted to her error by her sister, Ellen, who wrote her frantically, "am very sorry you made such a mistake. . . . It is too bad for Abbie [the second patient] and too bad for your reputation here if you cannot be depended when after you had made an engagement. . . . I do not know what you had better do—you and Abbie are the ones to agree upon something."[23] In a subsequent letter to Littlefield, her sister continued to voice concern about the problem, emphasizing the consequences that might ensue. "I <u>do</u> [underline in original] hope that Abbie will get along well and be able to get some good help that you may meet your engagement here—if you fail to meet it I am afraid it may do more harm than you could repair soon."[24] Ellen suggests and then rejects solutions to the problem, reasoning that sending for another nurse might be costly and that the doctor would be more likely than Littlefield to know about substitute nurses.

Littlefield arranged for her sister Mary to care for the second case but she remained distressed by her error. She asked Ellen to speak with the doctor involved to explain the situation, as it was too complicated for Littlefield to put in a letter. She also believed the situation required a personal response, even if it was from a third party, her sister. She acknowledged her responsibility, declaring, "The mistake made is very unfortunate I know, for all concerned & I can not [sic] account for it . . . if it were all explained to the Doctor he might think me the more stupid."[25] She advised Ellen that if the doctor did not know of a nurse, the patient might try to hire another nurse, Miss Hoag, a colleague of Littlefield's. Yet, Littlefield was reluctant to let Hoag know of her error, writing "Although I would much rather she know nothing whatever of the matter—only I feel obliged to do what I can to supply my place."[26]

Reliability in taking cases as promised was a hallmark of a good private duty nurse and continued as the standard of first-rate private duty practice. It was incumbent upon the nurse to arrive as arranged once engaged for a case. Patients depended on nurses appearing when they said they would. When they did not, the nurse, or, later, private duty registries, suffered potential loss of business. Littlefield weathered this professional storm without any apparent damage to her reputation. She remained in high demand with patients, yet her concerns and those of her sister were real and emphasized the precarious nature of the private duty market, which depended on a variety of factors and a nurse's ingenuity to maintain a successful practice. As self-employed independent contractors, they needed to assume all the skills required to run a good business. Customer service was essential for successful practice. And, as Littlefield knew, rumors and gossip held the potential to destroy a reputation.

Left obscure in Littlefield's writings are the ways in which she arranged the amount and payment of compensation for her work. Periodically, she reports receiving somewhere between $15 and $20 a week for her services, an amount typical for the time. The method through which she negotiated payment from patients is left unspecified. In one case, she records that the husband of a patient who had just given birth asked her to accompany the family from Springfield to

Middletown, Connecticut, for a period of two to three weeks.[27] She had already received $20 for her first week of work and the husband inquired what her terms would be for the extra time as he did not want to stand in the way of her earning more if she had another case. Littlefield did not reveal the outcome of her negotiations but as she did accompany the family to Connecticut, a suitable agreement was most likely reached.[28]

Littlefield's patient charges stayed within the same range over time, a pattern typical of nurse wages, which tended to remain stagnant with few increases in the price of private duty nursing occurring. She earned the same $15 to $20 a week in 1892 that she received in 1884.[29] Having their roots in nineteenth-century practices, stagnant wage rates persisted as a major problem for nurses throughout the twentieth century. The only way a private duty nurse could increase her income was by taking more than one case at a time, a logistical impossibility when caring for one patient on a twenty-four-hour basis. This dilemma plagued nurses over decades.

Littlefield's singular experiences display professionalism and pride in her care and a keen sense of business in making her practice a success. Late nineteenth-century families depended on a constellation of members to carry out tasks involved in sustaining a household. Both married and single women shared in household responsibilities, which kept family enterprises running, whether these included churning butter, milking cows, sewing clothes, or caring for children. Littlefield's choice of career allowed her to meet the multiple demands placed on her as well as providing her with an independent income. By navigating several roles at once she enjoyed a life filled with pleasure and achievement. Littlefield lived into her nineties and family reminisces of her recall a happy, thoughtful, caring woman who maintained delight in her work as a nurse.

Littlefield represents a pioneer private duty nurse entering the field on the cusp of professional nursing when trained nurses were rare and not yet accepted fully as necessary for illness care. In Littlefield's time there existed a good deal of ignorance and uncertainty about the trained nurse.[30] Doctors and patients lacked a consensus on what expectations trained nurses offered, thus permitting early practitioners freedom to create practice customs on their own with little fear of criticism or censure. Littlefield's early years as a nurse took place in a period before the rise of nursing's professional sensibilities. Professional associations, which promoted normative ideas about professional practice, did not begin organizing until the 1890s. Nurses completing their training in the very early years of professional nursing did so without the constraints of later practice. Nurses' professional aspirations and a growing market for nurse services created a need to define better the parameters of nurses' work and establish conventions that dictated normative behavior. As more and more graduate nurses entered the private duty field, the elements of an infrastructure that organized and systematized the work environment emerged.

Characteristics of the Emerging Nurse Labor Market

The profession of nursing saw significant achievements by the beginning of the twentieth century. There were somewhere between 549 and 867 schools of nursing operating in the country, descendants of the late nineteenth-century movement to educate a group of workers specifically for paid care of the sick.[31] Although national standards designating the components of an adequate nurse educational program did not yet exist, national nurse leaders pointed to some agreement on what comprised a good nurse educational system. Nurses also completed major organizational accomplishments with the formation of several professional associations. An ultimately successful campaign to obtain legal recognition and protection of nursing through the passage of state nurse registration acts was in its infancy. Further, professional nurses proved their worth and received national fame through participation in the Spanish-American War.

Accurate estimates of the number of individuals working as nurses at the turn of the twentieth century do not exist. Statistics kept on the nurse labor market for the first decades of the twentieth century tend to be inexact and confusing. The U.S. Census enumerated an occupational category of "nurses" beginning with the 1860 census, listing a total of 8,132 nurses in the thirty-four states and eight territories then comprising the Union.[32] Thirty years later, the 1900 census differentiated nurses into two categories: one for "nurses (trained)" and a second for "nurses (not specified)."[33] The term *trained nurse* applied to those who had completed a course of nurse training or education in one of the hospital-based programs cropping up around the country. The "nurses (not specified)" category pertained to individuals employed as nurses who did not possess formal education or training in nursing. Census officials noted that efforts to distinguish trained nurses from nontrained nurses were not always successful.[34]

Adding further to inaccuracies found in nurse census enumerations was the Census Bureau's practice of including student nurses in the trained nurse category. This convention, which continued through the 1950 census, inflated the number of nurses reported. A 1974 recalculation of census figures by the Department of Health, Education, and Welfare (HEW) corrected for the inclusion of student nurses and provides a more accurate accounting of the number of nurses for the years 1910–1960, although basic classification problems with nurse-related census enumerations remain.[35] Despite issues surrounding counts of nurses, a cautious reading of U.S. census data does offer some sense of the size, growth, and characteristics of the early twentieth-century nurse labor market, allowing identification of several salient features descriptive of the nurse workforce.

In 1900, the U.S. Census listed 12,026 trained nurses. It is unclear how the Census Bureau arrived at this number, although the bureau reported that "Effort was made to separately classify trained nurses."[36] Contemporaries generally considered this estimate too low. In a 1900 article in *Trained Nurse and Hospital Review*, Anita Newcomb McGee, assistant surgeon general of the U.S. Army, attempted to approximate the number of nurses then present in the United States. Basing her analysis on reports issued by the Bureau of Education, which tracked nursing education programs, and beginning with the first known schools of nursing in the country, dating from the 1830s, McGee concluded that the number of all nurses that had graduated from schools of nursing was somewhere between twenty-five and thirty thousand.[37] Of course, not all of these nurses were working or even alive in 1900, yet taking McGee's estimate as a highest number of possible nurses and using the census figures for 1900 as the lowest limit, there were somewhere between twelve and thirty thousand nurses, graduates of some type of training program, existing in the United States at the turn of the century—a wide and somewhat inexact range.

The remaining figures, provided by the 1900 census, which consisted primarily of data on the race, age, and marital status of nurses, grouped the "nurses (trained)" and "nurses (not specified)" categories together, making differentiations between the two impossible. Beginning with the 1910 census, not only is greater detail provided on nurses but "trained nurses" and "nurses (not trained)"—the former "nurses (not specified)" category—are treated separately, allowing a more refined picture of the nurse population to emerge.

Trained Nurses

The most notable, defining, and enduring characteristic distinguishing the nurse population in the twentieth century was its tremendous growth. By 1910, there were 50,476 nurses, an increase of 38,672 over 1900 figures. Ten years later, the 1920 population of nurses doubled to 103,879 nurses and doubled again in 1930 to 214,989. Even allowing for the inexactitude of the census figures, the nurse labor market demonstrated an early and persistent trend toward enlarging; achieving a 325 percent increase between 1910 and 1930. Schools of nursing, also experiencing significant growth, demonstrated ample ability to turn out larger and larger numbers of nurse graduates (see figure 1.1).

The phenomenal increase in the trained nurse population was the result of several converging factors that created high demand and also led to nursing's

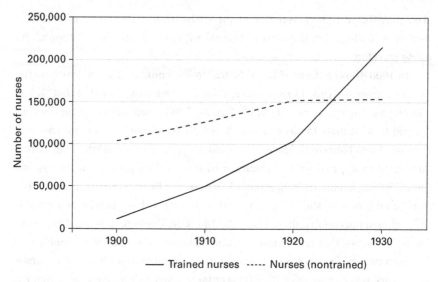

Figure 1.1. Trained nurses and nontrained nurses, 1900–1930. Sources: U.S. Department of Commerce and Labor, *Twelfth Census of the United States: 1900—Special Reports: Occupations at the Twelfth Census* (Washington, DC: Government Printing Office, 1904), xxvi; U.S. Department of Commerce 1913, 1923, and 1933.

popularity as a legitimate occupation. The main factor driving demand for nurses was the rapid growth of American hospitals during the last three decades of the nineteenth century. In 1873, there were an estimated 178 hospitals in the United States.[38] By 1904, the U.S. Census Bureau recorded 1,493 hospitals, a figure that included voluntary general, children's, specialty, and some tuberculosis hospitals but not sanitariums, psychiatric facilities, or private run-for-profit hospitals.[39] This number rose to 6,719 by 1930.[40] Included in that number were 4,302 general hospitals as well as psychiatric facilities, tuberculosis hospitals, children's hospitals, and other specialty institutions, all of which utilized trained nurses. Hospital expansion, attributed to the rise and success of scientific medicine as well as changing patterns of illness care, encouraged the middle class to seek out institutional care when ill. Changing illness care patterns required that hospitals hire caregivers competent and able to deliver increasingly more technical and complex treatments, a need met by opening schools of nursing. Hospitals found it expedient to use students to deliver care, solving their nursing care problems at a low cost. A simple equation developed: as the number and size of hospitals increased, so too did the number of nurses.

The second noteworthy factor driving the nurse population upward was the growing appeal of the occupation as a meaningful, remunerative form of work for women. In the late nineteenth century, women entered the workforce in larger numbers and began moving into jobs different from the domestic and manufacturing work that had previously employed the bulk of women workers.[41] Nursing was one of the occupations that offered different opportunities; these opportunities served as a reasonable alternative to more mundane jobs and carried some attractive characteristics for those needing to make a living. Nursing had shed its unsavory and largely undeserved reputation as an occupation filled with drunkards and loose women and became known as respectable. The required education was conveniently provided and paid for by the hospital-based school system. Further, its promise of steady work, a promise not always fulfilled, beckoned those dependent on outside income.

Schools of nursing experienced little trouble in finding, admitting, and graduating students, turning them out in droves. The relative ease with which nurse training programs accepted applicants represented an added advantage for those seeking an occupation. In general, schools looked for women with good health, a respectable reputation, no family responsibilities, willingness to work hard, sufficient education to read and write readily, possession of some mathematical skills, and the ability to produce letters testifying to their character. Educational requirements for the early schools were minimal; most accepted applicants with only an eighth-grade, or even lower, education.

An 1882 U.S. Bureau of Education circular of information on training schools for nurses reported that the highest educational attainment required by the sixteen schools surveyed was a common school education.[42] Educational requirements for admission to nurse training schools failed to rise even as more schools entered the market. Prominent nurse educator and leader M. Adelaide Nutting lamented the lack of higher educational standards, blaming the situation on the dependence of hospitals on students for patient care delivery and a willingness to admit all applicants regardless of educational background. Nutting's 1912 Bureau of Education report, *Educational Status of Nursing*, estimated that about 35 percent of schools required a high school education or equivalent, 23 percent required only one year of high school, 22 percent required a common school education, and 14 percent had no educational requirement at all.[43] Not only did this situation fail to improve over time, but it worsened. A 1923 Rockefeller-funded study, *Nursing and Nursing Education in the United States*, reported a decline in the percentage of schools requiring a high school education from 1912 levels to 29.1 percent in 1918, although the percentage of schools requiring at least one year of high school rose to 42.7 percent.[44] It was not until the 1930s that nursing schools began routinely requiring a high school education. In 1932, 90 percent of students surveyed by the Committee on the Grading of Nursing Schools entered their school of nursing with a high school diploma.[45]

Table 1.1.
Trained nurses living in cities with populations over 100,000, 1910–1930

Year	Percentage of nurses
1910	45
1920	45
1930	49

Sources: U.S. Department of Commerce 1913, 1923, and 1933.

Entry requirements for schools of nursing were relatively equal across the country, but the distribution of trained nurses was not. Most trained nurses congregated in large population areas; 45 percent of nurses in 1910 lived in cities of over one hundred thousand. This trend continued to characterize the profession over time. By 1930, the percentage of nurses living in cities over one hundred thousand rose to 49 percent (see table 1.1).

Nurses settled in areas in which job opportunities were higher or at least perceived to be higher. Logic dictated that cities with large populations offered greater chances of work. Given that early twentieth-century work prospects were closely tied to the hospital and school from which a nurse graduated, the vast bulk of nurses most likely hesitated to venture far from the schools they attended, most of which were located and concentrated in the major cities of the country. The concentration of nurses in large cities in conjunction with limited nurse availability in less populated areas led to the perception that the labor market was overcrowded rather than maldistributed, a complaint frequently voiced in the beginning of the twentieth century.

In addition to being in big cities, early trained nurses were overwhelmingly young, white, single women. The censuses of 1910, 1920, and 1930 showed that an average of 78 percent of trained nurses were between the ages of 21 and 44 years old. The inclusion of student nurses, who were traditionally younger, in these percentages biases the average age downward. The large percentage of nurses of young adult years indicates a relatively homogenous population age wise, reflecting primarily the large infusion of young entrants into the field. Older nurses were a smaller percentage of the population because of the heavy work and long hours. Comments in professional journals and at meetings often spoke to the length of a nurse's career, which spanned a relatively short ten-year period as the aging nurse would find herself not up to the tasks required as the years went by (see table 1.2).[46]

Table 1.2.
Ages of trained nurses, 1910–1930

	Percentage of nurses		
Age (years)	1910	1920	1930
16–20	10	7[b]	11
21–44	79	81	74
45–64	11[a]	11	12
65 and over	Not provided	1	1

Sources: U.S. Department of Commerce 1913, 1923, and 1933.
[a] Includes ages 65 and older.
[b] Includes ages 16–19.

Table 1.3.
Trained nurses by race, 1910–1930

	1910		1920		1930	
Category	Percentage	Total nurses	Percentage	Total nurses	Percentage	Total nurses
White	96	79,844	97	145,680	98	287,966
African American	3	2,433	2	3,324	2	5,728
Other	<1	50	<1	107	<1	484

Sources: U.S. Department of Commerce 1913, 1923, and 1933.

Between 1900 and 1930, the percentage of African American nurses declined from a high of only 3 percent of trained nurses in 1910 to a low of 2 percent in 1930. Even allowing for the fact that minority populations were often undercounted or miscounted by census officials, the number of African American trained nurses was abysmally low. Actual numbers of African American nurses remained constant throughout the first three decades of the twentieth century. In 1910, the first years for which the Census Bureau provided racial breakdowns on nurses, there were 2,433 African American nurses. This number rose to 5,728 by 1930, an increase of 135 percent—which fades in comparison to the 325 percent increase in white nurses over the same period (see table 1.3).

Limited opportunities existed for African Americans wanting to become professional nurses. Segregated conditions and racial bias denied African Americans entry into schools of nursing reserved for white Americans. In 1886, Spelman Seminary in Atlanta, Georgia, opened the first school of nursing for African American women, followed by others schools in the South exclusively for

Table 1.4.
Trained nurses by gender, 1900–1930

Year	Women (%)	Men (%)
1900	94	6
1910	93	7
1920	96	4
1930	98	2

Sources: U.S. Department of Commerce and Labor 1904;
U.S. Department of Commerce 1913, 1923, and 1933.

African Americans.[47] The segregated system of nurse education extended to the North. Chicago's Provident Hospital and Training School opened in 1891 in response to the lack of facilities willing to admit minority women to nurse education programs.[48] Other segregated northern schools initiated nursing education programs for similar reasons. The segregated nurse educational system persisted well into the middle of the twentieth century and was one piece of a system serving two divided populations of professional nurses, characterized not just by segregated schools but also by separate professional organizations, exclusionary licensing systems, and working opportunities that differed considerably for African American nurses.

The most striking characteristic of the trained nurse field was the gendered nature of the workforce in which women predominated. In 1900, the percentage of nurses who were men was 6 percent, rising slightly to 7 percent in 1910, then dropping precipitously to 3 percent in 1920 and bottoming out at 1 percent in 1930 (see table 1.4).

The percentage drop reflects a consistent number of men nurses in an overall enlarging population. The actual number of nurses who were men remained about the same throughout the first three decades of the twentieth century, totaling 5,839, 5,464, and 5,452 men nurses in 1910, 1920, and 1930, respectively.

Men and African Americans shared similar barriers to entry into the profession. A few schools of nursing did admit men and some, such as the Mills School affiliated with Bellevue Hospital in New York City, which opened in 1888, admitted men only.[49] Men who nursed were considered ideal for certain types of patients such as men with urogenital conditions, and psychiatric and substance abuse patients. In general, the design of the modern system of professional nursing assumed a women's workforce and the profession became percentagewise increasingly more woman-oriented as the century progressed.[50]

Table 1.5.
Marital status of trained nurses, 1920–1930

Year	Single, widowed, divorced, or unknown (%)	Married (%)
1920[a]	92.5	7.5
1930	87.5	12.5

Source: U.S. Department of Commerce 1933.
[a] Data for 1920 listed in the 1930 census report.

Stereotypical women's characteristics, such as gentleness, kindness, and warmth, which were believed requisite in caring for the ill, re-enforced the gendered nature of the workforce. The perceived submissiveness of women to authority was thought to be a plus in a workforce considered in need of discipline and control. The lower rate of pay for which women worked also figured into calculations of who made the best nurse.

Trained nurses were also predominantly single. Census figures for 1920 indicate that only 7.5 percent of nurses were married, with the remaining 92.5 percent either single, widowed, divorced, or of unknown marital status. By 1930, the percentage of married nurses increased slightly but remained low; only 12.5 percent of nurses were listed as married. (Prior to 1920 nurses' marital status was unrecorded; see table 1.5.)

Aside from social conventions which dictated that women give up work upon marriage, nurses were strongly discouraged from combining marriage and work. Nurses worked long hours and were expected to demonstrate total loyalty and responsibility to their jobs and their patients. The addition of marital responsibilities to an already busy working life, which often involved night work and spending days away from home, seemed incompatible with a nurse's professional career. For most nurses, it was one or the other, either a job or marriage, and this was reflected in a largely single workforce.

As the early twentieth-century nurse workforce developed, the characteristics of nurses changed little and resulted in a homogenous young, white, single population of women. Before 1950, recruitment centered on gendered and racial assumptions that re-enforced measures used to employ, control, and compensate nurses. The lack of diversity within the profession and the resulting image of the young, white nurse presumed to be a temporary worker committed to the labor force only until marriage intervened was not just accurate but difficult to challenge.

Trained versus Untrained Nurses

Nurses labeled "nurses (not trained)" by the Census Bureau coexisted and competed with trained nurses for jobs and patients. Known within nursing circles variously as practical nurses, experienced nurses, domestic nurses, nurse attendants, or just plain nurses, individuals in this category worked as nurses without having completed a training program or educational experience. Subsidiary worker was the general term used by professional nurses to describe this category of worker. The absence of rigorous licensing laws or regulatory processes allowed these nurses to enter the work force on terms comparable to that of professional nurses. The abilities of these workers varied. While many demonstrated proficiencies that met or exceeded those of trained nurses, others were less skilled; they were helpful only with mildly ill patients and a genuine threat to the safety of the chronically ill.

Professional nurses viewed subsidiary workers as competitors who threatened the not-yet-established dominance of professional nursing for nursing the sick and spent considerable time and effort in trying to control, regulate, or drive subsidiary workers from the field. Numerous causes in which professional nurses engaged in the first three decades of the twentieth century such as obtaining state regulated licensing, establishing systems of nurse procurement, and devising work conventions included measures meant to differentiate trained nurses from their untrained counterparts as well as drive the nontrained group out of nursing.

Because subsidiary workers were an unorganized and unregulated group, most of the knowledge about them comes from professional nurses who spoke only in pejorative terms about these workers.[51] Census data on this group provide some measure of identifying characteristics of the individuals comprising the "nurse (not trained)" category. As with data on trained nurses, census data regarding nontrained nurses must be approached cautiously as the Census Bureau failed to define nontrained nurses clearly and the category may have included workers such as nursemaids or child care workers. A careful reading of census data yields insight into the general characteristics of the nontrained nurse population.

The percentage of nontrained nurses was considerably larger than the trained nurse category, with 103,725 individuals listed as nontrained nurses in 1900. This number reflected growth in the number of nontrained nurses evident throughout the last decades of the nineteenth century. Unlike the trained nurse category, which experienced consistent growth, the number of nontrained nurses enlarged initially in the early decades of the twentieth century but then began stabilizing by the 1930s. Figures for 1910 indicate an increase to 126,250 and an equal second increase in 1920 to 151,936. By 1930 the increase in numbers was a mere 1,926 to 153,862 (see figure 1.1 earlier in chapter).

By 1940, the census category of "nurses (not trained)" had disappeared from census enumerations with two new categories, "practical nurse and attendants" and "hospital and other institutions," appearing. Neither of these categories, which represented a newer type of nurse worker, is comparable to "nurses (not trained)," limiting further efforts at tracking functional characteristics of this group.

Nontrained nurses differed from trained nurses in several important ways. The distribution of nontrained nurses around the country exemplified different patterns, and as a group, nontrained nurses were older, racially more diverse, and included more men than their trained nurse competitors. Fewer nontrained nurses were located in cities with populations over one hundred thousand but with less of a percentage difference between the trained and nontrained group. The percentage of nontrained nurses in cities with populations over one hundred thousand ranged from 35 percent in 1910 to 40 percent in 1930, whereas the percentages for trained nurses were 45, 45, and 49 percent in 1910, 1920, and 1930, respectively.

Nontrained nurses tended to be older than trained nurses. In 1910, 50 percent were in the 21–44 age range, a percentage that remained relatively stable until 1930. A larger percentage of nontrained nurses were in the 45–64 age range: 36, 35, and 41 percent for the years 1910, 1920, and 1930, respectively, than in the trained group (11, 11, and 12 percent). A small but noteworthy group of nontrained nurses, approximately 8 percent, were older than 65 in 1930, as compared with only 1 percent of trained nurses (see table 1.6).

The nontrained nurse workforce contained more men and was racially more diverse than the trained nurse workforce. Men made up 13, 13, and 9 percent

Table 1.6.
Ages of nurses (not trained), 1910–1930

Age (years)	Percentage of nurses		
	1910	1920	1930
16–20	13	3	5
21–44	50	56	46
45–64	36	35	41
65 and over	Not provided	6	8

Sources: U.S. Department of Commerce 1913, 1923, and 1933.

Table 1.7.
Nurses (not trained) by gender, 1910–1930

Year	Women (%)	Men (%)
1910	87	13
1920	87	13
1930	91	9

Sources: U.S. Department of Commerce 1913, 1923, 1933.

Table 1.8.
Nurses (not trained) by race, 1910–1930

Category	1910 Percentage	Total nurses	1920 Percentage	Total nurses	1930 Percentage	Total nurses
White	85	107,850	90	138,095	89	114,810
African American	15	18,902	9	13,798	11	16,265
Other	<1	86	<1	103	<1	583

Sources: U.S. Department of Commerce 1913, 1923, and 1933.

of nontrained nurses in 1910, 1920, and 1930, respectively (see table 1.7). Up to 15, 9, and 11 percent of nontrained nurses were African American in 1910, 1920, and 1930, respectively, reflecting a better match between the population of untrained African American nurses and the general population of African Americans (see table 1.8).

The strictly segregated nature of the trained nurse workforce in terms of race and gender forced both African Americans and men who worked as nurses into the untrained market. This provided work opportunities for minority populations, even if it was of a disadvantaged nature.

Nontrained nurses also differed in marital status: larger percentages of nontrained nurses were married (18.7 and 24.7 percent in 1920 and 1930, respectively) compared to trained nurses (7.5 and 12.5 percent, respectively, for the same years) (see table 1.9).

In the early twentieth century, women did both work and marry, although in much smaller numbers than they did later in the century. In 1920, the marriage rate was 22.8 percent for women in the workforce. This figure increased to 28.8 percent in 1930; this percentage aligns with that of married nontrained nurses.[52] The presence of a substantial subset of married nurses indicates that for some women, nurses' work and marriage was a reality.

Table 1.9.
Marital status of nurses (not trained), 1920–1930

Year	Single, widowed, divorced, or unknown (%)	Married (%)
1920[a]	81.3	18.7
1930	75.3	24.7

Source: U.S. Department of Commerce 1933.
[a] Data for 1920 listed in the 1930 census report.

Conclusion

From 1870 to 1900, women began seeking jobs that were considered socially respectable and intellectually challenging, and that required higher education than factory work; all of these characteristics were offered by nursing. The appeal of the profession to a wide variety of groups, each with their own agendas, solidified nursing as an alternative occupational choice for women. Nurses were welcomed by physicians as more capable caregivers of the sick and sought after by patients and their families as an expedient answer to health-related issues, and the nursing profession grew rapidly during the turn of the twentieth century. Women such as Chloe Cudsworth Littlefield entered the profession with high hopes that it would meet the need for meaningful, reliable, remunerative work; this hope was realized over her long career.

The profession spent its initial decades on the health care scene establishing its presence as a critical component of illness care but was stymied in developing a monopoly by having to share the market with a large group of untrained nurses. The two populations of nurses, trained and nontrained, one growing, the other declining, existed in an uneasy relationship to one another and to the sick public. Ill individuals were free to choose the type of nurse worker best suited for their circumstances. While the trained nurse category grew in numbers and secured a more reliable base of patients and institutions willing to employ its members, nontrained nurses survived in the nurse labor market, competing with their more educated counterparts and often driving the trained group to engage in tactics designed to limit nontrained nurse employment prospects. Competition and conflicts between the two groups escalated over the first four decades of the twentieth century. Later chapters address in detail the significance of the battles between trained and nontrained nurses.

Chapter 2

Starting Out

Organizing the Work and the Profession

Private duty nursing composed the predominant occupational field for professional nurses by the beginning of the twentieth century. Early chronicles of private duty nursing indicate that physicians or patients requiring the services of a graduate nurse relied on their local knowledge of which nurses were competent and available for taking patient cases. Key cities or towns, where a growing number of schools produced more and more nurses, required a more systematic method of hiring nurses. The emergence of nurse registries, agencies that served as the connecting link between nurses, patients, physicians, and hospitals, met the need of nurses to obtain patient cases and the need of patients to hire nurses. A plethora of different types of nurse registries began appearing throughout the country around the turn of the twentieth century, with each type exhibiting variations in the way it operated. In general, registries served as the main employment structure through which nurses found work. This chapter examines how and why registries emerged as the means through which nurses obtained jobs and the role of professional associations in their formation.

Commercial Employment Agencies

The first task in setting up an employment system for private duty nurses was establishing a means through which nurses and patients could find one another. Nurses needed a reliable way to seek cases; patients and physicians needed an easy way of obtaining and verifying the capabilities of the nurse. One means through which nurses could and did obtain jobs was via commercial employment agencies.

Commercial employment agencies, which operated as profit-making enterprises, placed nurses, both trained and nontrained, with patients, although many within the nursing profession discouraged trained nurses from using employment agencies for obtaining cases. Articles in professional nursing journals often referred to commercial agencies in scornful terms, citing their profit-making motive, the high fees the agencies charged nurses, and their practice of sending out nontrained workers as nurses, often with little differentiation from the trained group. Nurses criticized registries that placed nurses with other domestic workers, such as chambermaids and scrubwomen.[1]

Hospital-Based Registries

The employment agency model seemed ideally suited for the nurse labor market, in which patients in need of nursing care did not enjoy ready access to a supply of nurses and nurses in need of jobs required an efficient means of work notification. However, commercial agencies were not the main means through which nurses and patients connected with one another. Rather, it was through professional nurse registries, types of agencies similar to, although different from, commercial employment agencies, that nurses sought work.

Nurse registries were agencies that listed nurses who were available and met certain standards as defined by the registry for patient care. Patients or physicians notified the registry of the need for a nurse, initially in person or through a messenger system and later, as its use spread, via telephone; the registry then sent out a nurse suitable for the particular patient case. The initial impetus for establishing nurse registries began when student nurses were assigned to deliver care to private patients in their homes.

The Training School for Nurses at Bellevue Hospital in New York City provides an illustrative example of how initial nurse registries evolved. In 1873, a group of civic-minded, influential women dedicated to reforming American hospital care established Bellevue Training School.[2] The school, one of the first in the United States based on Florence Nightingale's ideas, consisted of two years of study and work in the hospital wards, after which the student received a diploma and was recognized as a trained nurse. One year after the program opened, the school began sending out students to deliver care to private patients, to "train nurses for the proper care of the sick in private families," and to "send nurses to the sick poor in their own homes."[3] The school, chronically short of funds from its inception, reaped a major benefit by pocketing the profits obtained from the service. Patients paid the school directly $16 a week for the services of the nurse, and students received $13 a month.[4] As the positive reputation of the school spread, demand for Bellevue's nurses grew rapidly and, in what would be a harbinger of things to come for the nursing profession, oftentimes exceeded supply. Two years after the training school opened, the governing body of the school decided to offer the services of graduate nurses, who received salaries of $18 to $25 a week dependent on abilities, age, and experience.[5] In 1878, after an embarrassing incident in which a Bellevue nurse stood accused of theft, the governing board established a more formal official registry that listed the names of nurses meeting specific standards and deemed eligible for sending out as a Bellevue nurse.[6] Nurses were required to comply with a set of regulations, provide evidence they met school standards, and wear a pin indicating their status as a Bellevue graduate.[7]

Other schools and hospitals established registries in patterns similar to Bellevue. By 1896, approximately forty hospital-based registries operated across the country.[8] Patients who wanted a nurse contacted the registry, which then sent out a suitable graduate. By sending patients only those nurses who held a diploma from the specific school, the registry verified that the nurse met school standards.[9]

Hospital-based registries operated within the hospital through the nursing superintendent or director's office. The office kept a list of nurses' names available for cases, assigning nurses as they received calls. The complexity of the registry varied with the hospital's size. In many cases, the registry did not exist as an organized separate entity as did Bellevue's, but was merely a function carried out by the nurse superintendent or supervisor, who kept an up-to-date list of available nurses, took calls for nurses, and notified nurses as they were needed. Hospital-based registries took on qualities more typical of a business enterprise when organizers developed rules and regulations governing how the registry ran and incorporated the registry as a business. In some instances, the hospital administered the registry, controlling its activity and ensuring that it operated to the hospital's benefit. Arrangements such as this sometimes caused conflict between nurses and the hospital administration. For instance, in 1896 the Alumni Association of the New York Hospital Training School for Nurses, in response to complaints about the methods used to run the registry, requested that the director of nursing accept registry control and that other changes take place to improve registry functioning.[10] The hospital's board of governors refused the request, leading the alumni association to organize a competing registry.[11] In a similar episode, the Bellevue alumni took matters into their own hands when the school's ladies board of managers, the registry's administering body, refused a request to install a telephone in the registry office to increase calls for nurses. Physicians joined the nurses in asking for the phone, yet the managers rejected the petition in favor of continued use of a messenger system. The dispute resulted in the establishment of a rival registry by the alumni association, which continued until the mid-twentieth century.[12]

Physician-Operated Registries

Hospital-based registries formed the backbone of the professional nurse registry system and would serve as the main type of nurse registry in the twentieth century. However, other types of registries organized outside professional nursing circles. In several localities it was physicians, not nurses, who recognized the benefit of such an operation and set up nurse registries. The Directory for Nurses of the College of Physicians of Philadelphia (CPP) provides one example of a physician-run nurse registry and also illustrates the close interest physicians demonstrated in the private nurse market. The CPP faced a nurse supply problem in the early 1880s. At the time, the largest source of trained nurses to the Philadelphia area came from educational programs attached to the Woman's and Lying-In Charity hospitals, both of which sent out their graduates to private patients but in numbers insufficient to meet physician demand for easily available nurses.[13] Physician complaints about nurses centered prominently on the inconveniences experienced in locating them for patient care. As one physician reminisced about his experiences in the 1880s, "Many was the time that I,—and every other practicing physician,—would have to employ a horse hack, often in the night time, and drive for miles in search of a nurse. Quite often, our first choice would be out of town, or sick, or engaged. Usually the next on our list would live in another part of the city, and so we might have to spend precious hours merely in the search for a second, a third, or even a fourth choice."[14]

Philadelphia physicians sought out the Medical Library in Boston (a nurse registry) for advice and determined that the CPP should set up its own nurse registry. Modeled on the Boston registry, the Philadelphia Directory for Nurses opened for business on May 14, 1882, and met with immediate success. By 1890, the directory listed over seven hundred nurses and emerged as the largest source of private nurses for the Philadelphia area until its closure in 1936.

Aware that the reputation of the nurses associated with the directory was critical, CPP required each nurse meet certain standards, thus serving as a basic credentialing system similar to that carried out by the Bellevue registry.[15] Certifying that nurses complied with the requirements of the registry became a hallmark of nurse registries and was particularly important before the enactment of state nurse licensing laws. Patients and physicians wanted some means of ensuring that nurses met minimum standards and that their nursing performance was credible.

Although its opening went smoothly, encountering few problems, the directory needed to address the immediate issue of what type of nurse, trained versus nontrained, to accept on the registry. In this 1880s, this issue had not yet emerged as controversial. Initially, the directory aimed to accept only nurses that graduated from a training program. In 1869 the American Medical Association called for the establishment of schools to train nurses "to qualify the student for the important, onerous, and responsible duties of the sickroom," recommending that trained nurses replace the "ordinary ignorant or uneducated nurse."[16]

The problem facing the directory was that few schools of nursing existed in Philadelphia in 1882. CPP physicians clearly favored trained nurses and sought out the cooperation and assistance of the Woman's and Lying-In Charity hospitals in setting up the directory. CPP agreed to the request that the directory send only graduate nurses and not students, a practice few schools at the time could claim they followed.[17] However, owing to the dearth of nursing educational programs in the Philadelphia area, accepting only graduated trained nurses proved impractical given nurse demand, and the directory accepted nontrained nurses based on recommendations from respected physicians.[18] The situation was relieved somewhat with the 1885 opening of a Nightingale-inspired training school at the Philadelphia General Hospital (formerly the Philadelphia Hospital). Subsequent openings of several other nursing programs in the Philadelphia area increased considerably the supply of trained nurses, leading the directory to alter its nurse acceptance practices in preference to trained nurses, although it continued to supply a certain number of nontrained nurses throughout its fifty-four-year existence.

Providing placement for nontrained nurses as well as trained nurses, a practice which later became extremely problematic for nurses and registries, presented a less severe problem in the 1880s. The small supply of trained nurses available made it inevitable that physicians would need to use nontrained individuals as the need arose. Relations between graduates of early schools of nursing and their nontrained counterparts were most likely more cordial than those that developed in later years as the numbers of both types of nurses increased and competition for patients rose. Early trained nurses were accustomed to working alongside nontrained nurses, because many of the first schools of nursing depended upon nontrained nurses for their operations. Sister Helen Bowdoin, the first superintendent of the Training School at Bellevue Hospital, relied on her experience as head of nursing at several English hospitals to qualify for the Bellevue position. The four head nurses originally working under her and responsible for supervising the students were experienced nontrained nurses.[19]

In addition, Bowdoin's successor, Eliza Perkins, was also a nontrained nurse.[20] The first two directors of the Boston Training School at the Massachusetts General Hospital were likewise not graduates of any nursing program. Rather, both possessed experience as nurses during the American Civil War.[21] Until the number of schools of nursing increased considerably with a corresponding increase in the number of graduate nurses, there simply were not enough trained nurses to meet demand. The shortage of qualified nurses meant that problems of competition between the trained and nontrained group did not develop until later. Furthermore, as seen in Littlefield's experiences, professional sensibilities, which pitted trained nurses against the nontrained group, had not yet awakened in the 1880s.

Physician-run nurse registries, such as the directory, met a need for efficient distribution of nurses to the public but required a critical mass of individuals willing to invest the time, energy, and money in administering a business enterprise. Most of the physician-run nurse registries were in cities such as Boston, New York, and Philadelphia that had substantial populations of organized medical groups. Such registries also situated nurses as dependent on and under the control of medicine. The development of other types of registries by nurses, particularly those administered and monitored outside of the hospital-based registry system, became a popular response to the problem of connecting nurses with patients in a way that let nurses take control of the working arrangements. These were known as central registries.

Central Registries

Central registries were designed to enroll nurses who did not belong to a local hospital or alumni association registry, were willing to travel distances for patient cases, and agreed to work in many different hospitals. Physicians and patients who needed a nurse could make one phone call to the central registry. The registry then assumed responsibility for locating and sending the nurse to the patient. The benefits of a centralized registry seemed obvious. The registry checked the credentials of the nurse much as hospital-based and physician-run registries did. Physicians invested minimal time trying to find nurses. By serving a larger area, the centralized registry presumably received more calls for nurses, thus ensuring steady employment for its nurse registrants.

By the turn of the century, the idea that central registries should be nurse-operated, noncommercial, nonprofit agencies became popular. The success of physician-controlled and other commercial nurse placement ventures led professional nurse leaders to recommend nurse-run registries as an expedient method of distributing private nursing services.[22] The practical aspect of using one agency to provide nursing services was the prime driving force behind the establishment of many registries, but the registry movement was more than just a handy way for nurses to acquire jobs.

Early twentieth-century nurse-run central registries were often associated with nurses' clubhouses or living quarters for nurses that provided a spectrum of services including meals, recreation, and educational opportunities.[23] Some believed a nurse registry should offer a variety of services to patients, in effect serving as a one-stop nursing shopping center for the community. Paying individuals could use the registry not just for nursing services when ill but they could also purchase special diets and sick room supplies.[24] For those who held this larger vision of registry services, the movement was a bridge between society and nursing, a way to educate the public to the ideals of the profession.

Although the primary job of the nurse registry was to connect graduate nurses with patients, leaders of the centralized registry movement also intended to categorize, distribute, and control all nurse workers based on qualifications determined by the registry. Expectations were that registries would resolve difficult problems surrounding nontrained nurses or subsidiary workers. Professional nurse leaders alternatively tried to control the unregulated growth of nontrained workers and, at the same time, recognized that many of these workers combined the provision of basic nursing skills with some household tasks and genuinely contributed to the care of the sick. Patients considered appropriate for the assignment of subsidiary workers or attendants were home-bound chronic, convalescent, or mildly ill individuals who also needed housekeeping services. Attendants charged lower fees than private nurse services, which kept health-care costs at an affordable level.[25] Leaders of the professional nurse registry movement advocated enrolling subsidiary workers as nurse attendants on registries and allocating them to appropriate patients as determined by the registry.[26]

Professional leaders did not limit the business of central registries to the private duty nurse market. Registries were encouraged to offer their services to hospitals, institutions, and other related agencies to fill staff and supervisory positions, serving as an early version of a nurse placement service. By providing a complete line of nursing services, leaders hoped the central registry would become the main distributor of nurses to all those needing nurses, whether at home or in the hospital. Some envisioned organizing central registries into a statewide network of registries with a headquarters connected to smaller centers. Nurses enrolled on the registries could be moved around and distributed throughout the state as local needs required, promoting more efficient use of nursing services and providing greater opportunities for nurses to obtain cases.[27]

Leaders believed connecting the nurse-run central registry to professional nurse associations such as state or local associations would achieve this wide array of goals. An already-organized nurse association offered a structure within which to readily establish a registry. Members of local nurse associations included nurse leaders, those who directed hospitals, schools of nursing, and related health care agencies, who could give the benefit of their experience to registry governance.[28] Contemporary journal articles reported the establishment of some nurse association–sponsored central registries in Boston, Denver, Washington, DC, Baltimore, Minneapolis, Philadelphia, Oklahoma City, and Kansas City during the first two decades of the twentieth century. These registries formed the nucleus of what were later known as professional nurse registries, which were directly connected with professional association activities.[29] The establishment of central registries and the formation of professional nurse associations took place concurrently and were closely related and dependent upon one another. The power of professional associations in mediating nurse employment situations grew significantly during this time.

Professional Nurse Associations

Nurses jumped into the professional association organizing movement in the last decade of the nineteenth century at a point when sufficient numbers of school of nursing graduates existed to ensure success. For the most part, organizing nurses into professional groups remained the province of nurse leaders who anticipated that professional associations would lead the fight for components considered essential for full professional status: better educational conditions and standards, state-mandated licensing of nurses, and the development of a code of ethics.

The formation of nurse associations was a contentious, byzantine process that pitted nurses against one another. The three associations that emerged from the competition were the American Nurses Association (ANA), the National League for Nursing Education (NLNE), and the National Association of Colored Graduate Nurses (NACGN). The ANA and the NLNE served as the face of white American nursing and controlled the direction and scope of activities for professional nurses throughout the twentieth century.

The earliest nurse professional organizations were nursing school alumnae associations. The New York Training School at Bellevue Hospital claimed the formation of the first alumnae association in 1889, and approximately thirty-one alumnae associations were in existence by 1895.[30] School of nursing alumnae associations formed for purposes similar to those of alumnae associations of other educational institutions. Alumnae associations instilled a sense of spirit and camaraderie among graduates of the same program and offered social and educational events of interest to members. Most significantly, school of nursing alumnae associations provided a mechanism for promoting issues of importance to working nurses, in particular setting up a means of obtaining and regulating conditions associated with employment and in arranging and overseeing the work parameters for private duty nurses through hospital-based registries. Alumnae held a vested interest in the establishment of efficient registries, whether administered by the hospital or the alumnae association. In either situation, the working arrangements made by the registry were of significant concern to alumnae members, who were often the main source of supply of private duty nurses.

For many nurses, alumnae associations provided the easiest way to maintain their professional and employment affairs. However, for others, such as those who moved away from the school from which they graduated or who graduated from a school without a functioning alumnae association, joining an alumnae association was not a possibility. By the 1890s, nurses began forming local nurse associations as either a substitute for or an addition to an alumnae association. Local nurse associations provided a means of organizing with other nurses from different schools within a particular area and provided benefits similar to those given by alumnae associations. They offered social and educational events in which nurses could gather. In several cases, local nurse associations developed plans for obtaining sick benefits for their members. Moreover, as with alumnae associations, local nurse associations monitored issues of importance for working nurses. Some operated registries for their members.[31]

During the 1890s, the *Trained Nurse and Hospital Review*, the sole nursing journal published at that time, reported on several local nurse associations organizing around the country.[32] Work issues figured prominently in the formation of these associations. In particular, local nurse associations portrayed themselves as one means for differentiating their members from nontrained nurses and were promoted as a way for trained nurses to capture a greater share of the private duty market. They would often distribute to physician group directories, listing nurse members who had completed a nurse training program and were available for patient care.[33] Local associations took seriously their mission to protect members from the nontrained. For example, by incorporating the word *protective* in their names, many local associations, such as the Spokane Protective Nurse Association, indicated that they were protecting their members against competitive inroads from the nontrained group.[34] Use of the term *protective association* mirrored the practice in other associations formed by nineteenth-century working women's groups who, barred from trade unions because of their gender, organized cooperatively to distribute available work and maintain wage rates, a mission similarly supported by working nurses.[35]

On a national level, nurses began organizing in 1893 with the formation of the American Society of Superintendents of Training Schools of Nursing (ASSTSN), an association of leaders of training schools and precursor of the National League for Nursing Education. The brainchild of Isabel Hampton Robb, the ASSTSN took an aggressive role in forming new organizations for nurses. As Robb figures prominently in early professional organizing activities, it is worth considering her career and the ideas on which she based the formation of the major twentieth-century professional nursing associations.

A Canadian by birth, Robb graduated from the New York Training School at Bellevue Hospital in 1883.[36] After a short period working in Europe as a nurse/companion to wealthy traveling Americans, she accepted a position as the superintendent of nurses of the Illinois Training School for Nurses (ITSN). The main hospital with which ITSN contracted for delivery of nurse services was Cook County Hospital, an institution firmly controlled by politicians. Robb's tenure at ITSN was short, only three years, and marked by difficulties working in the tough world of Chicago politics. Unhappy at ITSN and eager to advance her career, she accepted a position as the first superintendent of nurses and principal at the newly established Johns Hopkins School of Nursing in 1889. The prestige attached to the new school affiliated with the recently established Johns Hopkins University allowed Robb recognition as a leading nurse educator, placing her in a favorable position to influence nurse education as well as to play a major role in the formation of professional associations.

In 1893 Robb attended the International Congress of Charities, Correction, and Philanthropy, held during the Chicago World's Fair. The event included a special section on "The Hospital Care of the Sick, Training of Nurses, Dispensary Work and First Aid to the Injured." The secretary of the section, Henry H. Hurd, was the superintendent of Johns Hopkins Hospital and a colleague of Robb's. Her position at Hopkins, her connection to Hurd, and her reputation as a prominent leader made Robb the logical choice to chair the subsection on nursing. Robb took this opportunity to set forth her plan for organizing American nursing, which revolved around a two-step process and culminated in the establishment of two major national nursing organizations, the ASSTSN and the Nurses Associated Alumnae of the United States (NAA).

Robb believed in the primacy of bringing together regular working nurses, reasoning that "Superintendents being the heads of schools have a great deal of influence, not only among their pupil nurses, but graduate nurses, and until we can get superintendents united regarding the fundamental principles of the work, we cannot expect the nurses to work and to unite and to be as successful as they must be later on when we hold ideas in common."[37] This selective vision reflected Robb's beliefs that those in leadership positions possessed the aptitude to lead, strengthen, and reform the profession and especially to guide the less capable working nurses in their organizing efforts. Robb noted the benefits accruing to nurses of such an approach, remarking on the "advantage to the busy graduate nurses of having a body already organized to relieve them of the burden and responsibility of all the various details involved in the formation of an organization."[38] Robb was not just gathering together the best and the brightest of professional nursing, she was doing working nurses a favor by creating their association for them. Robb moved quickly on her proposal.

Robb's plan for organizing trained working nurses involved first encouraging the formation of school alumnae associations, a movement already in progress. Her design for the NAA, which organized in 1896, depended on using alumnae associations as the association's basic membership unit.[39] Robb's reliance on alumnae associations as the building blocks of the larger national group ensured that only nurses meeting the qualification of graduation from a school of nursing could join as a member in the national group, thus eliminating nontrained nurses. She argued that "the nurses can only be represented through their alumnae, so the organization of the alumnae associations and superintendents' society is necessary before we can have any qualified members for the larger national association."[40] The major caveat in Robb's plan was that the NAA should admit not just any alumnae association to the national group; only certain alumnae groups, designated as meeting defined standards set by the leadership group, were eligible. Initially, these standards stipulated that the hospital affiliated with the alumnae association contain no fewer than one hundred beds and that the students take a course of at least two years, later changed to three years, in the hospital without being assigned private duty cases.[41] These requirements eliminated not only nontrained nurses but also the substantial number of nurses who graduated from smaller schools with minimal standards. The NAA was designed not as an open organization welcoming to all nurses, but rather as an organization in which only those nurses who claimed graduation from a school that adhered to standards as promulgated by the national body could join.

Robb's influence on the way in which professional nursing developed was enormous. The top-down approach she advocated, in which elite leaders guided and set the course for the vast majority of working nurses, meant that the professional associations developed as exclusive rather than inclusive bodies. The rejection of graduates from small schools perceived to have lower standards

divided the profession into two camps: those from the elite leadership group
and others that rejected an organization that appeared not to want them.

Robb's and other nurse leaders' determination that organizing the profession proceed on a standard-based level was a serious attempt to impose needed
reforms in the nursing educational system and it was grounded in realistic fears
concerning the increasing number of hospitals opening schools. The increase
in schools alarmed those who witnessed nurses entering the labor market with
questionable credentials. There were long work hours, minimal theoretical preparation, and poor facilities where students lived. Training program educational
standards, never very high to begin with, seemed to erode over the decades as
any and almost every hospital jumped on the nursing school bandwagon. As
New York nurse Sylveen Nye observed in 1900, "Under present conditions any
person can organize a stock company, rent a house, put in half a dozen beds and
call it a hospital. Then in order to have the necessary work performed cheaply,
a training school for nurses can be established and incorporated, pupils admitted and for payment for their services give them what? A course of instruction
that enables them to properly and faithfully carry out the orders of any physician and give to every patient committed to their hands the best possible care?
No, they receive a diploma, Trained Nurse."[42]

As it was, even the most prestigious schools, such as Massachusetts General, Bellevue, Philadelphia General, ITSN, and Johns Hopkins, barely qualified
as educational institutions. The crux of the matter was how to convince hospitals, which ran the schools, to improve standards. Robb theorized that by making
high standards requisite for joining the national associations, hospitals would
enhance their educational programs and accept the expense as the price they
must pay to have their alumnae association align with the professional body.

The debate over how national nurse associations should organize erupted
in 1901 when nurses attending the Third International Congress of the International Council of Nurses argued over the appropriate organizational structure
for national nursing associations. Ethel Gordon Fenwick, British nursing leader
and president of the International Council of Nurses, encouraged the establishment of school of nursing alumnae groups as the core unit of national organizations, commenting that the strong bonds formed during students' educational
years provided the incentive needed for nurses to join in larger groups.[43] Sylveen Nye, by then president of the recently established New York State Nurses
Association (NYSNA), disagreed, stating that a nurses association organized
along alumnae lines would fail. "The very nature of such an organization is too
narrow. Nurses need to broaden, to mingle with those of other schools, and to
get out of the ruts. . . . It would be a mistake to make the State associations

dependent upon the success of the local organizations, which are too often fail-
ures, and kept in existence only through the indefatigable efforts of a few
women," Nye asserted.[44]

Disagreement over the top-down alumnae association approach raged for
years, consuming time and effort during the first decade of the NAA's existence.
Many nurses continued to question the rationale behind using the alumnae associations as organizing units and urged opening up the NAA to more nurses as a
better means of encouraging hospitals to adopt improved nurse education standards. ITSN graduate I. C. Rose raised this point at the NAA's Seventh Annual
Convention, arguing, "And right here we must ask ourselves the question, which
is more advisable, to put our standard so high that only the smaller percentage
of nurses can possibly meet the requirements, or at first shall we be content to
have a more elastic standard."[45]

Rose noted that not every nurse could go to the best schools, suggesting
that admitting nurses to the NAA from schools with lower standards would
encourage such graduates to work to improve their school's standing. She predicted defeat if the NAA stuck with high admission criteria.

Other problems directly connected to the alumnae association organizing
model confronted the NAA. First, not all nurses belonged to an alumnae association, either because their school did not have one or they chose not to join; this
automatically barred them from NAA membership. Nurses moved around the
country, and if they relocated away from their schools, many saw little need to
support an association that provided them with few benefits. At the turn of
the century, nurses had already organized other types of professional groups.
As noted, some local nurse associations were formed in the last decade of the
nineteenth century that provided the same, and in some cases more, benefits
for the individual nurse. Some alumnae associations simply did not want to the
join the NAA. For example, the New York City Hospital Training School Alumnae Association, affiliated with one of the oldest training schools in the country, initially decided that participating in the NAA was too costly with few
benefits, a decision that was reversed in 1903.[46] Further, the entry of state nurse
associations into the mix complicated an already befuddled situation.

New York State provides an illustrative example of just how convoluted the
formation of nursing associations became. Of the twenty-six alumnae associations attending the second annual meeting of the NAA, nine came from New
York, indicating strong statewide support.[47] However, the state contained several other nursing groups, such as the Buffalo Nurses Association, established
in 1895, and the Protective Association of Graduate Nurses of New York State
(PAGN), which formed in 1897. These groups held very different opinions on

how nurses should organize.[48] Both groups rejected the alumnae association model of membership, utilizing individual membership instead as the basis of entry into their associations.

In 1897 a group of New York State nurses aligned with the NAA began to agitate for a state nurse organization for the specific purpose of passing a state nurse licensing act. This group proposed organizing the state association along alumnae association lines similar to the NAA.[49] PAGN opposed the move and took action to draw up its own licensing act. The Buffalo Nurses Association, known to be independent of NAA, also resisted forming the state association on alumnae association lines. Reports of contentious nurse meetings, charges, and countercharges filled the pages of *Trained Nurse and Hospital Review.*[50] In the end, compromise won the day. PAGN failed to garner continued support and dropped out of sight after a few years. The Buffalo group continued to negotiate with those wanting a state association based on alumnae association membership. After numerous meetings, discussions, and debates, the New York State Nurses Association organized in 1901, which settled the issue for the state but created further turmoil in the NAA.

In 1901, the NAA, now eager to include various types of nurses' societies, such as state and local associations, appointed a committee to revise the bylaws to allow admittance of the state nurse associations now forming in greater numbers.[51] However, several states paralleled New York's example and had lower membership requirements that conflicted with the national body. State nurse associations, established with the primary purpose of passing nurse practice acts, aimed for larger memberships to convince legislators that a sufficient body of trained nurses supported proposed licensing acts.[52] This varied with NAA aims, which sought to limit membership to a more select group.

The NAA debated this issue until 1904 when it voted to change its bylaws to admit state nurse associations.[53] Even so, the membership issue failed resolution. At this point, state nurse associations weren't the only ones seeking membership in the NAA; local nurse associations at the county levels, which were eligible for NAA admittance based on the 1904 bylaws change, were also reaching out. Faced with a dizzying array of differently organized groups, the NAA, renamed the American Nurses Association (ANA) in 1911, engaged in a major reconfiguration and reorganization beginning in 1916 and ending in 1922. The reorganization resulted in a federated model composed of state nurse associations divided into local units called district nurse associations, which were the former county associations. A nurse choosing to join the ANA joined at the district level, which represented a component of the state nurse association. State associations replaced alumnae associations as the entry point for membership in the national ANA. Membership requirements varied from state to state and district to district. Any state or district could make it more or less easy for a nurse to join individually or require membership in a school alumnae association. Moreover, many states continued the alumnae association membership requirement, which was not officially abandoned by the ANA until 1944.[54] The retention of alumnae associations as significant components of the ANA up to the early 1940s created a collection of powerful interest groups within the main body. In states that continued the alumnae association model, alumnae groups held significant power and were able to prioritize issues of importance to them.

Structural changes implemented by the association's reconfiguration created a more logical organization but also held some long-term ramifications for the ANA. For African American nurses, state association control of entry into the ANA institutionalized racial barriers, exclusion, and segregation. In its early years, the NAA admitted alumnae associations affiliated with black schools of nursing, although in minuscule numbers. Chicago's Provident Hospital School of Nursing was admitted in 1903, followed by the District of Columbia's Freedman's Hospital School of Nursing in 1904.[55] Some state associations admitted African American nurses either individually or through their school's alumnae association. In 1905, the alumnae association of the Lincoln Hospital School of Nursing in New York City became a unit member of NYSNA.[56] The alumnae association for the Harlem Hospital School of Nursing was listed as a NYSNA member, and thus an ANA member, in 1928, shortly after its 1924 opening.[57] Giving state associations the authority to determine membership requirements meant that states could segregate with impunity and discriminate without reprisals. Any state could place barriers against a black school of nursing seeking admission. In most cases, state associations simply barred black schools or applied membership requirements intended to discriminate. Until the mid-twentieth century, when the ANA finally desegregated, many states' nurse associations existed for white nurses only.

African American nurses had already initiated a separate professional association before the ANA reconfiguration. The establishment of NACGN occurred in 1908. Founded by a group of leading African American nurses, NACGN organized with aims similar to those of ANA, including working toward better educational standards, keeping up to date on professional issues and concerns, and improving the status of nurses. Also, NACGN took on the difficult and challenging tasks of seeking interracial professional cooperation and fighting job discrimination based on race. As historian Darlene Clark Hine noted, "Though the notion was never overly articulated by black nurse leaders, they undoubtedly used these organizations as shields from the excessive racism, hostility, and denigration of their white colleagues, behind which they developed and honed leadership skills essential to attaining the ultimate objective of integration and acceptance into the mainstream of American nursing."[58] The existence of a small number of black alumnae groups in the ANA and the special status afforded the Freedman's Hospital alumnae association, which permitted that group entry as an individual unit of the ANA, the only alumnae association so treated once the federated model was put in place, meant white nurses could rationalize, as they did, that they had done the best they could under the racial conventions of the time.[59] The apathy African American nurses found among white nurses for addressing issues of racial justice and integration in the ANA continued even after ANA integration.

The trilevel division of the ANA into national, state, and district components also split the focus and interests of the association into varying levels of priority. The national ANA, in which nursing educators and directors predominated, tended to concentrate on educational issues and other programs intended to reform the profession. Divisions played out on the national level as the elite leadership group engaged in professionalizing endeavors to secure nurse licensing acts, upgrade standards for schools of nursing, and carry out curricular reform. However, these issues, highly valued by nurse leaders, appeared disconnected from the everyday concerns of the majority of working nurses. As Susan Reverby noted, "The concerns of such nurses—for improved working conditions, income, and recognition for their skills—were perceived as antithetical to the professionalizing effort."[60]

The emphasis on professionalization and the tactics designed to achieve it is very apparent when examining the national programs, aims, and actions of the ANA. However, when viewed from the state and district levels, a different picture emerges. District nurse associations, whose membership included larger proportions of working nurses as opposed to that of the leadership group, could not avoid dealing with nurses' issues. Working nurses attended district association meetings, lodged complaints, and made demands that districts address their concerns about employment. Moreover, when district nurse associations entered into the private duty registry business through the establishment of central registries, the work of nurses, specifically the work of private duty nurses, placed working issues at the forefront of district association activities. The nature of the relationship between a district, its members, and the district-run registry was complicated and intense. The district required the support of members to carry out successful registry activities.

Conclusion

The late nineteenth- and early twentieth-century proliferation of nursing schools releasing scores of graduate nurses into the job market and the growing acceptance of professional nurse services for illness care created a need to devise an orderly system of sending nurses to patients. At the same time, professional nurses began developing patterns of employment, which they hoped would lead to satisfactory working conditions and reliable income. Utilizing a third party to link nurses and patients was viewed as a practical means of job procurement. A number of agencies that served as connecting points between nurses and patients existed within the late nineteenth-century nurse labor market. For some nurses, control over their place in the labor market became of paramount importance. Professional nurse registries provided a way for nurses to promote professional aspirations, achieve professional goals, and shape the market.

In the same period that nurses came to the consensus that they should exert strong control over their work, the profession also began a complex movement to organize into professional associations. Taking control was no easy task and the three-organization structure that emerged dealt with rivalries, disunity and acceptance, and promotion of racial segregation built into the system. Despite its many flaws, it was a structure that remained in place through the first half of the twentieth century. It was also the structure that spoke for working nurses, addressing issues of concern for the nurse at the bedside. The national organizations often spoke with muted voices on nurse working conditions, preferring to concentrate on matters the leadership believed were of greater import. On local levels, district and state nurse associations did not have the luxury of avoiding issues members prioritized, such as conditions in the workplace.

In the next chapter, the experience of one New York City district nurse association in setting up and administrating a central registry will be presented, shedding light on how districts dealt with issues central to working nurses and also illustrating how early twentieth-century registries operated.

Chapter 3

Supplying Nurses

The Central Registry Business

A registry is a factor in the community; supplying nurses of all schools to rich and poor; helping to create uniform standards and wipe out class distinction; supplying nurses for institutional or public health nursing; a registry through which the problem of nursing those of moderate means has been met; which is controlling the attendant and wiping out the commercial registry.

—Elizabeth Burgess, "The Future of the Central Registry"

These words, spoken by Elizabeth Burgess, a prominent champion of professional private duty registries, summed up the characteristics of an ideal central private duty registry. Many in the professional nursing community shared and supported Burgess's conception of a central registry as one administered by and for professional nurses, standardizing delivery of nursing care, and functioning as a major distribution point for all nursing services. Central registries, also known as professional nurse registries, indicating their control by nurses, simultaneously offered a way for nurses to organize their work and manage their professional careers, deliver nursing care to patients, and impose a uniform set of standards delineating the qualifications of nurse caregivers. Their affiliation with professional association groups added further to their appeal. Such registries became agencies of choice favored by many practicing nurses and leaders in the nursing community as the best mechanism for supplying nurses.

The number of functioning central registries varied over time. Before World War II, the ANA recorded 145 active professional registries. This figure rose steadily after the war when 176 professional registries were in operation by

1956, after which time the number declined. In 1965, there were still 153 professional nurse registries listed with the ANA.[1] This chapter examines the experience of one of those registries, the New York Central Registry (NYCR), analyzing how it navigated the complex nursing business scene.

By the first decade of the twentieth century, New York state nurses achieved significant prominence, assumed major leadership roles in professional activities, and were at the forefront of nursing advancement. The distinction with which many in professional nursing circles held the state was due to the sheer size and scope of its nursing population. A 1903 U.S. Bureau of Education report listed seventy-nine schools of nursing in the state, the most of any state and ten more than Pennsylvania, in second place. Thirty-five schools of nursing were located in New York City alone.[2] The 1910 U.S. Census reported that 10 percent of the nation's nurse population resided in New York State, with 5 percent of all U.S. nurses living in New York City.[3] By 1904, a local group of New York City nurses was sufficiently organized to form a county nurses' association, the New York County Nurses' Association, later renamed the New York Counties Registered Nurses' Association (NYCRNA).[4] NYCRNA's location in the nation's most populous city, the site of many large hospitals and health-related agencies, an estimated 10 percent of the nation's hospital beds, as well as New York City's substantial professional nurse population, ensured its status as a leader in state nursing affairs.[5]

Much of NYCRNA was comprised of unit groups representing local school of nursing alumnae associations, a membership structure that continued after the 1916 ANA reorganization and persisted well into the middle of the twentieth century. NYCRNA's leadership, aware of the dominant status of alumnae associations, considered the wishes of the alumnae groups in all activities and often deferred to their interests when making decisions. This tactic made it easier for NYCRNA to stabilize and carry out its programs.

One of NYCRNA's member alumnae associations was an organization known as the Association of Graduate Nurses of Manhattan and Bronx (AGNMB). The AGNMB formed in 1902 to meet the needs of the growing population of graduate nurses moving into New York City and functioned as an alumnae association, offering services to graduate nurses not belonging to a local alumnae association.[6] Of concern for AGNMB members was the plight of private duty nurses, who were either left on their own to obtain cases or used commercial registries for work. Private duty matters remained a major focus of AGNMB throughout its existence, and the organization served as a driving force behind central registry and NYCRNA affairs.

Reports of flourishing nurse-run private duty registries in Boston and Buffalo convinced NYCRNA's membership in 1907 that a district-sponsored central registry was warranted.[7] In 1909 NYCRNA considered a report, compiled by the County Registry Committee, which investigated the New York private duty market. The report concluded that nurses unaligned with an alumnae association were forced to find cases through commercial profit-driven agencies, a situation considered by organized nursing as incompatible with professional ideals. The County Registry Committee determined that approximately six thousand trained and nontrained nurses registered for work at commercial registries throughout the city. In arguing for the establishment of a central registry, the committee noted it was both a privilege and a duty for NYCRNA to take on such a project, which carried the potential to better control the professional life of nurses and unify the strength of the graduate nurse group. The report recommended that the association establish a central registry.[8]

NYCRNA embarked on a plan to carry out the report recommendations by eliciting support for the core registry from hospital superintendents and physician members of the county medical and the county homeopathic societies as well as nursing school alumnae associations.[9] To dispel apprehension, NYCRNA promised alumnae associations that the proposed central registry would not interfere with the associations' registries work, but would be concerned with the "registration of the floating population of nurses now registering at undesirable bureaus: to respond to all surplus calls and to be a central bureau of information."[10] NYCRNA further distanced the proposed central registry from those of alumnae associations by offering an institutional nurse placement service in addition to private duty placement.[11] The institutional nurse placement service specialized in obtaining positions for qualified nurses in hospitals or other health-related agencies. A full-service nurse placement agency not only set the central registry apart from alumnae association registries, which only placed private duty nurses, but also fulfilled a goal set by nursing leaders that centralized registries serve as large-scale nurse distribution centers.

NYCRNA was successful at convincing the alumnae associations that the new venture would not threaten their registries. The alumnae associations demonstrated significant interest in the project, promising to refer surplus calls received from their registries to the central registry and in some cases offering financial aid during the initial organizational period. NYCRNA voted to establish the central registry (which became the NYCR), which opened for business on July 1, 1910. Twenty-two days later, the registry received a call for and sent a nurse to its first case, a patient with scarlet fever at Presbyterian Hospital.[12]

Registry Organization

The organization, administration, and policies of the newly organized central registry had much in common with other professional registries, reflecting contemporary practices by professional groups as the best way to provide private duty nurse services.[13] The NYCR had total control of the business vested in NYCRNA's executive committee as a membership corporation, an element considered crucial to achieving the aims of the professional group. A governing board selected by each affiliated alumnae association oversaw registry operations and reported directly to the executive committee. Administration of the registry fell to the registrar and an assistant.[14]

The registrar had a central role in directing the placement of nurses by using expertise as a professional nurse to evaluate requests from patients, and combining knowledge of the capabilities of each nurse enrolled in the registry to select the most appropriate nurse available. Women who had received some higher education, possessed vast experience in nursing, and had developed business acumen were found to be particularly well qualified for a registrar position.[15] NYCRNA appointed Pauline Dolliver, a graduate and former superintendent of nurses of the Massachusetts General Hospital School of Nursing, as the NYCR's first registrar. Dolliver was familiar with New York City, having worked as the assistant superintendent of St. Luke's Hospital School of Nursing. This was an important attribute, as knowledge of the local nurse labor market was considered essential to running the registry.[16] Dolliver received an annual salary of $1,500 and rooms at the registry.[17]

Since the registry was a district activity and purposely designed as a democratic organization, NYCRNA meetings included routine discussion of registry business during which members voiced approval or disapproval of policies. In general, the governing board presented decisions regarding the registry to the executive committee for approval. The executive committee then notified the membership of the action at meetings with no discernible dissent and little participation from members noted. The absence of disagreement over registry matters did not always indicate approval of policies by nurse registrants. In fact, nurse leaders active in association activities often complained that private duty nurses lacked interest in professional affairs.[18] A perceived lack of enthusiasm, coupled with poor attendance at meetings, made private duty nurses less of a factor in decision-making, their voices often silent. For private duty nurses, locked into a seven-days-a-week, frequently twenty-four-hours-a-day work schedule, nonattendance most likely reflected a lack of time. Although leaders were consistent in accusing private duty nurses of professional indifference, their absence at meetings allowed the operation of the registry to proceed with little interference from members.

Nurses seeking membership in the NYCR submitted credentials for approval and indicated which type of cases they preferred—or often registered against certain types of cases. Nurse leaders criticized nurses registering against cases, urging nurses to be available for all cases and to accept more difficult ones. Legitimate reasons for registering against cases included inexperience or unfamiliarity with a certain disease entity. Inconvenience was also deemed an appropriate reason for registering against cases. For example, for contagious cases, nurses sometimes underwent a period of quarantine afterward, thereby reducing their potential for income. For nurses who often existed on the margins of financial security, any loss of revenue spelled economic disaster.[19] The custom of registering against cases troubled both private duty nurses who needed work but wanted autonomy and registries obliged to send out nurses regardless of their condition or the case.

After acceptance as a registrant, a nurse agreed to abide by registry rules, which outlined procedures for placing her name on call, the manner of assigning cases, dues, working hours, and policies for a miscellany of situations she might encounter.[20] Nurses had their name added to a list of available registrants and agreed to remain within a two-hour contact area of the registry, receiving cases in rotation based on when they were added to the list. A variant of this was the selection method, which called for the registrar to evaluate the patient situation and assign the nurse most appropriate to the patient. Those who viewed the registry as a system linking the best nurse to each unique patient favored the selection method. Working nurses tended to be wary of the selection method, as it often resulted in favoritism by the registrar toward her preferred nurses.[21] Any violation of the rules, such as refusing to take an assigned case or being unavailable when called, resulted in the nurse's name reverting to the bottom of the list. The registry expected loyalty from registrants and urged them to promote its services whenever possible.[22]

In the initial years of operation, the NYCR adopted approaches and addressed problems typically encountered by related agencies serving the private nursing market. Solving problems persisted as an elusive exercise as the same challenges arose again and again. Examining how the NYCR dealt with challenges peculiar to the private duty business provides a picture of the workings of the early private duty registry system and issues involved in setting up a nurse distribution network. Three areas—registry membership, nurses' fees, and how well the registry carried out its business—are particularly relevant for consideration of later problems.

Registry Membership

One of the most immediate issues addressed by the NYCR was determining who was eligible for enrollment. Two factors complicated registry eligibility: the intricacies of the New York State Nurse Practice Act and NYCRNA's membership requirements. The New York State Nurses' Association (NYSNA), established in 1901, was the nation's first state nurses' association and took credit for passing one of the original and strongest nurse practice acts in 1903.[23] Leaders hoped that the Nurse Practice Act, when enacted, would lead to higher standards of nursing practice. However as historian Nancy Tomes noted, strict regulations and the nonmandatory nature of the act worked to lessen its impact and usefulness for regulating nursing.[24]

The act's restrictiveness related to the requirement that licensing candidates had to graduate from a school approved by the New York State Education Department. This regulation barred graduates of schools that failed to obtain education department approval from taking the registration examination. Tomes estimated that in 1909 a third of the schools operating in New York State were not approved by the state.[25] Education department approval applied to schools both in and out of state. Most schools failed to apply for approval so a substantial number of graduate nurses working in the state remained ineligible for New York registration.

Lacking a state license to practice nursing did not necessarily represent an impediment for working nurses. Licensing laws were both mandatory and voluntary. Mandatory laws require that anyone who practices the occupation be licensed and meet the requirements of the state's regulations or face penalties if found practicing in violation of the law. Voluntary laws applied only to those using the title of the occupation. Early state nurse practice acts protected only the title "registered nurse" and use of the initials RN after a nurse's name. State nursing associations lacked the political power to pass more desirable mandatory laws regarding education or work hour mandates. Therefore, they accepted the voluntary, less adequate form.[26] Voluntary status meant anyone could practice as a nurse if he or she did not claim to be a registered one. Licensing conferred no major benefit for graduate nurses. Tomes estimated that in 1910, registered nurses represented at most 60 percent of the state's graduate nurses.[27]

Incorporated shortly after the passage of the Nurse Practice Act, NYCRNA's original organizers deemed it inadvisable to demand state registration for members and did not require it. Expectations were that nurse members would become eligible for and seek out state licensing. The association welcomed alumnae groups from schools whose graduates lacked registration. As late as

1914 NYCRNA admitted three alumnae associations (for the Italian, Sydenham, and Flower Hospitals Schools of Nursing) even though their members were not all registered nurses.[28] This practice placed NYCRNA in a serious dilemma once the organization entered the registry business. Including unlicensed nurses meant the registry's standards failed to meet those of the state association. Further, excluding unlicensed graduate nurses meant NYCRNA operated a service unavailable to some of its members. There was also the threat that nurses who were unlicensed through no fault of their own might use commercial registries. Moreover, many nurses living in New York City were considered unlicensed as graduates of out-of-state schools or schools that were in-state but not approved.[29]

The issue of registry membership was part of a larger debate within organized nursing regarding standards and admittance into the profession. Nursing leaders engaged in a decades-long battle to regulate nursing practice via licensing acts believed to lead to higher standards for schools of nursing. However, hospitals saw nursing schools as an efficient and cheap way to deliver nursing care; therefore, they outmaneuvered such efforts by rapidly establishing a tremendous number of new schools. The number of schools skyrocketed from around 550 schools in 1900 to 1,844 schools in 1930.[30] Licensing laws often failed to meet leaders' expectations that state-regulated practice would uplift the profession. The dubious caliber of many nursing schools added additional concerns.

Facing the reality that state registration was still an undervalued commodity, the NYCR chose a middle route to registry membership by establishing three classifications of registry membership for graduate nurses. Class A nurses were members of an alumnae association affiliated with NYCRNA and members of its school registry if one existed. Class B members included individual members of NYCRNA. Class C members were unlicensed graduate nurses, not members of NYCRNA, who agreed to seek registration within a year of application to the registry.[31] Registry fees were $5 higher for Class B and C members, providing an incentive to those nurses still unlicensed to obtain registration. Still, the three-class system failed to resolve all membership issues completely.

The graduate/registered/nonregistered nurse membership issue represented only one perspective in determining the appropriate nurse worker to admit to registry membership. Debates on subsidiary workers demonstrated the other standpoint. Recognizing the value of providing less-trained employees and the NYCR's resolution to deliver a full range of nursing services, the registry established a category of skilled attendants.[32] The number of attendants joining the registry was never large, averaging 15 percent of the total membership. Further, registry commitment to these workers was less than complete.[33] In 1915, the registry

dropped trained attendants after NYCRNA learned that accepting only graduate nurses would make the agency exempt from taxation.[34] The registry reversed
this decision in 1921 upon the urging of New York City Commissioner of Public
Welfare Bird S. Coler, who asked the registry to admit graduates of New York
City schools as trained attendants. In addition, a revised 1920 state nurse practice act provided for a new category of licensed, trained attendants.[35]

The issues surrounding both trained attendants and nonlicensed graduate
nurses went to the heart of the problem of determining who was the real bedside nurse. Ultimately, efforts by the NYCR to control the practice of nonregis-
tered nurses through the registry system proved unsuccessful. In addition, new
challenges would arise with the implementation of fees.

Lavinia Dock credited the Lady Managers of the Bellevue School of Nursing with setting the first fee for trained nurses at $21 per week.[36] The fee-setting
process for private duty nurses considered customary fees, the general market
rate, and approval of nurse charges by hospital governing boards. Alumnae association registries commonly participated in determining fees to charge patients
in their home hospital. When an association desired a fee increase, the group
petitioned the hospital governing board, which retained the right to approve or
disapprove the request.

Fee setting for private duty nurses took on additional importance when hospitals considered the remuneration paid to nurses directly employed by the
institution. When the number of patients in a hospital temporarily rose beyond
the capacity of the student nurse–led workforce, hospitals hired private duty
nurses on a per diem basis as supplemental staff. Nurses working on a per diem
basis, a practice emerging in the 1920s, enabled hospitals to obtain a crew of
temporary expert general duty nurses without the obligations, such as room and
board, owed full-time staff.[37] When hired on a per diem basis, private duty
nurses expected to receive the customary daily private duty fee, a fee hospitals
often considered too high. Later, as hospitals employed more graduate nurses
on a full-time basis, they linked staff nurse salaries to private duty rates. As a
consumer of private duty services, it remained in the hospital's best interests to
keep private duty rates moderate over time. New York Hospital once more provides an illustrative example of how hospitals and nurses arranged this process.
In April 1920, the alumnae association appointed a committee to confer with
the hospital's governors about raising the remuneration of nurses employed by
the hospital to conform to the going local private duty rate of $6 per day.[38] The
governors agreed to this request, and by June nurse employees began receiving
the same rate as private duty nurses.[39] This equity in pay kept all nurses, whether

private duty or hospital employed, stabilized and standardized the costs of nursing care for hospitals and patients alike.

Private duty nurses seemed to accept the fee-setting mechanism, especially since they exerted a degree of control as they were party to initiating increases and demonstrated agency in determining their rates. More likely, they saw mutual benefits in the methods used to set fees. When alumnae associations requested fee increases, hospital boards inevitably consulted other hospitals regarding their private duty rates. Emerging from this practice was the institution of a local standardized private duty rate among hospitals within a regional area, preventing undercutting of fees between nurses. But the practice also set fees at the lower private duty rate and stymied benefits potentially gained from competition.

Some nurses disagreed with setting standardized fees. These nurses may have understood that standardized fees would not allow them to charge higher fees in times when demand for nurses rose. They could not profit from shifts that demanded services or confront the competition between nurses that might arise. Nurse administrator Christine Kefauver, writing in *Trained Nurse and Hospital Review*, challenged the standardized fee. Kefauver believed leaders erroneously let working nurses think higher fees would decrease work opportunities. In a blatant attack on nurse leaders, Kefauver observed,

> Furthermore there is a tendency to standardize the nurses wages and this standard is based on that which maintained twenty years ago. Any attempt to raise it is frowned upon by the leaders of the nursing profession (few of whom are engaged in private nursing themselves) and the general public. . . . The contention is made by the leaders of the nursing profession, and with truth, that if the private nurse raises her prices large numbers of people will be deprived of her services. It is however, equally true that large numbers have *always* [italics in original] been so deprived and that such would continue to be the case if nurses charges were reduced to *one* [italics in original] dollar a day, so this is no good reason why she should be required to accept a salary which is less than sufficient for her means.[40]

Standardizing nurses' fee within a locality, with hospitals consulting one another before contemplating changes to nursing remuneration, became a time-honored tradition and as nurses became hospital employees this was resorted to by hospitals for determining nurse salary levels and keeping them low.[41] This oligopolistic market structure, in which a few buyers of nursing services, the hospitals, determined a standard rate regardless of market demand, resulted in stagnant nurse salary levels that were nonresponsive to normal supply and demand mechanisms.[42]

The fee-setting mechanism is significant not just for its effect on nurse remuneration. The active participation of nurses in fee setting through their agents, either the alumnae associations or the central registry, challenges traditional stereotypes of nurses as helpless victims of more powerful men-dominated physician and hospital groups who set fees without input from nurses.[43] The negotiations in which registries engaged with hospital boards resembled those of trade unions' discussions with employers. Although hospital boards did not always grant fee increase requests, evidence exists to indicate the concerted action of organized groups of nurses was a source of strength and frequently success, such as in the NYCR's experience in determining and elevating private duty nurse fees.

The NYCR set initial fees for nurses at $25 per week or $4 per day, a standard private duty fee for 1910. Alcoholic, insane, and contagious cases, patients with nervous disorders, and the first two weeks of obstetrical cases were all charged $5 a week more.[44] Nurses charged higher fees for patients with certain disease conditions or health states, such as obstetrical cases, in which the nurse cared for two patients, not one, or in substance abuse or psychiatric cases, in which patient safety and well-being demanded the constant presence of the nurse without breaks. NYCRNA member alumnae associations recommended fees adopted by the NYCR, which reflected typical rates charged by city alumnae association registries. Vigilance on the part of member associations insured adherence to local rates and NYCRNA received challenges when members believed the association shirked this duty.[45] In May 1912 the AGNMB inquired of NYCRNA's executive committee as to why the NYCR rates did not rise to the amount set by a group of alumnae associations the past October.[46] Registry rates did rise the following November.[47]

The 1912 increase in fees applied to the weekly rate charged patients, which was raised from $25 to $28 per week. The fee increase and the united effort alumnae associations employed to achieve it received the attention of the local press. A *New York Times* article claimed that the actions of the "nurses trust," composed of hospital alumnae association registries and the NYCR, would cause a rise in the cost of illness.[48] The article resulted in a flurry of letters to the *Times* arguing for and against the higher fees. One physician wrote that in his experience nurses who charged higher rates were not more efficient and maintained lofty ideals of their value to patients.[49] A nurse responded that the rate increase was a necessity created by higher costs of living.[50] Another nurse challenged the notion that a graduate nurse in good standing would work for less than $25 a week, implying it was only untrained nurses who accepted lower fees.[51]

In 1918, the registry increased the daily fee to $5 a day.[52] Some hospitals refused to agree to the higher charge, maintaining the $4 rate as acceptable for their patients. At the 1919 annual NYCRNA membership meeting this issue received vigorous discussion, during which NYCRNA leadership noted that the association had approached hospital boards, which failed to approve the $5 rate, requesting a reversal of their decision. Several hospitals were willing to compromise on a $4.50 fee, but most wanted to keep the lower rate. NYCRNA appointed a committee of alumnae association members to formulate a plan to obtain compliance with the $5 charge. The meeting minutes noted an unusual degree of participation from the membership, which highlighted the comments of private duty nurses who all agreed the $5 daily rate was fair.[53] S. S. Goldwater, director of Mt. Sinai Hospital, chairman of the Committee on Hospitals, General Medical Board, and Council of National Defense during World War I, and former member of the NYCR's governing board, noted the success of the alumnae associations' efforts to increase private duty rates. He acknowledged justification for the increase but feared it would decrease enrollment of nurses in the army needed for war service.[54] The registry later instituted another increase to $6 a day in 1920.[55]

The Patient of Moderate Means

The $25 per week rate for private duty nurse care was widely accepted throughout the country up to World War I with professional journal articles frequently citing it as the standard rate.[56] Fees also customarily included the cost of the nurse's meals. The patient's family supplied meals to nurses who cared for patients in the home. Hospitalized patients paid a fee to the hospital for the nurses' meals, with the hospital supplying the meals. Hospitals raised revenue from this system by charging patients a larger amount for the nurses' meal than the meal cost and then pocketing any profits.

Charges for both the private duty nurses and the inclusion of her meals made the expense of private nursing care out of reach for most of the population. Estimates of who hired private duty nurses are difficult to make for the early decades of the twentieth century. One 1915 survey completed in New York State reported that of 113 women undergoing childbirth at home only one had the continuous care of a graduate nurse. Of those surveyed forty-nine received continuous care not from a professional nurse but rather from a practical (not trained) nurse.[57] Commentators acknowledged that wealthy people used private nursing, poor individuals used visiting nurse services, and middle-income patients worked out sick care arrangements as best they could.[58]

Nurses, aware that high fees limited their services to only the wealthy, searched for ways to increase the availability of care to those of more moderate means. Methods suggested included establishing special funds that patients could draw from to pay the regular private nursing fee, sick benefit societies to which patients could contribute and use in the event of illness, and free care supplied by nurses. One example of a special fund was the Crerar Fund of Chicago, established through a legacy left to the Illinois Training School for Nurses (ITSN). The Crerar Fund allowed low-income workers who required nursing care to contribute a portion of the nurses' fee while the school contributed the difference.[59] In another scheme tried out in Cincinnati, nurses registered with the central registry were required to volunteer a certain amount of time for free care. The Cincinnati registry envisioned eventually establishing a fund that would compensate the nurses for such care.[60]

The NYCR adopted a variation of the free care method, sometimes referred to as the Toronto Method.[61] The registry accepted charity cases, assigning nurses whose names were at the bottom of the list of on-call nurses and who agreed previously to take charity patients. The nurse accepted what the patient could pay. A nurse on a charity case was relieved when a regular case became available for her.[62]

Providing free or reduced-price nursing care was disadvantageous to nurses and was thought to be demeaning to patient recipients. Commentators on the subject in nursing journals presumed self-respecting workers would avoid any form of charity as a humiliating experience. Many expressed concern that providing charity care to self-supporting patients encouraged dependence.[63] One optional payment method for lower-income patients was the sliding scale, which referred to the adoption of a different rate of charges based on a patient's ability to pay, a practice often used by physicians. Sliding scales received extensive discussion at professional meetings and in journal articles. Editorials in the *American Journal of Nursing* (*AJN*), the official journal of the ANA, commended sliding scales as the best solution to extending nursing care to the middle class.[64]

Although physicians reported success with sliding scales, support for the scheme among nurses was lukewarm. Doctors who saw many patients in one day had the potential to make up reduced fees from poorer patients with visits to the wealthy. Private duty nurses who cared for one patient over extended periods of time might be locked in a low-income situation for weeks.[65] The practical aspects of determining which patients were and were not able to pay the regular fee baffled nurses, who seemed hesitant to investigate patient finances. Nurses were also suspicious that wealthy patients would unfairly claim poverty to reap commercial advantages from a sliding scale.[66]

The main opposition to sliding scales centered on the use of a local standardized rate of nurses' fees, which nurses maintained was essential in an unregulated, competitive market.[67] "The remuneration for the services of the thoroughly trained and graduated nurse is one of the most fixed, immutable and unalterable laws of mankind; it is $25.00 a week, including room and board," complained one physician in discussing the subject.[68] Nurses feared that if fees varied, the door would be open to price wars between professional graduate nurses and untrained nurse workers, with the eventual outcome of below-market rates for nursing care. Even those supportive of sliding scales cautioned that it required careful consideration when being instituted.[69] Lavinia Dock supported set fees, suggesting that sliding scales be limited to nurses enrolled in a strong central registry able to withstand any assault on charges from rival groups.[70] At a 1907 NYCRNA meeting, members voiced disapproval of sliding scales but noted the custom was in vogue. A committee appointed to investigate a sliding scale of prices subsequently determined it was not practical to institute.[71]

The frustration involved in devising a lower-cost solution to private nursing and the rigid pattern of nurses' fees led to suggestions for revision in the nurse remuneration system. Some believed it a poor economic practice to set an across-the-board fee for all practitioners regardless of experience or skill. Nurses newly graduated from schools of nursing could expect to command the same rate of pay as those who had been working for several years.[72] The only means private duty nurses had available to increase their income was to take more cases, a situation dependent on the supply of nurses and demand for their services.

A graded registry, which combined a sliding scale of charges for different types of nurses by categorizing nurse workers per schooling and skill, offered an alternative to the standard rate and relief for those with moderate incomes when confronted with nurses' bills.[73] Nurses with higher classifications charged higher fees; those with less training or experience worked for less. Proponents of graded registries envisioned an organized system in which the nurse educational system would graduate different levels of nurses; the registry system would then distribute them to patients appropriately, thus relieving some of the costs of nursing care. Yet, a graded registry had considerable flaws. Objections included the fact that those who could afford the higher-priced nurse might opt for a lower-cost one to save money. Less well-off individuals would be forced to choose the cheaper and less-qualified nurse regardless of their illness. This seemed unfair and incompatible with professional ideals, which dictated that patient need rather than ability to pay should determine patient assignment.[74]

The graded registry scheme was intertwined with the subsidiary worker problem and appealed to health-care leaders searching for ways to provide low-cost care. A 1908 American Hospital Association (AHA) subcommittee on nurse training, which examined the issue of providing care to the middle-class patients, blamed high-priced graduate nurses who adhered too strictly to set fees for denying care to the middle class. The subcommittee chairman, Rev. A. S. Kavanagh, superintendent of Brooklyn's Methodist-Episcopal Hospital, believed hospitals should adopt the graded nurse scheme to introduce a cheaper type of nurse worker. Chairman Kavanagh declared, "If nurses continue to consider $25 or $30 per week as part of the standard which they must always maintain to safeguard their honor, then our hospitals must remember their duty to the whole community and seriously take up the question of supplying this need."[75] The AHA subsequently appointed a committee that presented a plan in 1914 for the grading and classifying of nurses. The classification plan provided for three levels of nurse workers: Grade A, registered or graduate nurses; Grade B, attendant nurses; and Grade C, household nurses.[76] This plan received significant opposition from nursing groups and the AHA never acted upon it.[77] Opponents of nurse grading were concerned that no regulatory mechanisms existed for confining the lower-grade nurses to their intended patients.[78] Yet, the idea of different levels of nurses assigned to patients based on nursing care needs remained a favored approach to solving the problem of high-cost nursing care and rationalizing a confusing system of care delivery that relied on patient ability to pay as the prime determinant of who received a nurse.

The Nurse Registry Business

As a commercial enterprise, the first years of operations were disappointing for the new venture. NYCR membership increased only gradually and finances were poor despite strenuous efforts at promoting registry services and curtailing expenses. Survival of the registry depended on yearly subsidies from the alumnae associations. The situation changed around 1915, when the NYCR's prospects improved; expressions of confidence in the business from nurses, physicians, and the public were noted. By 1920, the NYCR was self-supporting, had paid back bonds to finance the initial operation with interest, and no longer requested subsidies from the alumnae associations.[79]

Registry productiveness can be evaluated by examining two aspects of the agency's operation: the number of patient calls received and filled, and membership totals. Although exact figures on the number of patient calls received and filled and membership statistics are sparse for the initial years of NYCR operations, data which do exist provide some understanding of how well the registry functioned. The number of patient calls received provides a rough indication of how much business the registry received by those requiring nursing services. Percentages of calls filled suggest how well the registry met demand for its services.

For the initial years of operation, from 1911 to 1915, patient calls averaged a meager 95.6 per month. A turnaround occurred in 1918, when patient calls received soared to 612 per month. The large increase in calls observed in 1918 was most likely connected to the deadly flu epidemic, which contributed to a greater demand for nursing services overall. By 1923 the NYCR was receiving an average of 433 calls per month (see table 3.1).[80]

By the early 1920s, greater consumer awareness of registry services and better publicity explains some of the increase in calls received. The governing board of the NYCR invested considerable time and effort considering how to more effectively inform the public of registry services, with circulars of information periodically passed out to groups thought good sources of business. As physician groups were the prime source of referrals for nursing services, the registry directed heavy publicity to them. A contemporary idea that individuals living alone in hotels were a population in need of nursing care when ill led registry officials to also distribute circulars at city hotels. The various advertising schemes put into action by the registry proved successful.[81]

Membership totals gauged registry effectiveness. Professional registries depended for income on yearly registrant fees, a practice that varied from that of commercial registries, which charged nurses a percentage of each case they received. Dependence on fees meant that registries relied heavily on increasing the number of nurse registrants enrolled on the registry rather than the number of patient calls for financial solvency.

NYCR membership increased slowly. Between 1911 and 1915 membership averaged 185 nurses a year. By 1923, the average number of nurses listed as members increased to 550.[82] Two factors—a general increase in the number of graduate nurses entering the labor market and an expansion of NYCRNA—led to membership growth. The tremendous increase in schools of nursing in the initial decades of the twentieth century led to greater numbers of graduates each year. The number of nurses graduating from schools of nursing nationally almost doubled in a ten-year period from 8,140 in 1910 to 14,980 in 1920.[83] In New York City, 827 students graduated in 1918.[84] Adding graduate nurses to the local labor market at the rate of almost 900 a year easily contributed to a significant increase in membership. A reconfiguration of NYSNA in 1919 replacing the

Table 3.1.

New York Central Registry patient calls received and filled, 1911–1915, 1918, 1923

Date	Patient calls received (average per month)	Patient calls filled (average per month)	Percentage filled	Membership
1911	113[a]	84[a]	74[a]	161[b]
1912	104[c]	84[c]	80[c]	186[d]
1913	94[e]	68[f]	87[f]	201[g]
1914	73[h]	63[i]	79[i]	196[j]
1915	94[k]	77[k]	81[k]	375[k]
1918	612[l]	376[l]	64[l]	418[l]
1923	433[m]	n/a	n/a	550[m]

Sources: Figures for 1911–1915: "Minutes, Governing Board, Central Registry, NYCRNA," 1913–1914, box 8, NYCRNAP; figures for 1918: "Minutes, Executive Committee, NYCRNA," 1918, box 15, NYCRNAP; figures for 1923: "Minutes, Registry Committee, NYCRNA," 2 November 1923, box 8, NYCRNAP.

[a] Average based on number of patient calls received and filled for February and May 1911.

[b] Based on membership totals for May 1911.

[c] Average based on number of patient calls received and filled for January, February, April, and November 1912.

[d] Average based on membership totals for April and November 1911.

[e] Average based on number of patient calls received for January, April, May, June, September, and October 1913.

[f] Average based on number of patient calls filled for January, April, June, September, and October 1913.

[g] Average based on membership totals for April, June, and October 1913.

[h] Average based on number of patient calls received for March, April, May, June, July, August, September, October, and December 1914.

[i] Average based on number of patient calls filled for March, April, May, June, July, August, September, and December 1914.

[j] Average based on membership totals for April, May, June, September, and December 1914.

[k] Based on figures for January 1915.

[l] Average based on patient calls received and filled and membership totals for March, May, and June 1918.

[m] Average as reported in minutes; based on unknown months.

county system with district associations further explains the registry's increased membership. NYCRNA became District 13 of NYSNA and included not just New York County and the borough of Manhattan, but also the counties of Bronx, Richmond, and Westchester.[85] The expansion resulted in new registrants becoming eligible for and enrolling in the registry.

Despite the increase in membership and generally upbeat reports of registry business, the registry varied in its ability to fill calls received for nurses.

Between 1911 and 1915 the registry had a decent call fill rate, averaging 78 percent. During the boom year of 1918, the registry filled only 64 percent of calls.[86] The rate of calls filled is a rough index of nurse supply and demand. In 1918, several events affected nurse supply. The most profound was the flu epidemic, which not only increased demand for nurses but removed many nurses from the labor market as they also fell victim to the flu.[87] World War I military service further decreased the number of available nurses.[88]

Given these two events, it is probable that the NYCR experienced more trouble filling requests for nurses. Although reports of nurse shortages surfaced nationwide, the NYCR reported its best membership totals to date. Tremendous increase in demand for nurse services in a market with fewer overall workers because of the flu epidemic and armed services requirements can explain some of the decreases in filled calls, although it is possible the registry used inefficient practices in distributing nurses.

Maintaining a high rate of calls filled could characterize a dependable service, one which would receive repeated calls from those in need of nursing care. The registry seemed oddly oblivious to this fact. In the early years of business, such as in 1913, a year when the registry filled almost 90 percent of calls received, records document concern over filling calls. Despite that excellent record, NYCRNA's executive committee called for greater effort on the part of the registry in meeting demand for nurses.[89] By 1918, the registry perceived unfilled calls caused by a scarcity of nurses as an operational crisis, but they did not outline plans for improving the matter.[90]

Although records for the next few years fail to include exact figures on patient calls received and filled and membership rolls, as the registry entered the 1920s positive reports of registry business are noted. Finances were good enough to increase the registrar's salary and hire additional staff for the office.[91] The 1920 nurses' fee increase to $6 for twelve-hour shifts indicated confidence that requests for nurses were adequate and permitted higher rates. The NYCR settled into the routine of running a professional nurse placement service. Registry officials expressed satisfaction with the progress of the venture.

Conclusion

By 1920, the private duty labor market had to respond and adapt as a different field in which many workers competed with one another for jobs and powerful interest groups, such as physicians and hospitals, influenced working conditions. Graduate nurses found limited work alternatives in other places. Private duty nursing was an expensive commodity that many people needed, but few could afford.

Professional nursing organizations viewed participation in the field through district association-run registries as integral to the interests of the profession, critical to the proper distribution of nurses to the community, and protective of nurse workers. When a district association operated a private duty registry, it consumed a significant amount of time and money and often required compromises in meeting professional goals. District-run central registries served as an intermediary between nurses, their patient employers, and hospitals, which forced professional associations to confront issues on a pragmatic rather than idealistic basis. The interest of rank-and-file nurses in obtaining favorable working conditions at a fair wage conflicted with that of registry leaders, who emphasized the dependable, professional nature of the service. When registries supplied nurse workers, deciding who was and was not eligible to nurse sick patients took on meaning sometimes incongruent with the values of the professional association. Further, the need to establish the worth of nursing care via private duty fees propelled districts into activities that resembled those of trade unions. Entering the nurse labor market as a distributor and quasi-employer of nurses introduced an element of commercialism into professional affairs that proved difficult for professional leaders to reconcile with their visions of self-sacrificing nursing service. In New York, alumnae groups gave support but continued to maintain their local hospital-based registries, restricting the market for the NYCR. The private duty market was, above all, a local service requiring knowledge of local practices.

Despite problems, NYCRNA claimed success in the first ten years it managed a central registry and pointed to growing numbers of patient calls for nurses as proof that the agency accomplished its intended purposes. Moreover, the steady increase in membership provided the income necessary to sustain operations and testified to critical support among graduate nurses for professionally run registries. Further, as was seen in practices revolving around fee setting, private duty nurses exerted a degree of control over their conditions of work.

Professional nurse registries were not the only agencies providing nurses to the general population. A collection of other registries of both a nonprofit and commercial nature competed with professional nurse registries for the same patients and nurse workers. The professional associations believed they were the best ones to distribute nursing services on a low-cost, nonprofit basis. They would spend over seventy years trying to find solutions to a competitive labor market plagued with problems of inefficiency, ineffectiveness, and obsolescence.

Chapter 4

Surpluses, Shortages, and Segregation

By the end of World War I, many stakeholders wanted to study the nursing profession. Professional leaders supported campaigns to investigate nursing issues, believing they could use such studies as a mechanism through which to achieve educational reform.[1] Professional working nurses, confronting an increasingly crowded labor market, searched for solutions to problems in obtaining and maintaining gainful, consistent employment. Coincidentally, health-care industry analysts and physicians awakened to the crisis surrounding payment of nursing care. Deciding who should deliver nursing care, the type of education received by those employed as nurses, and the means through which to finance nursing care were central in the ongoing debate regarding illness care.

Groups responsible for funding and carrying out studies on nursing represented a cross section of parties interested in nursing and health-care issues, such as professional nursing organizations, physician and hospital associations, public health groups, lay individuals, and charitable philanthropic foundations. For example, C.E.A. Winslow, an important twentieth-century public health analyst, and founder and chair of the Yale University Department (later School) of Public Health, was an early researcher on the wider concerns about health care delivery. In addition, M. Adelaide Nutting, professor at Columbia University's Teachers College program, had a long history of advocating improved educational models for nursing. New voices such as analyst Janet Geister, nurse, researcher, and future executive director of the American Nurses Association (ANA), and statistician May Ayres Burgess served in leadership capacities on several of the studies. Both Geister and Burgess epitomized the reform movement in nursing dedicated to designing innovative and efficient models of nursing care delivery.

Physicians who served on studies presented a more complex, self-interested point of view. William Darrach, dean of Columbia University's College of Physicians and Surgeons, served as chair of the Committee on the Grading of Nursing Schools (CGNS), a position that presumably called for a degree of neutrality. In a crucial encounter with the New York Academy of Medicine's executive committee as the CGNS was in its formative stage, Darrach placed his spin on the aims of the study, reflecting physician views of nursing. "The Committee was appointed with a two-fold idea," Darrach explained, "one to help the nurses and the other to keep track on the nurses, so that whatever they did would be supervised by the medical profession."[2] Darrach admitted that nursing education was in "an awful mess," and that "the main thing is to have nursing education on a sounder basis."[3] Members of the academy responded to Darrach's remarks with predictable candor. One physician noted that "nursing education is in control of women who will not brook any control from medical men. They have an exaggerated idea of their profession."[4]

Historians examining early studies into nursing tend to concentrate on their relevance for educational matters and reform, the areas on which the studies focused. Still, each investigation devoted considerable attention to the nurse labor market, making an examination of each study from a nursing workforce perspective both illuminating and necessary. Findings tended to be consistent and validated professional nursing leaders' ideas on the cause of nurse employment problems; they believed problems stemmed from the fact that the private duty/student system of care delivery was an inefficient, expensive, and poor distributor of nursing services, preventing nurses from securing stable jobs. Published recommendations echoed nursing leaders' assertions that extensive reform, reorganization, and redistribution of nurse workers were imperative. The key method suggested for improving care delivery involved substituting graduate nurses for students to deliver patient care in hospitals and requiring schools of nursing to exist solely as educational institutions. Staffing hospitals with a permanent corps of employed nurses would free students to learn, allow patients to receive adequate nursing during hospitalization, and ensure steady employment for graduate nurses.

The Post–World War I Nurse Labor Force

The 1920 U.S. Census figures listed approximately 301,124 individuals working as nurses, of whom about 149,128 were either graduate, registered, or student nurses.[5] Acute care hospitals, although major consumers of private duty services, did not employ many nurses; the clear majority of nurses, 80 percent in 1920, worked in the private duty field. Hospital or institutional nursing and the public area of health claimed the remaining 20 percent evenly divided between the two areas. Student nurses numbered about fifty-five thousand.[6] This contingent of graduate and student nurses comprised the professional nurse workforce employed in institutions, health care agencies, and private homes.

Hospitals and other medical establishments employed approximately ten to eleven thousand nurses, most of whom did not deliver direct patient care but worked as supervisors, administrators, or educators.[7] A survey published in 1920 on New York City hospitals completed by the Public Health Committee of the New York Academy of Medicine found that 36 percent of the nursing staff in hospitals with training schools or affiliated with training schools were gradu-ate nurses.[8] The Public Health Committee estimated that 3 to 37 percent of the graduate nursing staff were engaged in teaching and supervisory work, which frequently overlapped with bedside nursing care activities, making a clear delineation between the three tasks difficult. Reports on the nurse labor market during the 1920s consistently blamed nursing care delivery problems on a lack of graduate nurses for bedside care; assumptions were that fully trained gradu-ate nurses were in short supply for direct patient care.

In general, direct patient contact with graduate nurses was limited to those patients who hired private duty nurses. The use of private duty nurses for hos-pital care represented a transition from original models of home-based private nursing care established in the late nineteenth century. An abandonment of home care occurred during the initial decades of the twentieth century as patients and nurses began favoring institutions for sickness care. The emergence of private duty as a predominantly hospital-based service most likely took place over a period of years, appearing in different parts of the country at different times. In Illinois, for example, complaints that nurses were refusing home cases in preference for hospital cases emerged in the early 1920s.[9] Both the 1923 *Nurs-ing and Nursing Education in the United States* (Goldmark) report and the 1926 NYSNA study on conditions in the private duty market estimated that three-fifths of all cases taken by private duty nurses were in hospitals.[10] By the late 1920s, hospital-based private duty care was the norm.[11] The CGNS survey of two hundred professional registries in 1928 revealed that 79 percent of calls received were for hospital cases.[12]

Student nurses delivered most of the bedside nursing care in the 1,800 hos-pitals that operated schools of nursing.[13] The status of caregivers in hospitals without a school of nursing is indeterminate. Many of these hospitals may have used attendants trained specifically by the hospital or hired individuals who demonstrated some capacity for nursing. The 1920 New York City hospital study estimated that "trained attendants, ward helpers and so-called 'practical' nurses" delivered 7 percent of the care given in hospitals with training schools.[14]

Small fluctuations in the numbers of nurses could set off worries about nurse shortages and instigate actions to increase supply. An illustration of how a temporary change in supply created the perception of a crisis is found in the post–World War I era.

A Nursing Shortage

Following World War I, reports in professional journals indicated that the number of applicants to schools of nursing dropped slightly.[15] As the decline was in the number of entering students, decreases in the number of graduate nurses did not show up until 1922. The situation reversed quickly and by 1924 the number of graduate nurses was well above 1920 levels and continued to climb throughout the decade.[16] Despite increased numbers of nurses, reports of nurse shortages persisted.[17]

Uniform agreement existed that the shortage was of hospital bedside nurses, and that the shortage was relative and directly connected to an increase in demand for nurse services.[18] The heightened demand for bedside nurses was caused in part by factors such as increasing hospital use and construction, which increased space and the number of beds available. For instance, between 1918 and 1928 more than 1,500 new hospitals opened, with an expansion in bed capacity of almost 300,000 beds over 1918 levels.[19] In addition, the complexity of patients' hospital care increased. New treatments emerged. With these treatments, a broad range of newly introduced patient services such as radiological, laboratory, and therapeutic services consumed more and more nursing time.

Early twentieth century hospitals exhibited a sparse employee structure devoid of the multiple layers of workers seen in today's institutions. Student nurses had to be all-around hospital workers capable of performing any job, including nonnursing tasks such as food preparation, formula-making, messenger service, patient escort, and cleaning functions, further claiming student time.[20] One of the effects of more elaborate, labor-intensive hospitals was an overall increased demand for student nurse labor.

Student nurses also had increased demands in the classroom. Although schools of nursing remained focused on patient care delivery rather than student education, increased rigor in educational standards appeared in the World War I era. In 1917, the National League for Nursing Education (NLNE) released its first *Standard Curriculum for Schools of Nursing*, which outlined the components of a good nursing school and included recommendations on increased class time and decreased hours spent on patient care for students.[21] Hospitals were under no obligation to follow the standards and most did not. Even the NLNE failed to recommend wholesale adoption of the standards, recognizing that most schools were in no position to reduce hours spent by students in patient care. The *Standard Curriculum* foreshadowed a trend in which students spent more time in class and less time on patient units.[22]

Graduate nurses were a vast presence in the labor market, yet their services were unavailable to most patients. Fees charged by private duty nurses and the rigid method of providing private duty services, requiring that patients hire nurses for twenty-four hours, seven days a week, continued to place nursing care out of the financial reach of most sick people. The idea that private duty nurses were underutilized and spent an inordinate amount of time waiting for cases became conventional wisdom by the early 1920s. Determining how to distribute skilled nursing services and provide enough work for graduate nurses, while educating the nursing workforce, was the core problem. Proposed solutions can be classified roughly into two primary categories: the supply-side approach and the reform method.

Proponents of the supply-side approach held to the idea that nurses caused shortage conditions. Supply-siders thought nurse educators held impossibly high standards, which not only took students away from patient care for class activities but also created overeducated graduates who subsequently shunned careers as bedside nurses. Those graduate nurses who did work at patients' bedsides in the private duty field demanded exorbitant fees, which the average ill individual was unable to pay. Supply-siders advocated a system of short training courses in nursing for women willing to work for low wages.[23] Short-course nurses remained a mainstay of proposals to alleviate shortage conditions throughout the century. By 1934, ten states regulated the practice of subsidiary or short-course workers. These laws failed to achieve popularity, and few people applied for licenses. In four of these states, Michigan, New York, Virginia, and Pennsylvania, only 1,251 individuals received licenses under these laws.[24] Lost on many who favored such proposals was the fact that one hundred fifty thousand people, either untrained in nursing or trained with a short course, were already present in the job market. It was well known that this group of nurse workers charged and received fees not much different from those of professional nurses, eliminating any cost advantage to a short-course nurse. Lack of regulation and control over these workers continued to create problems.[25]

Not surprisingly, nursing leaders were in the vanguard of the reform movement, which focused on quality rather than quantity. Believing the problem was not a shortage of students but rather a shortage of qualified applicants to schools,

reformers held to the goal of establishing a true educational system that eliminated student labor, thus attracting higher-qualified candidates to schools.
Reformers wanted hospital reliance on student labor as a cost-saving measure
to cease. In reformers' eyes, student nurses deserved schools in which education was the priority. By replacing students with graduate nurses employed in
staff positions, students could focus on educative activities. Improving the educational experience would better prepare graduates for delivery of the complex
care that leaders thought represented the future of nursing and enable hospitals
to offer steady, reliable work to graduate nurses, eliminating the employment
problems experienced by private duty nurses.

Convinced their ideas were sound, logical, and practical, professional leaders promoted this general scheme throughout the early decades of the twentieth century, spending years seeking support for their plans.

"Your Money and Your Life"

On April 30, 1925, private duty nurses, frustrated over poor working conditions
in New York City, met at the Central Club for Nurses to map out a plan for shorter
hours and higher fees for private duty service in hospitals. Dr. Augustus Downing, assistant commissioner of education of New York State, attended the meeting, cautioning the nurses to moderate their demands so that higher fees would
not restrict nurse services to the wealthy. Newspaper reports of the meeting
noted the unhappiness of those in the audience to Downing's remarks. "Hisses
were sounded. . . . His [Downing's] remarks were interrupted often by cries from
the room."[26] Eventually, the nurses agreed to a proposal suggested by Downing
that further study occur. The result of the gathering was to request that the New
York Counties Registered Nurses Association (NYCRNA) conduct a study of private duty nursing within the New York City area. NYCRNA asked the registry
committee of the central registry to assume responsibility for the investigation,
which the committee was willing to do.[27]

A second NYSNA district in Buffalo appointed a committee to conduct
a similar type of study. NYSNA combined the two projects into one state-
sponsored survey on the economic conditions of private duty nursing, appoint-
ing Janet Geister as director.[28] Geister, a member of NYCRNA's registry committee,
was eminently qualified to guide the investigation because of her experience in
conducting field studies and surveys. Geister recognized that complaints of physicians and nurses differed.[29] Physicians were interested in obtaining nurses
easily and cheaply; nurses' concerns centered on low wages and poor working
conditions. Geister's announced goal for the NYSNA study was to generate information on actual conditions within the nurse job market, diagnose the exact

problems with private duty nursing, and formulate ways to distribute nurses better.[30] The study, carried out between 1925 and 1926, became a landmark investigation of conditions in the private duty market, exposing extreme working conditions for nurses and validating a need to reorganize the job market.

The NYSNA study consisted of questionnaires completed by nurses on a variety of factors such as the number of days and hours worked, patient charges, income, type and location of cases obtained, and years spent in private duty nursing.[31] Nurses completed the questionnaires during a one-week period in February 1926. The study provided a plethora of data on critical components of private duty work and investigated demand for nurses, how well the market met nurse employment needs, and the difficulties physicians claimed they experienced in obtaining nurses.

The first and most significant indicator of how well the private nurse job market operated was the number of days spent by nurses on call without cases, a value providing some measure of how successfully the market met nurse demand for work. Some explanation of the way private duty nurses obtained patients clarifies the significance of days on call.

Nurses signified availability for cases by placing their names "on call" at their registry. Once a nurse notified the registry she was on call certain obligations ensued, such as being available by telephone for messages, notifying the registry when leaving home for any reason, and promising to be ready to travel to a patient's home or hospital within a reasonable period from the time she received a case.[32] A nurse on call was considered ready and anxious for work. A day on call was not comparable to a day off but resembled more a day in which a worker might show up for work but receive neither a job nor pay. Of the total number of possible days of work the nurses included in the study could work, 72 percent were actual working days. Sickness accounted for 5 percent of the possible days of work. Days listed as not worked accounted for the remaining 23 percent. The high rate of days of work spent waiting for new patients and not working, amounting to almost a quarter of the possible days of work, pointed to a very inefficient job market (see table 4.1).

The second measure of private duty employment level is days spent on cases. Unlike traditional jobs that involve a specified number of work days per week with designated days off, private duty nurses worked each day continuously from the start of a case to its termination. Nurses preferred long cases, which provided reliable income and reduced time spent in waiting for new patients. Nurses in the study worked an average of five days a week; this period was considered less than ideal for private duty nurses. Geister highlighted 47 percent of nurses who worked less than seven days a week as evidence of

Table 4.1.
Average private duty nursing workweek in New York State, 1926

Category	Value
Average number of days worked	5 (72% of possible work days)
Average fee charged patients	$5–7
Average weekly earnings of nurses	$31.26

Source: Janet Geister, "Report of a Survey of Private Duty Nursing," in *Proceedings, Official Meeting, New York State Nurses Association, 24th Annual Meeting, 1925,* ed. NYSNA, NYSNAP, AC-2, box 5, Bellevue Alumni Center for Nursing History, Guilderland, NY.
Note: Averages based on one workweek in February 1926.

Table 4.2.
Number of days per week private duty nurses employed, 1926

Days per week	Percentage of nurses worked
5–7 days	68[a]
3–4 days	13
1–2 days	7
Did not work	12

Source: Janet Geister, "Report of a Survey of Private Duty Nursing," in *Proceedings, Official Meeting, New York State Nurses Association, 24th Annual Meeting, 1925,* ed. NYSNA, NYSNAP, AC-2, box 5, Bellevue Alumni Center for Nursing History, Guilderland, NY.
Note: "Employed" means spent on cases.
[a] Forty-seven percent of nurses worked six days or less.

low employment. Nurses working seven days nonstop comprised 53 percent of the respondents. Sixty-eight percent of nurses worked at least five days a week but more than 30 percent of nurses studied were well below acceptable levels for days of work (see table 4.2).

Geister's concerns about days per week worked reflected contemporary understandings of special duty conventions. When looked at from the perspective of hours worked per week, a different picture emerges. Given that 80 percent of the cases worked by nurses in the study entailed twelve-hour shifts, a five-day workweek equaled sixty hours. Estimates of the average weekly hours of work for general workers in 1920 and 1930 are 49.8 and 47.7 hours, respectively.[33] Despite the higher number of weekly hours worked by nurses in comparison to other employees, Geister interpreted a five-day workweek as an indication of

Table 4.3.
Private duty nurses' hours of work, 1926

Hours of work	Percentage of nurses
12	80
24	20

Source: Janet Geister, "Report of a Survey of Private
Duty Nursing," in *Proceedings, Official Meeting, New
York State Nurses Association, 24th Annual Meeting,
1925*, ed. NYSNA, NYSNAP, AC-2, box 5, Bellevue
Alumni Center for Nursing History, Guilderland, NY.

nurse underemployment. However, about 75 percent of the nurses worked at
least as many hours per week as the average worker, and 68 percent worked
sixty hours or more (see table 4.3).

Overall, the two measures, days on call and length of cases, substantiated
the argument that the job market failed to achieve full employment. For Geister, the persistence of conventions and practices used by nineteenth-century private duty nurses was the main culprit in this failure. Private duty nursing
remained a twenty-four-hour, seven-days-a-week service delivered from the
beginning of illness to its conclusion. The custom made sense when patients
requiring constant attention received care in their homes. It seemed practical to
bring the nurse to the patient. As patients sought out hospital care, private duty
nurses simply transferred their conventional home-based practices intact to
institutional settings. However, hospital care was different. Unlike private homes
where patients were isolated, hospitals grouped sick people together and possessed the potential, which Geister believed was yet unrealized, to develop
distinct and improved nursing care delivery models. Geister challenged the
notion that ill individuals required continuous nursing care. Such care was
prohibitively expensive for most patients and frequently unnecessary. Patients
locked into twenty-four-hour nursing care paid for more care than most needed.[34]

Results of the NYSNA studies confirmed the belief that private duty nursing was in serious difficulty, as 40 percent of the respondents indicated that they
planned to leave private duty in the future, demonstrating nurses' discontent
and suggesting to Geister that private duty required fundamental changes. She
cited the number of nurses not working a full week, irregular employment, the
short working life of private duty nurses, and uncertain and low income as proof
that reform was essential.

Geister advised a radical reorganization of nursing care delivery service,
promoting as a first step the distribution of nurses into central clearinghouses

or registries. Adopting the early twentieth-century idea of a central registry as a community center for all nursing needs, Geister recommended the expansion and standardization of such agencies as an efficient method of dispersing all levels and types of nursing services. Centralized registries could offer alternatives to traditional care delivery patterns, decrease nursing care costs, and enable more people to avail themselves of private care when sick. Geister proposed diversification of nurse services into group nursing, which entailed the assignment of one nurse to more than one patient, each paying a portion of the nurses' fee, and hourly nursing, which referred to the employment of a private nurse for short periods of time. For those nurses wishing to continue in the traditional one-to-one nurse-patient mode, Geister saw no difficulty. She noted that there would always be patients preferring full-time nurse services and advised those nurses interested in providing private services to affiliate with a registry.

Geister's reasonable solution was not implemented. Despite complaints and discontent over working conditions, nurses demonstrated allegiance to the private duty system. Accounting for this loyalty is not difficult: nurses faced limited occupational choices, and private duty, although unattractive, was the one employment option open to most graduates.

The NYSNA study also revealed an additional reason private duty remained a major field of employment. The average weekly salary of $31.26 indicated to investigators the low general income of private duty nurses with a mean hourly wage of 49¢ an hour, which Geister claimed was about even with charwomen, servants, and unskilled laborers.[35] A review of the data from a different perspective reveals, however, that 41 percent of the nurses made over $41 a week, a not inconsiderable sum. Nurses earning higher incomes might still have spent substantial time out of work, reducing their annual salary, but the number of nurses commanding weekly salaries greater than the average indicates that the potential existed for better compensation than the norm. Nurses were aware that earnings varied, and some may have entertained thoughts of joining higher income ranks.

Other employment opportunities, such as institutional work, provided regular salaries but were dependent on hospital-controlled rates. Moreover, private duty nurses lived independently, unencumbered by the needs, oversight, and paternalism of the hospital administration. The practice of including maintenance costs (such as the cost of meals, uniforms, etc.) as part of institutional nurses' remuneration, because these nurses were required to live within the confines of the hospital grounds, lessened the appeal of hospital employment.

Less evident and determinate is the number of nurses that either wished to engage in full employment or were dependent on a twelve-month income. Were some nurses more interested in part-time or sporadic employment, for which private duty offered a flexible schedule? What was an acceptable rate of employment for a predominantly women's occupation in 1926? A nearly full week of work for almost 70 percent of the nurses studied may or may not represent a satisfactory rate of employment given the population.

Comments elicited from nurses completing the 1925 survey shed light on their perceptions of private duty. Many complained of the long hours, which caused some to leave the field. Others spoke of their preference for private duty. "I prefer private duty because I would rather do regular bedside nursing. It is more interesting to myself, more to the patient in the case and more serious illness where attention is required," remarked a nurse. Another explained her dislike of hospital work. "I specialize in obstetrics and like it. Like nursing better than anything else I have ever done. Don't like hospital positions. Too much like training days. As my specialty in obstetrics as well as private duty in house, home cases is my work."[36]

The results of the NYSNA study received wide coverage in professional journals and meetings and hit a nerve in professional nursing and medical groups. In 1926, as the Committee on the Grading of Nursing Schools (CGNS) was getting organized, Mary Roberts, editor of the *American Journal of Nursing* and a member of the committee in charge of CGNS's national study of the nursing profession, met with the Rockefeller Foundation's president, George Vincent, to ask his advice as to how to proceed. Roberts reported that the newly formed committee believed in the importance of the NYSNA study but did not want to investigate issues deemed unfriendly or politically sensitive to the hospital and medical groups. Nurse leaders in New York City at the time were acutely aware that physicians were eager to solve nurse supply problems to their advantage. The subcommittee on nursing of the New York City Medical Society was campaigning for a plan to institute a new categorization of nurse workers. NYSNA officials were invited to meetings to discuss the plan, which included adding a less-trained nursing tier, but found the physicians' ideas professionally threatening.[37] The prestigious and powerful New York Academy of Medicine was also deeply involved in efforts to reconfigure the nursing profession, holding conferences on the "Nursing Situation" and releasing recommendations on how to enlarge the supply of nurses.[38] Roberts asked Vincent his opinion on involving other groups, such as doctors, hospitals, and patients, in the new study. Vincent advised Roberts to involve hospital and physician groups interested in nursing issues.[39] This advice was accepted and relayed to other nurse leaders. The CGNS included medical hospital and public health groups (see Appendix).

The Committee on the Grading of Nursing Schools

In 1911, the NLNE sought to develop a method of grading or classifying schools of nursing, believing such a classification scheme, like the approach used by Abraham Flexner in his study of medical schools, was an essential first step in improving nursing education. Carrying out such a project entailed considerable expense, requiring funds the NLNE did not possess. Adelaide Nutting appealed to the Carnegie Foundation in 1911 for financial aid, but it denied the request.[40] For years the project languished. Convinced the project was fundamental to reforming nursing education, the NLNE continued to solicit support from nursing and hospital groups. In 1925, substantial donations from the three national nursing organizations and a gift from Frances Payne Bolton, a wealthy and influential philanthropist to nursing and later a member of Congress, allowed the project to commence. The resulting undertaking, formed as the Committee on the Grading of Nursing Schools (CGNS), would carry out the largest nationwide study of the nurse job market to date.[41] CGNS appointed statistician Dr. May Ayres Burgess as its director, with the membership representing leading national health care associations and experts in the field of education.[42]

The committee intended to accomplish its original goal, which was to study and ensure a steady stream of nurses by carrying out three related projects: a study of supply and demand, a job analysis, and a grading of schools of nursing.[43] The first project, the analysis of the supply and demand for nursing services, was the CGNS work most concerned with the nurse labor market; it involved surveys and questionnaires given to nurses, physicians, and other related groups. The study, published in 1928 as *Nurses, Patients, and Pocketbooks*, was a compilation of each survey's findings.[44] The results of each survey tended to verify the CGNS's ideas regarding problems in the nurse labor market.

In 1928 the professional nurse population in the United States had grown to 197,198. Private duty nurses continued to dominate the profession, claiming 54 percent of nurses. The percentage decline in nurses practicing private duty from 1920 levels reflected both a decrease of approximately thirteen thousand private duty nurses and an increase of fifty thousand total nurses over an eight-year period. The fields of public health and institutional nursing also expanded.

The total number of nurses increased rapidly during the 1920s because of larger numbers of students graduating each year and an increase in the number of schools, which rose from around 1,800 in 1920 to 2,155 in 1928. With the exception of 1922, when the number of graduates declined, approximately 1,200 more nurses graduated each year between 1920 and 1928. The investigators estimated that if the rate of growth continued, sixty thousand nurses would graduate in the year 1965, adding up to a total of 716,794 professional nurses. Many nursing leaders considered this number of nurses unacceptably high given the population of the country and future job prospects for the profession; they could not have predicted the changes occurring in health care over the next decades, or the increasing acceptance of a hospital-based nurse workforce.

Questionnaires completed by 3,392 private duty nurses during one week in March 1927 revealed that the average private duty nurse worked 5.1 days (similar to the findings of the NYSNA survey), waited on call 1 day, and spent 0.9 of a day either resting or sick. Many nurses, 55 percent, worked seven days during the week. Nurses working five days or more accounted for 68 percent of those surveyed. During the week of study, 86 percent of the nurses cared for one case each. Hospital cases accounted for 53 percent of the patients treated by the nurses. For the remaining proportion of patients, care occurred in the home.

The investigators grouped physicians answering questionnaires by specialty, providing an idea of the type of case referrals nurses received. The four types of specialist most commonly using private duty nurses in rank order frequency were surgeons, obstetricians, internists, and general practitioners. The average physician using private duty nurses reported that of three patients requiring a nurse only two patients obtained one. Physicians attributed failure to obtain a nurse to the cost of nursing services. Interestingly, when patients answered a similar question, they identified their inability to find the right kind of nurse, rather than expense, as the greatest problem.

Fees and salaries varied little for private duty nurses. The major difference in private duty fees related to an extra $1 earned by nurses working twenty-four hours (nurses' fees averaged $6 for twelve-hour cases and a bargain $7 for twenty-four-hour care). Private duty nurses averaged a salary of $1,311 per year, which was less than that of nurses in the fields of public health and institutional work, where nurses averaged $1,720 and $2,079, respectively.[45]

The CGNS's private duty nurse registry survey provided the first thorough analysis of nurse registries. Although private duty registries operated in several parts of the country for many years, the workings of these organizations remained unknown. The CGNS located 879 agencies operating private duty registries for nursing services.[46] Of these, 389 returned usable questionnaires and were categorized based on a governing body operating the registry (see table 4.4).

The registry study revealed a weak business performance for registries overall. Only 17 percent of registries made a profit, with 28 percent unaware of their financial status. Registries operated by district nurse associations or commercial enterprises were both more likely to run a profit or break even. Registries operated

Table 4.4.
Registry categories

Category of registry	Percentage
Hospital or alumni	63
District association, nurses club, or commercial	24
Individual or small firm	10
Other	3

Source: May Ayres Burgess, ed., *Nurses, Patients, and Pocketbooks* (New York: Committee on the Grading of Nursing Schools, 1928), 70–71.
Note: Percentages are per the controlling body operating the registry.

by hospitals or alumnae associations, run mainly as small companies, exhibited less familiarity with their financial situation and more than half did not employ a full-time administrator. Only 200 of the 389 registries could answer questions regarding calls received and filled for patients. Of those registries that kept records on patient calls, the vast majority of calls received (79 percent) were for hospitalized patients. During a one-week period in January 1928, the registries received 9,696 calls for nurses and filled 9,574 of them, a 98 percent fill rate. Although 84 percent of the registries reported that hospital calls were easier to fill, the high fill rate for both home and hospital calls pointed to the ease patients had in obtaining nurses. Requests for nurses for home-based cases in larger cities were easier to fill. The investigators concluded that the number of nurses flocking to the major cities in search of work overcrowded the job market in those areas, creating a need for nurses to take any available case even if it was in the less desirable home setting.

Over 50 percent of the registries placed those who were not registered nurses. Practical nurses headed the list of subsidiary workers placed by registries, with an assortment of other workers such as orderlies, hospital maids, and domestics also placed. Most registries that placed subsidiary workers were in the district association, commercial, and individually run categories. A small number of hospital-based registries, 12 percent, reported enrolling practical nurses, demonstrating that a market for subsidiary workers, particularly practical nurses, existed. Investigators concluded that the need for practical nurses was not high, basing their conclusion on the fact that 93 percent of the total number of registries reported a greater need for graduate nurses than for practical nurses. The investigators de-emphasized both the use of and need for practical nurses, estimating that the number of practical nurses in proportion to registered nurses was steadily decreasing.

The CGNS investigators concluded that registries' need for nurses was declining, with most registries (325) expressing no need for additional nurses. Fifty-six percent recorded declining calls for nurses. Hospital-based registries performed better than district association or commercial registries. They reported increasing numbers of calls and fewer nurses waiting on call for new cases. The ability of hospital-based registries to efficiently respond to nursing demand helped them support operations. Nurse leaders, many of them critical of hospital-based registries, often called for them to affiliate with the preferred district-operated centralized agencies. Hospital registries persisted. Many factors, such as the desire for control over and familiarity with nurses, explain why alumnae associations and hospitals continued to operate local registries. The mere fact that hospital-based registries were doing what they were designed to do, that is, supply private nurses to hospitalized patients, made them viable agencies that felt less pressure to cease operations.

The success of hospital-based registries negatively affected district association and commercial enterprises, which were unable to meet patient demand for nurses from their registrant list as nurses saw the hospital agencies as providing greater access to patients. The growing use of hospital facilities for illness care and declining number of calls received for home-based care further constricted business for district association and commercial registries even as the nurse supply increased. Dependent as they were on home-based patients and overflow calls from hospitals, nonhospital-based registries experienced downturns in the private duty market first. This situation seemed to be developing in the winter months of 1928. The continued flow of graduate nurses into the job market each year added to crowded conditions, particularly in areas with populations over five hundred thousand known to attract large numbers of nurses.

The CGNS highlighted two main findings as particularly relevant for future planning. The first was that equilibrium existed between supply and demand as reported by nurse registries in the private duty market. The second was evidence of a severe oversupply of nurses in a job market that offered few job prospects for new entrants. Not only was the market reaching a saturation point for workers but the sufficient labor numbers already present in the field were meeting demand. The CGNS blamed the situation on a common cause—the use of students as a cheap source of labor by hospitals. The practice not only deprived graduates of hospital jobs but also created gridlock in the job market by pouring out enormous numbers of new nurses each year. Based on the findings, the CGNS passed two key resolutions, both of which concerned the nursing education system. The first was that hospitals should not have to absorb the cost of educating nurses, funds for which should come from private or public sources. The second stated that schools should not exist for cheap labor, but should "be based solely upon the kinds and amounts of educational experience which that hospital is prepared to offer."[47]

The registry study led the CGNS to conclude that existing registries suffered from severe deficiencies, requiring a complete reformulation of the system. Hospital-based registries were too narrow, district association registries too inefficient, and commercial registries lacking in professionalism. A professional nurse registry where private duty nurses could organize in central groups would solve contemporary nurse distribution problems. A new type of registry where nurses received salaries and worked eight-hour shifts would improve employment conditions for all. The proposed registry of the future would classify nurses by their capabilities and make patient assignments based on the capacities of each nurse. Complicated patients would receive experienced nurses; less experienced nurses would concentrate on moderately ill individuals with general nursing needs. Nurses' classification would determine salaries. Patients requiring help with housekeeping would receive domestic servants, thus eliminating the need for practical nurses.[48] Offering different schemes, such as hourly and group nursing, would allow patients new choices in how much nursing care they might purchase. Working under improved conditions with professional leadership would eliminate the dissatisfactions expressed by private duty nurses. Although seemingly reasonable, these strategies proved difficult to implement.

Nurses, Patients, and Pocketbooks received a mixed response. Clearly, telling hospitals to change the educational system was not a strategy designed for success. Nurses also seemed skeptical that hospitals would follow recommendations, as hospitals were very powerful. "It is about as easy to put into practice the implications of the report as it is to enforce prohibition," wrote one reviewer.[49] Hospital and physician groups tended to concentrate on the educational suggestions, particularly the suggestions to decrease the number of students and increase the use of graduates. Opposed to any plan that even hinted that some schools of nursing should close, hospital groups defended student service as the best way to deliver nursing care to hospitalized patients.[50] Their commitment to student service was not based solely on lower costs. Nursing schools, especially those in small communities, brought community cachet, but were particularly threatened by hints of cutting back on the production of students.[51] Communities took great pride in their hospitals, and hospital boards pointed to schools of nursing as proof their hospitals were in the mainstream of medical care.

The legacy of the CGNS is discouraging and complicated. After the publication of *Nurses, Patients, and Pocketbooks*, the CGNS continued to function until 1934, releasing two more volumes published with financial assistance from the Rockefeller Foundation.[52] As the work of the CGNS ended as funding ceased, the NLNE addressed the committee's uncompleted business. The original goal, grading schools of nursing, never reached fruition. *Nurses, Patients, and Pocketbooks* failed to galvanize the nursing community to call for radical changes. The CGNS did amass a tremendous number of facts, and nursing leaders used the data collected to argue for better educational standards and more secure employment opportunities for nurses. Further, the CGNS served as an accurate predictor of future events in the nurse job market. Employment of graduate nurses in permanent hospital positions eventually occurred. The Great Depression served as the economic catalyst responsible for modifications in the nursing care delivery system. As the country entered the Depression years, the difficulties in the private duty market would continue to worsen. Conditions that appeared negative in 1928 would be catastrophic by 1932.

Black Private Duty Nurses

Despite the prodigious amount of information on the nursing profession and nurses gathered by the aforementioned investigations, one group of professional nurses, black nurses, remained invisible as segregation dealt a cruel blow. Educated in a separate system and denied jobs in white institutions, black nurses forged career paths both similar to and different from those of the majority of white nurses. Historian Darlene Clark Hine noted that in the mid-1920s more than two-thirds of black graduate nurses worked in either private duty or institutional settings.[53] Hine also suggests that, at least in the South, many black nurses avoided private duty and worked in hospitals before embarking on careers in public health. Public health, considered a more prestigious field, provided a degree of autonomy missing in other areas of nursing for both black and white nurses.[54]

The limited mention of black nurses by officials of professional nurse registries under study in this investigation is notable. In New York City, the alumnae associations of both Lincoln and Harlem Hospital Schools of Nursing, both all-black institutions, were members of NYSNA and NYCRNA. Membership within NYCRNA presumably carried entry to the central registry. NYCRNA's central registry records do not mention the presence or absence of black nurse registrants. The establishment of a separate registry in New York City, affiliated with the National Association of Colored Graduate Nurses (NACGN), for black nurses suggests their exclusion from other registries, including the central registry.[55] In Chicago, black nurses were refused outright the services of the Nurses Professional Registry. Minnie Ahrens, executive secretary of the First District, rationalized the exclusionary policy by explaining, "because we cannot place them, the social differences are too great."[56]

Shortly after its founding in 1908, the NACGN established as a major aim the organization of a registry specifically for black nurses.[57] In 1917, NACGN's executive board officially voted to create a national registry in one of the larger black hospitals to register and place black nurses in both private duty and institutional positions.[58] NACGN's membership agreed with this plan at the next annual convention, approving the opening of the National Nurses Registry at Lincoln Hospital in New York City, one of the oldest and most prestigious black schools of nursing.[59] A year later, Adah Thoms, the registry's director, reported success in placing nurses in both private duty and permanent positions.[60] By 1920, reports of registry operations indicated placement of nurses in a variety of posts; the registry also served as a clearinghouse for potential jobs around the country.[61] The accomplishment of the National Nurses Registry in placing nurses in institutional positions is noteworthy given that even though a major aim of the ANA was to use nurse registries for that specific purpose, most registries failed to do so.

By 1925, the National Nurses Registry numbered eighty registrants, with its nurses charging the same fees as white nurses. As with white nurses, black nurses held to the necessity of maintaining a standard fee. A discussion on nurses' fees at a 1918 NACGN executive board meeting indicated that members were overwhelmingly supportive of a standard fee for nurses, although one member noted that black nurses often received lower fees than white nurses and another member preferred a fee-setting strategy that reflected the condition of the patient.[62] The registry received 80 percent of its calls from white patients. Contemporary nurses considered black patients too poor to employ graduate nurses. Black nurses enhanced their employment opportunities by readily accepting chronic cases that their white counterparts avoided.[63] The record is silent on how black nurses felt when relegated to the less desirable patients.

The Rockefeller Foundation, interested in the plight of minority nurses, gathered information on working conditions for early twentieth-century black nurses. In 1925, John Rockefeller told foundation secretary Edwin R. Embree his desire that the Rockefeller Foundation pursue any opportunity for improving the conditions for training of black nurses. Embree subsequently appointed

Canadian nurse, Ethel Johns, to conduct a study of black nursing in the United States. To prepare for this project, Johns consulted a study completed in 1924 by the Hospital Library and Service Bureau, a Rockefeller-funded organization, which collected and disseminated hospital information on educational conditions for minority nurses. Both the Hospital Library and Service Bureau report and Johns's report focused mainly on educational matters, but both studies also solicited data on working conditions for black nurses. Although the Hospital Library and Service Bureau report confined itself to summary statistics, Johns's report is mainly impressionistic, with an emphasis on obtaining "a sympathetic understanding" of the southern point of view.[64] The stereotypical racist assumptions contained in Johns's report make its findings suspect, and its conclusions must be approached with great caution.

The Hospital Library report compiled statistics on more than 1,600 accredited hospitals. Of these, only sixty used black private duty nurses; they limited those nurses to caring for black patients.[65] Johns's study did not estimate the use of private duty nurses but did include data from five hospitals surveyed that kept statistics on the employment status of their graduates. Of 827 graduates, approximately 60 percent worked. Of these, 224 nurses, 67 percent, were employed in private duty in 1925.[66] The study results indicate a higher percentage than the estimated 54 percent of nurses overall working in private duty, raising questions about the assertions that black nurses favored public health positions.

Johns noted regional differences in the employment of black private duty nurses. In the South, physicians expressed a preference for black nurses, noting that they adapted well to the domestic situation and gave excellent bedside care. White private duty nurses were resentful of black nurses, viewing them as a possible source of competition. The refusal of professional nurse registry service to black nurses made case referral difficult. Working within a stratified system, professional black nurses faced limited opportunities.

The CGNS reviewed the status of black nurses briefly, noting it had been unable to make an adequate study of the employment possibilities for them, although it recognized the need for more black nurses.[67] Still, the committee limited this need to areas of the country with large black populations. The CGNS expressed little hope that increasing the supply of black nurses would resolve any nursing care problems experienced by black patients. Expressing traditional views, the CGNS asserted that few black patients possessed the funds to pay for graduate nursing care. The committee, indirectly as a way to circumvent the issue of segregation, expressed the need for further study of the nursing needs of black populations. However, members seemed dismayed by the complexities of the segregated system, dismally concluding, "The social, educational, and economic problems involved in the question of the negro [sic] nurse are so difficult and so involved that the Grading Committee is not in a position to make recommendations concerning them."[68]

Conclusion

In the post–World War I era, high demand existed for one type of nurse worker: the acute care bedside nurse. The difficulty in obtaining enough bedside nurses created havoc in the nurse employment field. Hospitals continued adherence to an outmoded apprentice system of nurse education and were unable to devise a method of financing hospital nursing care without using students and producing scores of underused graduate nurses. The result was a job market with two separate yet interconnected sectors. In the hospital sector, demand for bedside nurses continued to rise and led to continuous efforts to increase the supply of students. Each year, an augmented number of student nurses graduated and was released into the private duty market, in which low demand for workers created overcrowding and oversupply. The isolation of graduate nurses in the small private duty sector resulted in underemployment and stagnant earnings. Nurse leaders understood the problem but, being unable to garner strong backing for change from nurses themselves, physicians, or hospitals, they preferred to focus on reforming the education system.

Consistently repeated throughout 1920s reports on nursing was the theme that private duty was an inefficient method of delivering nursing care to modern patient populations in both acute care and home settings. Leaders found some solace in the larger percentage of nurses employed by institutions in the late 1920s. However, the transition to staff nursing was occurring at a glacial pace. Little support existed for instituting radical transformations. While nursing waited for a stronger stimulus for change, the problems within the private duty system cried out for a solution.

The studies discussed in this section identify four main issues plaguing the private duty labor market: competition, maldistribution, underemployment, and segregation. Too many graduate nurses sharing the market with large numbers of subsidiary workers severely overcrowded the labor market. The two groups of workers performed similar functions with little distinct differentiation between them. The distribution system failed to provide enough work for nurses and enough nurses for patients. The expense involved for patients who wanted and needed care created unnecessary restrictions in nursing care use. Moreover, one group of nurses, blacks, was effectively separated from the larger nurse job market. Although private duty nursing had seemed a logical way to deliver professional nursing care at the beginning of the century, the rigid method of care delivery was making less sense for contemporary sick care practices.

Each of the reports discussed in this chapter focused on a specific aspect of the private duty situation and suggested solutions centered on that issue. The NYSNA study revealed the inherent rigidities of private duty, recommending diversification of the care delivery model. The CGNS specified nothing less than the total reorganization of the registry system, with the aim of control over the distribution of nurses. The two studies on black nurses bore witness to issues of injustices in the profession and confirmed the disinterest of white nurses in addressing the problem of segregation. Regulation, diversification, and control would comprise the cornerstone of solutions suggested by those interested in resolving private duty issues, although these solutions would come too late to preserve the private duty nursing profession.

Chapter 5

Private Duty's Golden Age

The studies and investigations carried out in the 1920s provided strong evidence that the nurse labor market possessed serious difficulties resistant to solution. Strong evidence did not necessarily convert to action. Even as the ink dried on the studies, the role of private duty nurse continued to hold a prominent place, employing substantial numbers of professional nurses up to and beyond 1930. Much of private duty's attraction as a professional choice for nurses was credited simply to its default status—there were few other employment opportunities for graduate nurses. Hospitals continued to cling to the student nurse care system and avoided hiring graduate nurses as employees, and nurses persisted in shunning hospital employment, viewing private duty as their best hope for employment. Although viewed by multiple groups as dysfunctional, disorganized, and disordered, private duty endured.

Criticisms of private duty nursing came from nursing and health care leadership groups who believed that only radical reorganization and hospital employment would rationalize the system. However, individual private duty nurses and the registries that placed them formulated strategies at the local level, away from the leadership, designed to ameliorate problems, make sense of the market, and respond to changing demands for nursing service. Examining the daily work of the private duty nurse and the functioning of the registry system sheds light on a good part of the durability of the market.

Many private duty nurse registries dealt effectively with nurse employment issues. Many worked hard at and delivered on their goal of distributing nurses to the sick public and providing nurses with work. Moreover, registries often took on challenges offered by a system that demanded twenty-four-hour service by modifying delivery aspects to meet changing circumstances. This chapter examines two registries, in Chicago, Illinois, and Brooklyn, New York, that determinedly defied obstacles and succeeded in connecting patients with nurses and nurses with patients. Their success offers a more nuanced, complicated image of a labor market riddled with difficulties, demonstrating that even as the nursing situation faced enormous problems, nurses engaged in concerted efforts to meet demand. Furthermore, as working conventions changed to meet market conditions, the contemporary contours of nurses' work regarding hours of work, payment for services, and personnel policies emerged. The story begins in Chicago.

A Bustling Registry in a Bustling Town

In 1923, Lucy Van Frank, head registrar of the thriving Chicago Nurses Professional Registry (NPR)[1] described the importance of private duty registries, specifically central registries, noting, "They are now considered as much a necessity in the nursing world as are commercial bureaus in the business world, and as essential a part of the great plan of caring for the sick, as is the system of Training Schools in the hospital."[2] Based on Van Frank's experience as registrar of one of the largest and most successful central registries, this was not an overstatement.

The NPR, which opened in 1913, resembled in many respects the New York Central Registry (NYCR). Established as professional nursing began dominating sick care work, the NPR, unlike the NYCR in New York City, succeeded in capturing a large share of Chicago's private duty market and operated for over seventy years, an astounding record in a field mainly known for reports of its demise. It was one of the largest and longest-operating central registries in the country. In 1923, the same year that the Goldmark Report reported severe underemployment of private duty nurses, the NPR recorded its busiest year to date.[3] Although twenty-five commercial registries competed with the NPR for nursing business, the registry continued to be the premier Chicago nurse agency for professional private duty nurses, and remained an example of an efficient, stable professional nurse registry.[4] The NPR found its success in the circumstances of the registry's organization as well as the peculiarities of the local Chicago market.

Professional nursing in Illinois developed similarly to that in New York State.[5] The Illinois State Nurses' Association (ISNA) formed in 1901, shortly after NYSNA organized.[6] In 1912, nurses in the counties of Cook, DuPage, and Lake established the First District of the ISNA, which included the city of Chicago and became the major center of nursing activity in Illinois. Due to its central location, Chicago's First District exerted the same influential position in state nursing affairs that NYCRNA did in New York State. The First District took on the job of entering the nurse labor market by opening the NPR in 1913.[7] The registry achieved immediate success in delivering private duty services to patients in the Chicago area and experienced tremendous growth in a very short period. One month after the NPR opened for business, it claimed 150 members, averaged 8 nurse placements a day, and ended its first year of operations with 500 members.[8] Between 1917 and 1923 the number of registrants rose to 957 and yearly calls averaged 11,028 by 1923.

Several factors account for the NPR's success. Once opened, the registry quickly mobilized and capitalized on considerable financial and moral support extended to it by the nursing community in Chicago. Chicago school of nursing alumnae associations donated substantial amounts of money to cover initial NPR expenses.[9] In addition, agreements worked out with several Chicago school of nursing alumnae associations resulted in the merger of their registries with the NPR, substantially increasing the number of nurse registrants. By the mid-1930s, the NPR listed the participation of twelve alumnae association registries, representing some of the greatest hospitals in Chicago and the surrounding area.[10]

Acquiring hospital-based registries on its membership rolls was crucial to NPR's success. Many guaranteed fee-paying members (each nurse paid a yearly fee to the registry) ensured financial solvency and reaped advantages for the alumnae associations who were spared the expense and effort of running a registry. The system worked in a simple manner. When an alumnae association joined the NPR, it prioritized the association's members for calls received from their hospital. Such arrangements improved work opportunities for all registrants and increased chances of filling hospital calls. This type of system mirrored the centralized registry system nursing leaders advocated (see chapter 4). Centralized systems consolidated calls for nurses within a local area, ensured an adequate supply of nurses available for demand, and rationalized the market.

The NPR's head registrar, Lucy Van Frank, added further to the success of the NPR with her strong management style and background in both nursing and business.[11] Van Frank was a notable figure in registry circles, serving on the ANA's Special Registry Committee in 1915 and also speaking and writing extensively on registry and private duty issues.[12] Much of her commentary illustrated how registrars approached the job of distributing nurses, identified basic problems in managing a registry, and depicted the relationship between the registrar and nurse registrants, which was a frequently negative one.

Van Frank identified private duty nurses as the "most discontented and unhappy group of all nursing groups."[13] Among criticisms Van Frank lodged against private duty nurses were their unavailability when called for cases, unwarranted complaints and misunderstandings over how nurses were assigned, nonpayment of registry fees, refusal to take unpopular cases, particularly those in patients' homes, and a tendency to disregard registry rules. Particularly irritating to Van Frank were nurses who refused cases, especially cases that involved patients with cancer, tuberculosis, or venereal disease, and those involving tiny infants with feeding problems.[14] Blaming the poor behavior of working nurses on the hospital training system, which accepted unqualified students, Van Frank urged private duty nurses to provide a good example for student nurses by exhibiting strong bedside care and keeping abreast of new procedures.[15] Communication gaps and different perspectives of private duty work between private duty nurses and registry leaders troubled relations between the two groups and placed obstacles in the way of solving problems for years, even as the NPR flourished.

Each year between 1923 and 1929, the NPR recorded significantly higher monthly patient assignments, as well as doubling of its membership (see table 5.1).[16] The NPR's widespread membership represented a significant portion of graduate nurses in Illinois: approximately 9 percent of the state nurses and 17 percent of the city nurses were enrolled in the NPR in 1930.[17] The NPR provided a solid number of registrants and served as a reliable source of patient calls in the Chicago area. Enough confidence in business existed to permit a private duty fee increase from $6 for twelve-hour cases to $7 in 1927.[18] Registry records indicated a financially robust enterprise. In 1929, the NPR recorded an impressive profit of $10,905.92.[19]

To manage a large number of members and patient requests for nurses, the NPR increased its staff, secured larger quarters for offices, and installed a switchboard service during the 1920s.[20] By 1930, a registrar and five assistants, all of whom were registered nurses, comprised the registry staff.[21] The NPR developed plans to expand services offered to patients, nurses, and health-care agencies: it provided hourly nursing services through which patients hired nurses by the hour as opposed to full twelve-hour shifts, and institutional placement services that offered nurses a means to obtain permanent positions.[22] First District took pride in the NPR, reporting on tributes received, such as when the Illinois Central Hospital expressed warm appreciation for the promptness with which NPR nurses responded to and cared for victims of a 1926 train wreck.[23]

Chicago private duty nurses joined the trend to hospital-based practice in the 1920s, clearly indicating their preference for hospital work by refusing home cases with great frequency. Van Frank admitted that home cases were not ideal,

Table 5.1.
Nurses Professional Registry patient assignments and membership,
1917–1940

Year	Monthly patient assignments (average)	Yearly membership (average)
1917	400	530
1918	337	482
1919	400	390
1920	574	620
1921	860	976
1922	882	982
1923	919	957
1924	1,117	1,157
1925	1,327	1,233
1926	1,752	1,489
1927	2,304	1,733
1928	2,384	1,744
1929	2,555	1,921
1930	1,996	1,806
1931	1,548	1,622
1932	1,326	1,457
1933	828	1,149
1934	1,265	1,203
1935	1,316	1,147
1936	1,658	1,197
1937	2,075	1,279
1938	2,121	1,327
1939	2,385	1,369
1940	2,758	1,515

Source: "Nurses Professional Registry, Average Number of Registrants and Average Monthly Number of Private Duty Assignments, 1917–1946," 26 July 1948, box 1, CNRC, Midwest Nursing History Resource Center, College of Nursing, University of Illinois.

stating, "Often the home conditions make nursing difficult."[24] However, her position required she find nurses for all requests and the extra time spent by registry staff placing a nurse in the home was burdensome. Physicians criticized nurses severely for refusing home-based patients, sometimes threatening to withhold hospital cases from nurses who refused to care for patients in the home.[25] Moreover, although nurses complained about unemployment during slack periods when patients were scarce, the ease with which they refused home cases indicated a degree of satisfaction with the amount of work received.[26]

Long hours of work, particularly the custom of working twenty-four-hour cases, was a dominant complaint of private duty nurses. Nationwide campaigns to reduce nurses' hours of work were ongoing throughout the early twentieth century, although initial drives for work hour reduction centered on student nurses.[27] For private duty nurses the effort to reduce hours focused on eliminating twenty-four-hour workdays.

The arguments advanced against twenty-four-hour shifts were extensive, with the fatigue experienced by nurses working excessive hours heading the list. Nursing required careful attention to patients' conditions; mistakes due to sleepiness after remaining awake for extended periods of time could result in disaster.[28] There was general consensus that most patients did not require constant attention. The presumption was that patients in need of around-the-clock care were so critically ill that a nurse would quickly tire out if she attempted to work twenty-four hours straight. In such cases, hiring two nurses, each working one twelve-hour shift, was considered more appropriate. Continuous work deprived nurses of free time associated with normal working hours, adding to nurses' dissatisfaction with the job.[29] The practice of a set fee per shift also meant long hours lowered the hourly rate of pay to an average of 30¢ an hour. The general unattractiveness of twenty-four-hour shifts detracted from nursing's appeal to well-qualified recruits.[30]

Patients cared for at home over long shifts needed sufficient sleeping spaces for the nurse. In the hospital, twenty-four-hour workdays presented complications as nurses remained with their patients throughout the night, requiring that hospitals supply cots in patient rooms for private duty nurses. Both patients and nurses complained about restless sleep under such arrangements. Reports that private duty nurses roamed hospital corridors at night dressed in their nightclothes, their hair tied up in curlers, attire considered inappropriate for professionals, filled nursing journals.[31]

Twenty-four-hour shifts did have some adherents. Such duty did not always demand continuous wakefulness on the part of the nurse. When assigned to twenty-four-hour cases, nurses were entitled to six hours of sleep and two to four hours of recreation time.[32] How this worked out in practice depended on the patient's condition and availability of relief for situations that required the patient receive constant attention. A nurse on a twenty-four-hour case might expect to be alert for the entire time, or she might engage in actual work anywhere from fourteen to sixteen hours. The extra dollar received for twenty-four-hour shifts could seem worthwhile if the nurse worked only two hours more than when on twelve-hour duty.

In rural areas with few hospital facilities, nurses feared fewer calls and reduced income if twelve-hour shifts became standard, particularly if patients felt they had to hire two nurses. The early twentieth-century association of twelve-hour shifts as appropriate for critically ill patients only made older nurses wary about shift reductions.[33] Others nurses simply preferred longer shifts and did not see a need to change.

Some nurses reasoned that twelve-hour shifts were not cost effective. Nurses working twelve-hour shifts often complained that travel time to and from patients added up to two hours a day, elongating the working day and giving nurses little time to rest before returning to duty.[34] Other factors added to the time spent on the job. Early twentieth-century nurses did not travel to work dressed in uniforms as it was customary to arrive at the hospital in street clothes and change into a uniform before reporting for duty. To take advantage of the hospital-provided meals, nurses had to allow enough time to change, eat, and be ready for duty at the start of their shifts, stretching twelve-hour shifts to fourteen to sixteen hours. Some believed it was more expeditious to remain on duty over twenty-four hours, save on travel time, obtain three meals, and earn extra income.[35]

Nurses working in private homes did not have a means of obtaining meals, so patients' families were expected to supply them. A nurse in meager financial circumstances could save significant money on food by accepting twenty-four-hour duty that included full board.

The tradition of including meals as part of the nurses' remuneration carried over from home-based to hospital care with a major modification. Hospitals charged the patients who hired private nurses for the nurses' meals.[36] In turn, the nurse received a meal, not money, for her board. The hospital used this as a revenue source, pocketing the difference between the fee charged the patient and the cost of the meal.

Despite reservations about shorter work hours, opposition to twelve-hour shifts among private duty nurses was limited. Resistance came mainly from physicians. Illinois physicians broadly expressed dissatisfaction with the move to shorter hours. They believed the increased cost of care would cause patients to avoid using private nurses. Other physicians objected because they would need to discuss patients' conditions with several nurses, leading to confusion regarding care.

Hospitals contested shorter hours for student nurses but muted their opposition to reduced hours for graduate private duty nurses. Institutions may have welcomed twelve-hour shifts as one way of relieving institutions of responsibility for providing sleeping arrangements for private duty nurses. Twelve-hour arrangements required no financial cost to hospitals and carried the potential for profit. When patients hired two twelve-hour nurses, hospitals charged patients for three additional meals for the second nurse, thus profiting from higher revenues.

The NPR was concerned about work hours from its founding in 1923. Many graduate nurses expressed less interest in the private duty field and reasoned that hospital mandates limiting nursing shifts to twelve hours might force physicians and patients to accept the practice.[37] This strategy had proven successful in Evanston, Illinois, where they established twelve-hour shifts for private duty nurses.[38] Aligning with hospitals to institute a contractual matter between nurse and patient underscores nurses' recognition that hospitals held greater authority to institute change, while also illustrating nurses' power to influence their own work. Working together made common sense and increased the chance of success.

Still, cooperation from hospitals was not easily forthcoming. By 1925 the NPR, frustrated over the slow pace of change to shorter hours, decided to take matters into its own hands and instituted a policy of assigning nurses on hospital cases to twelve-hour shifts only, resulting in a quicker method for gaining shorter hours.[39] Although physicians continued to voice opposition, by the end of 1926, NPR nurses were working twelve-hour shifts of hospital duty, and illustrating the importance of the alliance between nurses and hospitals.[40] In 1929, Van Frank confidently declared, "Today the modern Private Duty Nurse has become the Special Nurse in the hospital and seeks a twelve-hour service or less. This makes it possible for her to have more time for rest and relaxation and an opportunity to lead the life of a normal person."[41]

As the twelve-hour duty model gained traction with institutions and nurses, the NPR saw continued expansion of calls for nurses, although they were less robust than before the twelve-hour model was in place. Average monthly assignments showed a yearly increase of 198 cases between 1923 and 1924. Between 1926 and 1927, the year twelve-hour shifts became normative for hospital cases, the increase in average monthly assignments climbed to 552. Average cases increased only to 80 per month between 1927 and 1928. The following year recorded an increase in monthly assignments of 171.[42]

Because the NPR did not formally evaluate the change, the case numbers cannot be wholly attributed to demand. Many factors contributed to private duty nurse demand, such as incidence of illness and the financial state of those needing services. Determining the impact of one change on the private nursing service given the data available is impossible. Still, a 65 percent increase in the cost of private duty nursing, based on a difference in cost of one twenty-four-hour nurse at $10.50 a day versus two twelve-hour nurses at $17 a day including the costs of meals, most likely deterred some private duty use. Moreover, as the country entered an economic downturn in the late 1920s, raising the cost of private nursing services threatened to wipe out the market for private duty services no matter how the registries tried to remain solvent.

A Registry Grows in Brooklyn

In 1926, the year that Janet Geister's study of conditions in the private duty market recorded large amounts of underemployment among private duty nurses, District 14 of the New York State Nurses' Association opened a new professional nurse registry, the Nursing Bureau of District 14 (NB14).[43] Although 1926 was not a particularly auspicious year for entering the private duty field, it was precisely the maldistribution problems so clearly documented by Geister that led to the NB14. The NB14 was intended to improve the delivery of nursing care by having the registry serve as the main distribution center for nursing services for the New York City borough of Brooklyn.[44] The district received strong support for the endeavor from the Medical Society of Kings County's Committee on Nursing, which encouraged and supported setting up the NB14 as a means of improving dispersal of nursing services throughout the community.[45]

Despite reports of generally dismal prospects for private duty nursing, the NB14 recorded immediate success. Considerable support for the new venture came not only from the medical community but also from nurses. Seven alumnae associations helped launch the registry by either endorsing or offering financial support to the district for initial start-up costs.[46] Three alumnae association registries joined the NB14 immediately, with another three hospitals using the services of the registry at a high frequency.[47] In January 1927, after only nine months of operations, the NB14 listed 631 nurses as registrants. Furthermore, in a telling demonstration of the potential power of well-organized registries, registry officials proudly claimed their efforts in obtaining an increase in hospital private duty fees from $6 to $7 for twelve-hour duty enabled nurses to secure a living wage.

The events surrounding the rise in fees provide an illustrative example of how concerted action on the part of nurses in improving their working conditions via an organized body such as a registry contained the seeds of victory. Before the establishment of the registry, individual Brooklyn alumnae association registries unsuccessfully petitioned hospital boards for a fee increase from $6 to $7 for a twelve-hour shift. Once the NB14 opened, the registry set initial hospital fees at the preferred $7 for twelve-hour duty. Brooklyn hospitals, not pleased with this higher rate, suggested through the local Nursing Committee of the Hospital Trustees Association that the public address the question of nurse fees, but a public outcry never emerged. The NB14's support of higher fees as well as its robust membership rolls convinced hospitals to reconsider and accept the new rates, which quickly became the standard throughout the district within a few weeks.[48]

Under the careful management of Executive Director Emma Collins, the registry flourished. Collins, who wrote and frequently spoke on private duty nursing matters, used her position as director to implement ideas she believed critical to successful registry management.[49] Two main areas concerned Collins. She believed professional registries should capture as much of the work available for nurses by responding to community needs for nursing services and cultivating alternative nursing schemes. Additionally, Collins recognized the importance of registrants to registry functioning. She advised easy discussion of issues to resolve difficulties, advocating registry policies that improved working conditions for private duty nurses and, as discussed below, illustrate the NB14's commitment to registry services that met both patients' requests for nursing care and nurses' need for secure work.

From its inception, the NB14 offered services designed to meet the full range of nursing services in the community. The registry provided nursing for home and hospitalized patients and included in its membership not just professional nurses but also nonprofessional nurse workers such as trained attendants and practical nurses. Approximately 30 percent of the registrants fit into the functional, or nonprofessional, nurse category.[50] Their inclusion was intended to secure a larger share of the home-based nursing care market and purposely keep fees for home-based patients low as a further inducement for attracting home calls.[51]

Registry reports indicate that the NB14 was notably different from other professional registries in maintaining a larger home-based market. In 1933, 40 percent of the calls received by the NB14 were for patients at home.[52] Though the percentage of home calls declined in 1939 and 1940 to 20 percent, the number of home calls received by the NB14 continued to be higher than numbers reported by other professional registries.[53] Professional nurse registries nationwide reported that approximately 10 percent of the calls they received were for home cases in the same period.[54]

The NB14 also offered an array of alternative nursing schemes to patients. An hourly nursing service, providing private nursing care for short periods at hourly rates, functioned throughout the life of the registry.[55] In 1934, the registry inaugurated a home delivery service for birthing women. Nurses made prenatal visits to expectant women and were present at the time of delivery. The NB14 rented sterile maternity supplies to those patients requiring them.[56]

The NB14 made several attempts to enlarge the patient base for private duty services by providing nurses at reduced rates to individuals unable to afford the cost of regular private duty. First, in 1936, the registry hired a salaried community nurse to care for patients who needed private nursing care but were unable to afford it. Patients paid fees to the registry based on the patients' estimate of what they could afford. Difficulties in administering the program led to its termination in 1937.[57] A second attempt at providing professional nursing services to those of moderate income was more successful. In 1938, officials of the NB14 expressed concerns that the passage of the New York State Nurse Practice Act (the Todd-Fell Act) licensing practical nurses would result in acutely ill patients hiring lower-priced practical nurses in place of registered nurses. The registry established a fund supplementing the fees of registered nurses for select patients deemed in need of professional nursing care.[58]

The NB14 did not limit services to delivery of personal nursing care. It offered programs helpful for families in times of illness. The registry furnished loans of sickroom equipment such as bedside tables, bedpans, basins, and other supplies used for patient care to patients of limited means. The registry arranged a nursing resource file for patients and families who required additional caretaking services. The file contained information on facilities for convalescent care, day nurseries, and boarding homes.[59]

The Registry and Registrants

Officials of the NB14 recognized that patient needs imposed arduous working conditions on nurses and sometimes caused nurses to reject patient cases. Night duty, considered by nurses to be a particularly unpleasant line of work, led the list of cases nurses refused to take. Private duty nurses easily enumerated the disadvantages linked to night duty cases. Nurses complained of getting inadequate rest during the day when assigned to night cases. Accepting night cases often became a self-fulfilling prophecy. Nurses agreeing to take night cases soon found themselves offered patients only during the evening hours and seldom saw physicians, limiting their chances to build up a practice through physician referrals. Further, night duty nurses experienced greater difficulty in collecting fees from patients or families. Another reason was the sheer boredom of having to remain on duty during times when most patients slept.

The NB14 addressed the issue by creating policies designed to ease the burden of nurses on night cases and at the same time improve acceptance rates for night calls.[60] Registry regulations required that nurses rotate from day to night shifts.[61] Sharing night cases seemed fair to all and decreased the practice of registering against certain cases. The NB14 also did not demand that nurses follow the traditional practice of remaining at home throughout the day when waiting for night duty and promised not to call nurses before 4 P.M. for night cases, allowing them more free time during the day. The registry provided further assistance to night nurses by arranging for transportation to emergency cases after 11 P.M.[62] Rotating shifts and other amenities accorded night nurses proved to be successful but did not completely eliminate problems surrounding night duty, as the NB14 continued to periodically experience shortages of nurses available for night cases.[63]

For many nurses, trouble encountered in collecting fees when on night duty was enough reason to avoid less-popular hours. Nurses described the issues involved in fee collection through letters written to the registry. Several nurses claimed that after unsuccessfully sending bills to patients' homes, they spent time and money traveling to collect fees in person. In some cases, the hospital collected fees for night nurses but made it difficult for nurses to pick up the money when convenient for them. One nurse noted it was not unusual for her to have three or four uncollected fees at any one period. The problem of uncollected fees grew worse when caring for patients close to death. One nurse bluntly described the dilemma in the following way: "Sometimes we are told we are unethical when we request our fee of the family when the patient is critical and we are sure we will not be needed the next night, however, the night nurse who is timid may have a long wait until an estate is settled and an irregular $5 per day does not permit of much saving."[64] In response to nurses' complaints, the NB14 developed a policy that parties responsible for the nurses' payment sign a form before the nurse arrived on duty that they would indeed pay the fee.[65] Complaints about noncollection of fees decreased immediately after the institution of the new policy.[66]

The registry had a vested interest in keeping night nurses paid and happy. The NB14 recorded a notable increase in the number of night duty calls in the late 1930s. In 1938, 50 percent of the calls received were for night duty. A year later, 74 percent of the calls were either for night or evening cases.[67] Providing nurses to patients at undesirable hours would assume a growing importance in the private duty field, especially as nurses moved to eight-hour shifts.[68] Assuring nurses that the registry met their needs when assigned to night shifts lessened the chance they might seek to avoid cases that were becoming a significant share of the registry's business.

The NB14's demonstrated attention to registrants needs in other ways. The profession depended on practitioners who were expert and familiar with new techniques. After graduation from school, the opportunities to learn new methods lessened; nurses' skills sometimes became rusty, and graduate nurses benefited from the review of nursing procedures. To keep the nurses up to date with changing skills and therapeutics, the registry sponsored educational programs designed to introduce or review knowledge and expertise for nurses beginning in 1938.[69] Programs covered a broad range of topics, from review of medical care and procedures to demonstrations and practice of nursing techniques. By 1939, educational programs, known as the first Thursday lectures, were popular events.[70]

Providing educational programs met the needs of most registrants for continuing education, but some nurses required different measures. Sending competent nurses to cases assured the NB14 of repeat customers and represented an ethical responsibility of the agency. The registry was keenly aware that not all nurses met standards considered acceptable for patient care. Registries referred to problem nurses as nurses who "failed to give satisfaction" and found such nurses difficult to place. Because the likelihood of work was sparse for many of these nurses, registries displayed a reluctance to sign them up and to take their membership fees without hope of providing them with cases.

Two types of problems caused the registry to question a nurse's ability to provide private duty services. Nurses either created difficulties for registry operations or demonstrated incompetence in the delivery of care. The Registry Committee discussed problem nurses at meetings and made decisions to either remove them from registry enrollment or allow them time to improve their performance. In 1929, twenty nurses did not have their membership renewed because the registry believed their skills were so poor.[71] Nurses failing to cooperate with registry policies also ended up losing registry privileges. Some nurses placed themselves on call and then were unreachable when cases became available. Other nurses refused cases located at long distances from their homes.[72] The abilities of a nurse who did not comply with registry policies factored into whether she was asked to stay or leave the registry. In one instance a nurse, even though considered a good nurse, was accused of flagrant disregard of the rules of the bureau and dismissed. A year later she asked for reinstatement. The registry decided to give her one more chance based on the quality of her nursing care.[73]

Nurses posing threats to patient safety were generally but not always removed from the registry. In 1931, a graduate nurse failed her state board licensing examination three times. She was placed in the nonprofessional category of registry membership but retained registry privileges. The registry gave her one more opportunity to pass the licensing examination even though the hospital from which she graduated refused to permit her to nurse their patients.[74] The registry removed a trained attendant after receiving complaints that she was impudent and lazy, slept while her patient was in a coma, and borrowed money from other nurses without repaying.[75] Nurses sometimes offered justifications for behaviors considered unacceptable. A nurse accused of sleeping in the second bed of a two-bedroom house while her patient's fever rose to 105.4° Fahrenheit explained she was completing her second shift of work, needed the money, and fell asleep by mistake. The nurse received a suspension from the registry.[76] Extenuating circumstances could result in less-harsh penalties for nurses. A nurse who came to the registry with proper credentials applied a hot water bottle to a patient, causing burns to the skin. The nurse was dismissed from the case, apologized profusely, but remained on the registry.[77] In another situation, the registry received complaints about a nurse who was new to the registry. On her first case, the registry received reports that she did not care for her patient. On her second case, when assigned to a burn victim, hospital staff accused the nurse of sleeping during the night and failing to change her patient's dressings. Because the nurse had appropriate recommendations and a shortage of nurses existed, the registry continued to place her with patients.[78] In 1938, a practical nurse was dismissed from the registry when she fell asleep on a case, had a nightmare, and woke screaming, frightening her patient. The nurse reapplied for membership in 1941. The registry refused. Registry officials had received reports that the nurse was seen wearing a uniform and insignia like a navy nurse and was posing as a registered nurse.[79]

Nurses with health complications also created several issues. In one situation, a nurse with a severe lung condition that caused her to hemorrhage was required to pass a physical examination before returning to duty. Based on this situation, the registry instituted a policy that nurses posing a threat to patients' health obtain medical clearance before returning to duty.[80] Sometime later another nurse who developed a psychiatric illness required a referral to a psychiatrist. The registry removed the nurse from the registry, but upon her recovery a year later she asked for reinstatement. The registry re-enrolled her on the registry, but limited her to hospital cases on day shifts only.[81]

Support

The NB14 received endorsement for its operations from groups relevant to the nursing business. Nursing, hospital, and medical groups actively cooperated with and became involved in the administration of the NB14. Representatives from district alumnae associations were members of the Registry Committee and consistently attended and participated in registry governance.[82] District 14 solicited assistance from hospitals for the new registry as part of establishing the enterprise. Reports indicated encouraging cooperation from hospitals.[83]

Support given by physicians, the individuals from whom it was presumed most calls for nurses were received, was critical to registry functioning. Physicians demonstrated support in a variety of ways. The chair of the Kings County Medical Society's Committee on Nursing was a member of the Registry Committee and attended meetings regularly. Physician representatives advised registry officials on how to promote and publicize the NB14 to area doctors, sometimes offering hints on ways to improve services.[84] In 1930, the Medical Society, after a request from registry staff, eliminated commercial registry advertising in the society's bulletin. Registry officials perceived this action as a strong moral statement and advocacy for the NB14.[85] Physicians were also instrumental in offering educational programs to nurse registrants as a means of keeping private duty nurses informed of current medical advances.[86] The efforts of the NB14 to provide services considered by physicians to be essential to patient management resulted in patronage received from doctors. The Medical Society approved registry enrollment of multiple types of nurse workers, efforts at providing a broad range of services, and attempts to enlarge the agency's patient base.

No one action taken by District 14 insured the success of the registry. The series of decisions made regarding the policies of the registry, combined with much cooperation from groups relevant to the private duty nurse business, helped District 14 launch a stable center of nurse distribution. In many ways, the NB14 resembled the model of centralized nurse registries proposed earlier in the century. The NB14 was close to serving as a center for all community nursing needs. It provided nurses, supplies, education, and resources, and served as a demonstration of how a professional nurse registry could prosper.

Conclusion

Explanations for why Chicago's NPR and Brooklyn's NB14 succeeded in delivering private duty services are easy to enumerate. Both registries were in large population centers with ready access to patients, hospitals, and nurses. They practiced superior management styles. They received support from the local community of nurses and physicians that created an atmosphere that guaranteed growth.

Still, accounting for the success of the two registries represents only one part of a complicated story. The second part relates to how the two registries put in place measures designed to make sense of the labor market characterized by deficiencies, disorders, and disruption, and ensured reliable delivery of nurse services. Both the NPR and the NB14 invested considerable time and effort in developing reasonable working conditions under which nurses labored. The days were long gone when early private duty nurses, such as Chloe Cudsworth Litttlefield, could leverage their pioneer status to fashion their conventions of work. By the 1920s, such arrangements were no longer feasible or operative. The modern practice of private duty demanded a different, more standardized approach that included recognition that delivery of a twenty-four-hour service required reasonable working standards for nurses.

Both the NPR and NB14 focused on issues of prime importance to working nurses. These seemingly mundane matters, which leaders of the trade unions, such as Samuel Gompers, would have called "bread-and-butter" issues, most likely ranked high in importance among private duty nurses. This was a different perspective from that of the nursing leadership. Nurse leaders used the findings of the major studies on nursing to call for a radical reformulation of the private duty market and encouraged nurses to leave the field for hospital employment. Such exhortations may not have been particularly welcome or even of consequence to average nurses. Rather, knowing that working hours were standard, that periodic fee increases occurred, and that a process existed for the collection of fees were powerful incentives. They might determine who entered, remained, or left the private duty field as well as how well the field met the demand for nurses.

Moreover, the NPR and the NB14 took steps that went beyond simply defining basic working conditions. They also proactively engaged in tactics designed to improve, control, and determine nurses' conditions of work. Two situations discussed in this chapter, the institution of the twelve-hour day in Chicago and fee-raising in Brooklyn, highlight the power registries exerted in negotiating improvements in conditions of work. In both instances, each registry attempted traditional approaches used by earlier nurses, which included back-and-forth negotiations between nurse alumni associations and hospitals. When those negotiations broke down, both the NPR and the NB14 took matters into their own hands and acted.

The two registries' success in those situations was not surprising. When the registries spoke to the hospitals, they carried a power unavailable to individual nurses. The central registries represented many associations and several hundred nurses on whom the hospitals depended for patient care. Both registries enrolled large numbers of nurses, presenting a critical mass difficult for hospitals to ignore. Each registry also enjoyed good support from the medical community, providing a powerful ally group. Hospitals could not isolate one nurse or a single alumni association. Individually employed nurses negotiated on their own, unable to speak with the voice of hundreds of NPR or NB14 nurses behind them. As will be discussed later, this strategy was lost to nurses once they turned to hospital employment.

Not all registries replicated the success of Chicago and Brooklyn agencies. As will be seen in the next chapter, the New York Central Registry was unable to survive in a climate far more competitive and cutthroat. Moreover, the economic turmoil brought on by the Great Depression held the power to undo even the most carefully managed registry.

The next chapter examines how the private duty market fared during the Great Depression, examining the changes forced by the cataclysmic economic event. During the 1930s, private duty nursing underwent tremendous changes that affected the construction of the post-Depression nurse workforce market. Chapter 6 will explain why working nurses of 1940 looked very different from those of 1930.

The Great Depression

Collapse, Resurrection, and Success

Financial exigencies took center stage during the 1930s, requiring nurses to adapt and adjust to changing workforce circumstances. These changes tied them closer to hospital employment and altered the nurse supply/demand dynamic. At the same time, nurses' continued allegiance to the private duty nursing sector allowed them, at least in their eyes, a degree of independence and choice in their working lives. In the 1930s, many nurses remained unconvinced that giving up private practices and accepting hospital employment was to their advantage. The result was that during the nation's worst financial crisis, a labor market characterized as defunct and obsolete continued to thrive and new agencies emerged while older ones closed.

On December 31, 1932, after twenty-two years of distributing private duty nurses to New York City patients, the NYCR of New York Counties Registered Nurses' Association (NYCRNA) closed. The immediate precipitating cause was financial insolvency. Given the timing in the midst of the Great Depression, the closure was not surprising. What happened next, however, was unexpected. Nine months later, on August 1, 1933, a new registry, the Nursing Bureau of Manhattan and Bronx (NBMB), rose from the ashes of the defunct NYCR, assuming the mantle of the professional nurses' registry of note in the greater Manhattan area. As with its sister registry across the East River, the NB14, and Chicago's NPR, the NBMB offered nurses a professional venue owned and operated by and for nurses. Through NBMB nurses could obtain patient cases, and as with the other two registries, it achieved a significant amount of success, remaining in business until the early 1980s.

Table 6.1.
New York Central Registry patient calls received and filled, 1926–1932

Year	Patient calls received	Calls filled (%)	Membership
1926	13,000	85	727
1927	10,500	90	803
1928	12,000	83	789
1929	N/A	N/A	N/A
1930	8,000	88	760
1931	6,250	96	575
1932	3,000[a]	83[a]	455[a]

Source: "Graph Showing Calls Received and Filled by Registry Form," 1 September 1925–31 August 1932, box 8, NYCRNAP.
Note: Figures are unavailable for the year 1929; a change in the fiscal year for the registry made data collection of patient calls received inaccurate.
[a] Figures are for the first eight months of the year only.

The years between 1923 and its closure in 1932 were not easy ones for the NYCR. Numerous bad business decisions, poor managerial oversight, stiff competition from other private duty registries, and altercations with both the New York City Licensing Bureau and the New York County Medical Society over the type of health care workers sent to patients sapped the strength of the registry. These issues carried a financial cost and distracted registry officials from the ultimate purpose of the registry: connecting patients with nurses.

By the early 1930s, NYCR business conditions were at their lowest level, with the number of patient calls received falling precipitously from 13,000 in 1926 to 6,250 in 1932, a 50 percent drop.

The decrease in calls had consequences. Between 1928 and 1932, membership, which brought in income through fees and represented the sole registry revenue, dropped 42 percent (see table 6.1). In 1931, registry receipts just barely met expenses, and there were insufficient funds to meet expenses for the rest of the year.[1] Because it was a NYCRNA-operated entity, it was up to the membership to decide the registry's fate. In September 1932, NYCRNA's board of directors recommended closure. The membership agreed, voting in October to terminate the NYCR.[2]

NYCRNA was well prepared to shut down NYCR operations, settling all transactions necessary to conclude business by the end of the year.[3] However, concern over the destiny of the remaining registrants complicated the process. NYCRNA members weighed different options for those nurse registrants still enrolled in the NYCR and now left without a professional registry, including having NYCR nurses join Brooklyn's NB14, asking other alumnae association registries to take on former NYCR nurses, and amalgamating all professional sponsored city registries into one central registry.[4] The last-resort option, to do nothing and let the registrants find work on their own, raised fears that registrants would join commercial registries, a fate considered by nursing groups equivalent to professional death. This option was rejected outright by the NYCRNA leadership.[5]

The Association of Graduate Nurses of Manhattan and Bronx (AGNMB), which continued to function as it had since the beginning of the century as an alumnae group within NYCRNA for nurses from out-of-town schools, emerged out of a void. The AGNMB, a major supporter of the NYCR, felt a special responsibility to the remaining registrants who were also AGNMB members. It actively worked for the establishment of a new professional registry under its auspices.[6]

The ideal professional registry was believed to inspire professional pride, standards, and status, fulfilling multiple purposes. It provided adequate nursing service to the community and met the needs of physicians, its main clientele. Furthermore, it ensured the distribution of the most highly qualified nurses through membership requirements, as promulgated by the professional group, and provided nurse registrants, who governed their registries through committee membership and participation in decision-making; this control over practice was unavailable through other means.[7]

The themes identified as important for a professional registry echoed the ideas proposed for central registries at the beginning of the decade; these ideas had been re-emphasized by the CGNS's conception of the registry of the future (see chapter 4). In the committee's final report released after the founding of NBMB, the CGNS reiterated a commitment to distributing graduate nursing service through well-organized, sizable, central nursing bureaus that would employ private duty nurses on a salaried basis and eliminate uncertainty over income for nurses. Despite an emerging trend toward hospital employment of graduate nurses for general duty positions, nursing groups continued to advance the image of an all-purpose placement agency meeting the varied nursing needs of the community and operating under the control of nurses.[8] Professional nurses, such as those who comprised the membership of the AGNMB, persisted in trying to achieve this goal despite the significant difficulties encountered in operating a nursing business.

Ultimately, the NBMB owed much of its existence to working nurses' commitment to a professional registry. The AGNMB did not begin a serious effort to establish the new registry until receiving assurance of available financial support from interested nurses in the form of contributions. In one month, between December 12, 1932, and January 3, 1933, private duty nurses raised over four

thousand dollars.[9] A significant amount of money quickly obtained in the middle
of the Depression convinced the AGNMB that the project was worth pursuing,
and represented perhaps the most vital reason the AGNMB decided to take a
chance on the professional nurse registry business. Nurses simply wanted their
registry. As in Chicago and Brooklyn, working private duty nurses in Manhattan and the Bronx demanded a registry that not only provided a means of obtaining patient cases but also fulfilled their professional aspirations.

In its initial years of operation, the NBMB flourished. It finished its first year
with significant increases in all indices of registry effectiveness. The registry
recorded a 72 percent increase in the total number of registrants and a 154 percent
increase in the number of private duty calls received. The rate of unfilled calls
was high, at 23 percent, but the following year saw marked improvement in this
area.[10] Financially, the NBMB prospered, earning a substantial income. After just
one year of operation, registry staff received considerable salary increases; salaries were again raised the following year.[11]

The NBMB ended its first decade fiscally stable, with calls for professional
nursing services continuing to grow. Still, problems persisted. The NBMB had
trouble securing a wide-reaching share of the New York City private duty market, as had its predecessor, the NYCR. The NBMB's ability to fill calls, a prime
marker of registry effectiveness, did not match national statistics. Further, the
registry had to contend with considerable changes in the working patterns of
professional nurses. By the end of the decade, the effects of the Great Depression, changes in work hours, and greater hospital employment significantly
changed the market for private duty nurses, which was very different from the
one in which the NBMB was established.

Chicago's NPR was also experiencing difficulties for some of the same
reasons. In 1930, NPR's Van Frank reported, without hyperbole, that the unemployment situation among private duty nurses was the worst she had ever
encountered.[12] The next three years, the height of the Depression, witnessed a
continued deterioration in the employment prospects of private duty nurses.
The NPR recorded a 30 percent drop in patient assignments in 1931.[13] By 1932,
nurses registered with the NPR averaged 8.75 days of work per month, or 80 days
for the year.[14] As can be seen in table 6.2, for the years 1930 to 1936 the registry
sustained significant declines in profits. After 1936, the NPR began running
profits once more, although they were never as large as those recorded before the
Depression. Between 1937 and 1943, yearly profits were averaging $1,478. In 1943,
the NPR went into a financial slump and began to run deficits once again.[15]

NPR's dependence on membership dues for operational costs explains some
of the decline in profits. Membership dropped from 1,921 members in 1929 to

Table 6.2.
Nurses Professional Registry
profit/deficit, 1930–1936

Year	Profit/deficit
1930	+$6,865.63
1931	+$4,044.16
1932	+$86.18
1933	+$2,329.61
1934	+$12.09
1935	−$190.19
1936	+$77.60

Source: "Income over Expenses,"
n.d., circa 1947, box 1, CNRC,
Midwest Nursing History Resource
Center, College of Nursing,
University of Illinois.

1,149 in 1933. Adding to registry financial woes were some nurse registrants' delinquency in paying membership dues, as they were also affected by the economic downturn of the Depression. Attempts made to secure funding for registrants wishing to remain affiliated with the registry helped some; a $5 reduction in contributions helped others. The NPR also instituted more liberal payment plans that allowed nurses to spread payments over the year or register for membership privileges for short-term service.[16] Despite these measures, in 1932, the NPR began dropping nurses from the registry list for delinquency.[17]

To provide some immediate help, First District (Chicago) instituted several initiatives. It established a nurses' exchange in which nurses sold articles of handiwork.[18] A loan fund provided small amounts of money to those in need.[19] The NPR gave attention to nurses in high need, calling them out of turn for cases.[20] The registry relaxed policies that required nurses to reside within the Chicago area when on call. Nurses with families living some distance from Chicago were allowed to return home to reduce expenses, provided their name be close to the bottom of the list of on-call nurses.[21] The nurse received notification to go back to the city when her name reached a position on the list where it was probable she would obtain a patient case.[22] To preserve morale, First District encouraged nurses to keep busy by maintaining an interest in professional affairs, studying new methods in medicine, pursuing higher education, and developing recreational interests in areas such as music and art.[23] The NPR also sought to decrease the number of nurses seeking private duty work. Nurses graduating from schools outside of the Chicago area were first discouraged to register on the NPR, then refused registration. The registry implemented a policy requiring nurses who had not been actively employed for two years to enroll in a refresher course in 1932 before being allowed registry membership.[24]

More ambitious workforce projects were aimed at increasing the employment of graduate nurses by hospitals in any capacity. For example, hospitals were asked to hire only licensed personnel, rather than unlicensed and less-trained attendants.[25] First District appealed to hospitals to offer registered nurses postgraduate courses in which the nurse could review new techniques and procedures and, at the same time, become eligible for hospital room and board. Hospitals were urged to limit student enrollment and hire graduate nurses in students' places. Private duty nurses were asked to give volunteer service to hospitals one day a month as a help to those institutions willing to cut student enrollment.[26]

In May 1932, the Illinois State Nurses Association (ISNA) petitioned hospital superintendents, directors of nursing, and presidents of hospital boards of directors to limit the number of students admitted for the coming year.[27] Many hospitals in the Chicago area complied—they were also financially strapped—and reported admitting smaller classes of students in 1932; several schools closed.[28] Private duty nurses in First District gave a month or more of free service to Chicago hospitals as an aid to institutions that promised to reduce enrollment; hospitals were quick to accept the offer.[29] Hospitals also offered nurses a variety of schemes that provided small amounts of remuneration, maintenance (e.g., room and board, uniforms), or a combination of both in exchange for work. Some hospitals offered nurses compensation ranging from $1 a day to $20 a month with maintenance for four hours of work a day. In other cases, hospitals provided nurses who were willing to work as general duty nurses for a varying number of hours full or partial maintenance with no salary.[30]

These efforts were intended to ameliorate the worst effects of the Depression but exerted little influence on the core working conditions of most nurses. Nurses waited out the bad economic times as best they could. The measure that contained the greatest potential for making inroads into improving nurse employment was the institution of the eight-hour day, a Depression-era spread-the-work scheme that significantly changed job opportunities for nurses and transformed the nurse supply/demand ratio for decades to come.

The Standardized Eight-Hour Day

The effort to reduce working hours, begun in the 1920s with twelve-hour shifts, continued to absorb private duty nurses' attention into the 1930s. Twelve-hour shifts improved working conditions but failed to satisfy fully private duty nurses' expectations for reasonable hours. The severe unemployment during the Depression gave nurses a persuasive argument to use in the battle for a shorter working day.

California launched the first eight-hour plan for private duty nurses in 1929; the movement advanced across the nation as the Depression deepened.[31] Between 1933 and 1935, a torrent of articles describing successful eight-hour plans for private duty nurses appeared in professional journals. These articles credited the eight-hour day with increasing employment, improving the quality of care, lowering the cost of private nursing, enhancing patient satisfaction, and promoting healthy living for nurses.[32] They resonated with the nation's private duty nurses and employers. Shorter working days gained ground in the nation's hospitals, anticipating future trends in hospital staffing, and increased the number of days private duty nurses worked from around 10 to 35 percent.[33] More than 150 hospitals nationwide adopted the eight-hour day for private duty nurses in 1933.[34] By 1937, the number of hospitals reporting eight-hour days for private duty nurses rose to 855, representing 20 percent of the nation's hospitals.[35] Of the hospitals reporting eight-hour plans, 679 limited private duty nurses exclusively to that shift. The eight-hour day spread to 1,039 hospitals by 1940.[36]

The professional association for nurses, the American Nurses Association (ANA), held a vital interest in the eight-hour day but considered working conditions a local matter better settled by district nurse associations; the association initially rejected active involvement in the movement on a national level. This attitude changed in 1933 when the ANA weighed in on the matter by issuing a pronouncement outlining the association's general position, which was that nurses should not be expected to work more than eight hours out of twenty-four.[37] The 1933 entry of the ANA into the discussion coincided with the passage of the National Recovery Act, which provided for federal regulation of work hours via a code system in selected industries. Hospital industry and professional nurses were exempt from the provisions of the act. However, there were numerous calls to the ANA from its members, 65 percent of whom were private duty nurses, demanding action from the organization to help underemployed working nurses. The outcry made the conservative ANA board of directors address the situation formally.[38] In 1934, the ANA house of delegates passed a resolution firmly supporting eight hours of work as the regular working day for nurses nationwide.[39]

Reports from professional nurse registries tracked the progress of eight-hour duty beginning in 1934.[40] From 1934 to 1940, the percentage of calls for eight-hour shifts out of the total number of calls received climbed from 24 percent in

1934 to 78 percent in 1940, during which time the total number of calls and days worked by private duty nurses increased. Although several factors, such as improved economic conditions and higher hospital bed occupancy, played a role in the overall growth in private duty calls during the second half of the 1930s, reports uniformly attributed the improvement in employment for private duty nurses to adoption of the eight-hour day.[41]

Patients also reaped benefits. The eight-hour day increased private duty employment by lowering the cost of one unit of private nursing service. Typically, an eight-hour nurse charged fees $1 to $2 lower than those working twelve-hour shifts. The elimination of extra meal charges for nurses added to patients' savings. When patients hired three eight-hour nurses, they paid for only three meals as opposed to six meals for two twelve-hour nurses. Three eight-hour nurses cost $16.50 per patient based on a cost of $5 per shift plus 50¢ for meals for each nurse. In comparison, two twelve-hour nurses cost an average of $17 a day.[42] The 50¢ savings, while not large, seemed sufficient to increase patients' use of private nursing services. Further, reducing the cost of private nurses contributed to changing practices in private duty use and promoted increased employment of nurses. Many patients, including those who previously could not afford around-the-clock private nursing, chose to use nurses for just one or two eight-hour shifts, rather than hire nurses over an entire twenty-four-hour period. A larger pool of patients using some degree of private nursing increased the total number of nurses employed.

Not all registries experienced an easy transition to eight-hour shifts. Chicago's NPR made its first foray in June 1932 when it initiated eight-hour private duty nurses as an additional choice for patients. This effort met with little success, and a year later First District joined the NPR in planning a wider, more vigorous crusade. The district reasoned that, because it was consumers who employed private nurses, it was important to get information on working hours for nurses before a general audience. Involving consumers in the campaign to shorten nurses' working hours was a tactic commonly used by nurses in other localities. The Chicago movement included publicizing the benefits of eight-hour care through radio announcements, newspaper articles, and talks to women's clubs and civic organizations.[43] Progress was still slow, with only sixteen hospitals in Chicago permitting eight-hour shifts for private nurses by 1934.[44] Even as yearly national reports on the increasing popularity of eight-hour duty continued to appear, by 1940 just twenty-three Chicago hospitals required eight-hour shifts exclusively for private nursing services.[45]

The introduction of eight-hour shifts by the NPR did not result in an immediate increase in patient calls. The raw number of patient calls for shorter shifts

veraged between 19 and 174 per month for the years 1933 and 1934, respec-
ively, representing less than 1 percent of calls received for 1933 and a mere
2 percent of calls for 1934.[46] In 1936, the NPR received 3,100 eight-hour calls,
n average of 258 calls per month, or a 50 percent increase from 1934 levels.
Measured against the total number of calls for nurses received by the NPR, eight-
our calls were only 16 percent of the total calls received in 1936 for eight-hour
urses.[47] This trend reversed over the next several years as the NPR witnessed
reater movement to eight-hour calls. In 1941 calls for nurses to work eight
ours represented 80 percent of total calls. The following year the percentage
f calls rose to 87 percent; this corresponded with national figures, in which
0 to 85 percent of calls received by professional registries were for eight-
our nurses.[48] Although the eight-hour day for private duty nurses predomi-
ated by the early 1940s, reports persisted of nurses working twelve-hour and
ven twenty-four-hour shifts into the 1940s. By 1945, the ISNA reported a
icroscopic percentage of twenty-four-hour duty, but a small percentage of
welve-hour duty was still requested in some areas.[49]

Significant opposition from three groups—physicians, hospitals, and
urses—delayed acceptance of an eight-hour working day for private duty
urses across the nation. Physicians repeated familiar arguments regarding the
ncreased cost to patients via having to pay more nurses. They predicted mis-
ommunications when several nurses took care of one patient and feared care
vould deteriorate.[50] The traditional practice of supplying nurses with meals
aid for by patients complicated the eight-hour issue for hospitals, making them
nore formidable adversaries to shorter hours.[51] When hospitals transitioned to
welve-hour shifts, they merely added on to patient charges three meals for the
econd nurse. However, charges for additional nurses' meals were less easy to
ationalize when each nurse was only in the hospital eight hours and reduced
our plans stipulated charging patients for only one meal per nurse. Some of the
arly successful eight-hour programs reported eliminating nurse meal charges
ntirely as part of the scheme.[52] Estimates of income received by hospitals for
urses' meals are sparse. Some reports indicated hospitals made from eleven to
ifty-two thousand dollars a year from nurses' meals. Many hospitals were reluc-
ant to reduce an easy source of income.[53]

Proponents of eight-hour plans argued that the increase in nurses used by
atients would cancel out losses incurred by reducing the meals per nurse.[54]
Others called on hospitals to end the practice of charging patients for meals.[55]
As the eight-hour day gained ground, the debate over nurses' meals escalated
nd was a catalyst for discussions on professionalism.[56] Discontent expressed by
rivate duty nurses over the inclusion of meals as part of their compensation

stemmed from hospitals' efforts to limit losses incurred from shorter working shifts. Many hospitals simply transferred financial responsibility for meals from patients to nurses, billing nurses for meals during their shifts whether they ate the meal or not. Nurses themselves were divided over the issue.[57]

In 1938, the ANA recommended the elimination of meals as part of private duty nurses' fees and advised hospitals not to force nurses to buy hospital meals, a recommendation which received slow acceptance.[58] In a 1940 study of 1,039 hospitals that implemented an eight-hour day, at least 83 percent required either the patient or the nurse to obtain and pay for hospital meals.[59] It was not until 1945 that Illinois's First District established a policy of eliminating meals as part of private duty charges.[60] Although mention of meals was dropped permanently from fee schedules, nurses were asked to cooperate with hospitals who claimed hardship in adhering to the changed policy.[61] Later reports still referenced the fact that nurses' wages included meals."[62]

The most serious opposition to eight-hour duty came from nurses who viewed shorter hours with suspicion. Fear of reduced income, altered meal policies, and simple resistance to change headed the list of nurses' complaints about eight-hour shifts.[63] In Illinois, opposition from or apathy exhibited by private duty nurses led to slow acceptance of eight-hour shifts, with resistance to eight-hour duty being more of a problem outside the Chicago area.[64] Private duty nurses in support of eight-hour work schedules accused the opposition of selfishness. However, opponents attributed the resistance to eight-hour duty to the fact that some private duty nurses had extensive, reliable patient bases and sufficient employment. Rather than recognize the severe financial plight of most nurses, some nurses chose to oppose change rather than help their colleagues.[65] For the most part, all of these charges were unsubstantiated and ignored a counter argument that each nurse should have the liberty of deciding hours of work.[66] A united front of a large proportion of nurses eventually prevailed in promoting the eight-hour shift.[67]

Patients accepted eight-hour shifts with more ease than any other stakeholder group and their use of private duty services changed with shorter hour nurses.[68] The choice of hiring a nurse for anywhere from eight to twenty-four hours at a reduced rate opened up the possibility of more patients obtaining private nursing. Articles in professional journals indicated that shorter hours did introduce private duty to a different patient population, such as patients who were unable to afford the cost of twelve-hour or twenty-four-hour nurses but who could more readily finance one eight-hour nurse.[69] A 1935–1936 study on consumer expenditures found that private nursing services were limited primarily to individuals in high income brackets—those earning over three thousand dollars a year—determining that only 40 percent of the population could afford private duty care.[70] Data collected at the time did not account for the impact of health insurance plans, which expanded in popularity as the eight-hour shift became more common. Demand for private duty nurses rose consistently into the 1940s during the same period that the number of people with health insurance also increased. Hospitals also expanded, due to the availability of funds through the Hill-Burton Hospital and Construction Act.[71]

Patients may also have appreciated the ability to choose from a variety of private duty service shifts, such as those at night when hospital staffing was low. Data on which shifts patients preferred to hire nurses for is minimal for the late 1930s but some reports indicated a growing preference for private nursing services during night shifts, contradicting a popular belief that patients preferred private nursing during the day. Patients recognizing differences in staffing levels between the three shifts may have felt more comfortable with individualized nursing care during the night hours when number of hospital-employed personnel on duty was typically low.[72]

Shorter Hours, Substantial Changes, Same Pay

The general satisfaction with eight-hour duty downplayed one critical outcome of reduced hours—shorter hours did not improve nurses' incomes. Nurses received more cases, worked more days, and increased their hourly rate of pay, but remained locked in a very low-paying job.[73] Several factors complicate estimating the impact shorter workdays exerted on income levels. Appraisal of nurse income levels during the Depression is problematic to evaluate in general, given the abnormal economic conditions overall. Studies analyzing the effect of eight-hour duty on nurse earnings do not exist. Private duty nurses failed to keep accurate accounts, making self-report of income suspect. Nurses claimed they did not know how much money they earned. Both Janet Geister, in her studies of New York private duty nurses during the 1920s, and the CGNS commented on nurses' incomplete knowledge of their yearly income.[74] Several authors during the 1930s noted that attempts to estimate nurse earnings were inexact, as most nurses did not keep adequate records.[75]

Two 1930s studies shed some light on private duty nurses' yearly income levels. In 1938, the ANA published an extensive study of salaries and employment conditions affecting nurses. The *Study of Incomes, Salaries and Employment Conditions Affecting Nurses* surveyed nurses from twenty-three states working in institutions, and as private duty and office nurses. Over 11,000 nurses, including 245 private duty nurses in Illinois, reported on their income and working conditions for the years 1934 and 1935.[76] Although the small

Table 6.3.
Salaries and days worked for nurses nationally and in Illinois,
1934 and 1935

Year	Nationally		Illinois	
	1934	1935	1934	1935
Median yearly salary	$733	$810	$763	$798
Median number of days worked	157	174	141	157

Source: American Nurses Association 1938.

number of nurses surveyed both nationally and statewide limits the applicability of the results of the study, the results provide an idea of trends in income for
private duty nurses, indicating abysmally low yearly revenue. The results
also showed Illinois nurses worked fewer hours for more pay, an indication of
geographic variations that are difficult to explain (see table 6.3).

A second survey of working conditions for private duty nurses, completed
by the ISNA in 1939, resulted in similar findings. A total of 659 private duty
nurses completed questionnaires on annual salary, days, and shifts worked and
a variety of other employment conditions.[77] None of the nurses in the study
worked more than a total number of days equal to six months of a year. The average income reported for 1937 was $560.95. In 1938, nurses averaged $663.14.[78]
The results of the two studies demonstrate a bleak picture for private duty nurses
overall. Despite high hopes for improved working conditions from a shorter
working day and the reported increased demand for private nursing services,
they were still earning about 50 percent less than the $1,311 average yearly
income estimated by the CGNS in late 1920s.[79]

Even though the shift hour change did not increase their income, the eight-
hour day's significance for private duty nurses was substantial. On several different levels the shorter workday exerted a profound influence on employment
conditions for working nurses in general. Historian Marilyn Flood noted that
efforts to obtain eight hours of work for private duty nurses predated those for
staff nurses—private duty nurses were trendsetters. Flood claimed private duty
nurses set the standard for hours of work for both general and private duty
nurses.[80] The ground that private duty nursing laid further explains why hospitals actively opposed or reluctantly approved shorter hours for private duty
nurses. Hospitals feared that if one group of nurses within an institution, such
as private duty nurses, worked only eight hours, all nurses would ask for a similar privilege, driving up hospital costs overall.

Private duty nurses experienced different patterns of work after the introduction of eight-hour days. When nurses worked twelve to twenty-four hours, they often took extended periods of time between cases to rest and recuperate. Less fatigued from eight-hour shifts, nurses returned to on-call status faster.[81] The increased demand for private duty nurses, believed to be the result of eight-hour duty, challenged the market to supply sufficient nurses. Without market stresses, which were lacking in the mid-1930s, supply and demand balanced each other.

Perhaps the most critical outcome of reduced work hours for nurses was not apparent to most. Shorter hours of work for private duty nurses broke the model of continuous nursing care of patients from the initial onset of illness to its termination. Eight-hour shifts empowered patients to employ private duty nurses in a myriad of ways. Patients might hire nurses for only one or two shifts as opposed to a whole illness. Private duty nursing became episodic rather than a continuous model of nursing practice, with mixed results for nurses. Nurses achieved regular working hours with a chance for a greatly improved quality of life, but this accomplishment came at the expense of their commitment to close personal care. Sharing patients with other nurses eliminated the unique nature of the private duty nurse-patient relationship. When nurses gave up the one-to-one nurse-patient relationship over the course of a patient's illness, they lost a very particular and valuable aspect of professional nursing.

As the economy improved after the height of the Depression in 1933, professional nurse registries reported better employment conditions beginning as early as 1934. Nationally, registries received across-the-board increases in calls for the years 1935–1937. Decreases occurred in 1938 and 1939 as a result of the 1937–1938 recession. By 1940, business rebounded, and professional registries reported a slight increase (3.5 percent) in calls received.[82]

Reports of sporadic nursing shortages began appearing in professional journals as early as 1936 and were discussed intently at the June 1936 ANA board of directors meeting and American Hospital Association conference.[83] Hospitals blamed the shortage on greater demand for nurses after institution of the eight-hour day, stabilization of the economy enabling patients to afford to hire private duty nurses once more, and a pronounced expansion in hospital use.[84] Hospital occupancy rates for general hospitals rose from 64 percent in 1935 to 70 percent in 1940.[85] Improved medical techniques and increased medical specialization accounted for some of the increase in hospital utilization but a more obvious reason was enrollment in hospital insurance plans that permitted more people to afford institutional care.[86] In 1935, there were approximately 75,000 subscribers to insurance plans; by 1939 the number jumped to 2,900,000 nationwide.[87]

Controversy existed over whether there was a real shortage of nurses. Many nurses were suspicious, believing hospitals were using talk of shortages as an excuse for admitting larger student classes in their training schools, which decreased the need to hire graduate nurses. Hospitals began to hire less-trained workers such as nurse aides and assistants. Nurses believed such workers threatened their livelihoods by offering hospitals a low-cost solution to staffing problems.[88] Some employers believed better working conditions would cure any shortage problems. "I think the secret of getting nurses is to pay a living wage, give them good conditions of life and good food," remarked one hospital administrator at an AHA convention.[89] Other contended that the increased revenues hospitals were receiving from a sudden influx of insured paying patients should be used to attract nurses via higher salaries to institutional jobs.[90] In the private duty market, supply and demand conditions argued against a nursing shortage. The high fill rate for calls reported by professional nurse registries for the second half of the 1930s, which ranged from 96 to 99 percent, indicated a market in equilibrium between supply and demand.[91]

Despite the improved overall conditions, data from the NPR and other indices reveal a less positive picture. The average daily number of private duty nurses on call dropped from 434 in 1934 to 325 in 1936.[92] This represented a 25 percent decrease in nurses waiting on a call. To the more than three hundred nurses not working daily, this may have seemed small comfort. In 1937, the NPR reported no nurse shortage in Chicago.[93] A year later, conditions deteriorated again, although not to Great Depression–era levels. Because so many nurses were waiting for calls, the NPR temporarily limited registry membership to graduates of hospitals affiliated with the registry.[94] Over the next two years, NPR records reported a supply of nurses adequate to demand. At times, scores of nurses moving into the Chicago area made it difficult for nurses to obtain enough work.[95] The available work seemed to ebb and flow, according to nursing supply.

Despite what appeared to be a labor market trying to equilibrate, reports of private duty nurse shortages persisted. The explanation for why such reports appeared at the same time the private duty market was meeting demand can be found in the changing nurse labor market. It was general duty nurses, not private duty nurses, who hospitals hired in the late 1930s. A growing movement for hospitals to use private duty nurses as general duty staff nurses attests to the increasing interest of hospitals in nurses who would care for many patients, not just one patient. In 1936, reports from professional nurse registries noted an increase in the number of calls from hospitals for nurses for temporary general duty, now referred to as staff nursing. The percentage of calls for temporary staff nurses, also known as per diem nurses, received by registries rose slightly between 1937 and 1940, from 5 to 5.7 percent. The small percentage increase that corresponded with a simultaneous increase in the total calls received overall concealed a significant rise in the actual number of calls for general duty. In 1937, professional registries received 29,658 calls for general duty; by 1940 it increased to 38,089.[96]

Using private duty nurses intermittently as staff nurses was an easy way for hospitals to supplement insufficient staffs.[97] Private duty nurses could be hired and dismissed as patient occupancy rates rose and fell. This opened an additional source of calls for private duty nurses, but did not have universal appeal. Problems, such as setting the rate of pay, hours of work, and reprisals against private duty nurses who refused to comply with hospital requests for temporary help, marred the relationship between the two parties.[98]

Professional registries reported more difficulty filling calls for temporary staff nurse positions than for private duty calls. Between 1934 and 1940 registries filled regular private duty calls 100 percent of the time. The percentage of calls filled for temporary staff nursing ranged from 87 percent in 1937 to 91 percent in 1940. Nurses cited the long, strenuous hours of work and inadequate remuneration as reasons for refusing temporary staff nurse positions.[99] The *American Journal of Nursing*'s 1940 report on professional nurse registries attempted to rationalize lower rates of filling calls for temporary staff nurse positions by using the obvious and circular reasoning that nurse registrants preferred private duty to staff nursing, which was why they registered at private duty registries and did not work as hospital staff nurses in the first place.[100] But this explanation underplayed the significant problems private duty nurses experienced when they accepted temporary staff nurse positions.

Wages received for temporary staff nurse positions, considerably lower than the fee charged for regular private duty, presented the greatest source of discontent for private duty nurses.[101] Hospitals typically offered private duty nurses a daily fee prorated from the monthly schedule rate of pay for permanent staff nurses. Hospitals still included maintenance (e.g., meals, uniforms, laundry, or a combination) as part of staff nurse compensation; this wasn't part of the daily prorated fee. The 1938 ANA study on incomes, salaries, and employment conditions found that 65 percent of 6,790 institutional (staff) nurses surveyed received full maintenance as part of their remuneration. Another 28 percent received partial maintenance. Only 4 percent of institutional nurses did not receive maintenance.[102] In 1938, a study of general duty nurses carried out by the ISNA found that of 628 institutional nurses, 52 percent received full maintenance as part of their salary, and 37 percent received partial maintenance. Only 9 percent of the nurses received a full cash salary (without maintenance).[103]

The practice of assigning nurses to split shifts (nonconsecutive hours of duty) represented another irritant for private duty nurses. A nurse might be hired from 7 A.M. to 11 A.M., receive a four-hour break during a slow period of the shift, and then return to duty from 3 P.M. to 7 P.M.. Hospitals used split shifts as a means of providing coverage at busy times without hiring additional staff. Private duty nurses, who were accustomed to working consecutive hours, resented split shifts. Because they lived outside hospital grounds, private duty nurses who wished to return home during their break period made four trips to and from work over an eight-hour day.[104]

A significant cause of dissatisfaction with temporary staff nursing occurred in institutions that required private duty nurses to provide service supplementing the regular staff as general duty nurses. Some hospitals refused to allow nurses who refused temporary staff positions to receive private duty calls in the institution.[105] The ANA considered these complaints in its 1938 study of working conditions for nurses and made several recommendations designed to relieve some of the worst aspects of temporary general duty care. These included asking hospitals to pay temporary staff nurses based on location, to assign private duty nurses to consecutive hours only, and to ensure that nurses not be denied private duty privileges if they declined temporary staff nurse positions.[106]

In Chicago, nurses registered at the NPR who filled calls for temporary staff nursing echoed the complaints of unfair treatment by hospitals found in national reports.[107] By the early 1940s calls for temporary staff nurse positions increased dramatically in response to a general problem of staffing hospitals related to wartime needs for nurses.[108] Even as they requested more and more temporary nurses, hospitals paid them below typical fees for private duty nurse service. Some hospitals paid staff nurses only $3 to $4 a day at a time when private duty nurses received $5 a day.[109] Usually, nurses were required to work split shifts as part of staff nursing service. Some hospitals allowed the nurse to retain her position on the registry list while on a staff nurse assignment, releasing her when she received a case; in others, nurses had to give up their places on the registry list when filling temporary staff nurse positions. Many nurses reported that hospitals discriminated against them if they refused temporary staff nurse jobs. Even in hospitals that did not discriminate, there were warnings to nurses that temporary staff nursing was expected and that refusing requests for temporary service would not be overlooked by hospital authorities. Troubles between nurses and hospitals over filling temporary staff nursing positions continued into the war years.[110] The punitive, authoritarian approaches devised by hospitals to engage nurses for patient care defied logic and failed to result in satisfactory responses to staffing issues. Private duty nurses continued to resist filling temporary staff nurse positions, and hospitals persisted in devising solutions designed to alleviate nurse shortages but failing to resolve them in the long term.

Conclusion

As the country entered the war years, conditions for nurse employment improved. In 1940, the NPR reported its busiest year on record. The registry reported proudly that twenty-two hospitals used the NPR exclusively for private nursing services. Another forty institutions used the registry as needed. The registry felt comfortable enough with economic conditions to raise membership fees.[111] NPR finances improved; the registry showed one of the highest post-Depression profits.[112] Reports of registry effectiveness in meeting demand for nurses began to resemble those of the late 1920s. Demand for nurses was high, membership was up, and profits were good. The NPR continued their well-deserved claim as the premier distributor of professional private nursing services in the Chicago area.

In New York, the two major professional registries, the NBMB and NB14, mirrored patterns seen by the NPR in both private duty nurse use and nurse membership, testifying to a stable private duty nurse business that on the surface appeared much as it had in the late 1920s. At the same time, significant alterations occurring within the private duty market indicated a labor market in considerable flux.

During the 1930s, nurses achieved a beginning step to a more normative working life with the institution of the eight-hour day. Although not completely accepted across the nation as standard hours of work, eight-hour service for private duty nurses represented major progress in regularizing nurses' labor with that of other occupations and considerably transformed private duty nurses' relationships with their patients. Shorter work days also contributed to increased demand for nurses, a trend already underway as hospitals began to need more graduate nurses available for patient care.

The growing demand for nurses came at a steep price, creating an adversarial relationship between nurses and hospitals. Accustomed to using more pliant and obedient student workers, hospitals approached nurses' reluctance to take on staff nurse work with punitive measures that worked to repel nurses rather than attract them to hospital employment. The actions of hospitals foreshadowed trends used by hospitals over the next decades as they attempted to address increasing nurse shortages. The situation posed serious problems as the country faced World War II minus a sufficient supply of professional nurses. Conflicts between nurses and hospitals over whether nurses should continue to work as independent private duty nurses or employed staff nurses highlighted the growing control hospitals exerted over nurse work. The next chapter examines the how the nation grappled with a supply of nurses insufficient to meet demand, the solutions proposed, and the effects on nurses in the private duty market as they increasingly sought employed hospital positions.

Chapter 7

More and More (and Better) Nurses

> If you say more and better [nurses] that's just wonderful but [first] it has to be more.
>
> —Surgeon General Thomas Parren's response to
> Nursing Chief Lucile Petry Leone's wartime plans
> to both increase the number of nurses and upgrade
> nursing education

The most pressing issue facing the nursing profession from 1940 to 1950 was supplying care sufficient to meet institutional and patient demand. Developing tactics to meet nurse demand outlasted World War II, consumed the attention of nurse and health-care leaders, and shifted the employment patterns of nurses. This period saw the implementation of three main strategies: an increase in the number of nurses graduating from schools of nursing, installation of a three-tiered hierarchy of hospital nurse workers to rationalize the nurse labor market, and improvement of the distribution of nurses by replacing independently employed private duty nurses with institutionally employed staff nurses. Improvement of nurse working conditions did not figure into these strategies. Concentrating on the supply of nurses and new types of nurse workers without attending to the working environment failed to solve the shortage issue and created significant tensions within the market. For private duty nurses, the changed circumstances significantly altered the way in which they practiced nursing.

As the country entered World War II, the nursing profession faced the significant challenge of supplying nurses to care for the extraordinary needs of both the military and civilian population. Surgeon General Parren's response typified what many in the medical field assumed would provide the solution to the wartime nurse shortage—produce more and more nurses. After all, since the beginning of the twentieth century, the nation's health-care system demonstrated a robust and remarkable ability to increase the number of nurses, enlarging the professional nursing workforce from a mere 11,000 in 1900 to approximately 284,159 by 1940. Producing more nurses seemed a strategy assured of success.[1]

Expanding the nurse workforce met some of the immediate demand but failed to ensure a stable workforce for a more technologically advanced health-care system than had been present in the pre-war period. Solution by numbers proved insufficient to the war and postwar shortages. Even as more nurses graduated from nursing educational programs, nurse shortages persisted and threatened the safe delivery of patient care in the nation's hospitals.[2]

Yes, Virginia, There Is a Shortage of Nurses

The nursing profession acknowledged the existential threat of worldwide war and recognized the critical role nurses would play in the conflict. In 1940, even before the bombing of Pearl Harbor, several leading professional organizations formed the Nursing Council on National Defense (NCND), which eventually became the National Nursing Council, an organization composed of six major nursing associations and several federal agencies central to nurse utilization and resources.[3] The council was a voluntary body designed to coordinate and develop plans for nursing's response to the war emergency. The council also represented a major and unprecedented cooperative effort on the part of organized nursing to work together on issues of national import. Its members seized the war situation not only to carry out the profession's patriotic duty but also to advance professional aspirations designed to improve and reform nursing.[4] Significantly, the council included as a full partner the National Association of Colored Graduate Nurses (NACGN), which waged a contentious but ultimately successful battle to include African American nurses in the war effort, presaging the later racial integration of the profession. A second governmental entity, also set up in 1940, the Subcommittee on Nursing, a subcommittee of the Health and Medical Committee to Advise the Council on National Defense, handled nursing matters with federal agencies and worked in close cooperation with the council.[5]

The council's first order of business was to carry out a national inventory of registered nurses.[6] The 1941 inventory, conducted through the United States Public Health Service, laid to rest skepticism raised in the late 1930s that the country had a nursing shortage. Results indicated that the country had about 289,286 registered nurses, of which approximately 173,055 were actively engaged in nursing practice. Of these, 89,327, or 51.6 percent, met the primary requirements for potential military duty. Another 25,252 inactive nurses indicated availability for duty if needed. Given that not all nurses available would meet military standards, the inventory estimated there were 75,000 nurses eligible for armed force service but that a total shortage of 76,000 nurses for combined military and civilian needs existed.[7] Approximations of nursing shortages fluctuated over the course of the war, climbing to over 100,000 by the end of the hostilities.[8]

The situation was dire. Even if nursing schools accelerated their programs to less than the traditional three years, a limit existed to how fast the system could produce one nurse, let alone 76,000 of them. Furthermore, as the draft kicked into high gear, removing many men from the workforce, employment opportunities for women and the better pay that went with them cut into the pool of nursing's typical recruits of young white females. As one author noted: "The nurse shortage was not met in 1941. It is not being met in 1942. And, if the war continues, it seems evident that it will not be met in 1943 or 1944 on the present basis of operation."[9]

Initially, nursing and government leaders hoped that somehow more nurses would be located to mitigate the crisis. Some believed that large numbers of "hidden" nurses who failed to answer the 1941 inventory could ease the shortage.[10] One commentator lamented that nurses tended to marry and raise families, dropping their actual workforce rate to only 60 percent; this, if the commentator thought about it a bit, was a remarkable rate for a predominantly female occupation.[11] The war placed nurses in a gender bind. At a time when other American women were urged to keep the home fires burning till the men returned, nurses received admonishment for not signing up for military service abroad.

Private duty nurses received criticism for not contributing more to the war effort. In 1942, the council's *Distribution of Nursing Service during the War* provided guidelines for determining the most efficient use of wartime nurse resources. The council recommended that private duty nurses should be reserved for "acutely ill patients, for those requiring special treatments, and for patients in situations where the limited amount of nursing service available make it necessary for private duty nurses to be employed."[12] The recommendation preceded the War Manpower Commission's 1943 *Procurement and Assignment Services for Physicians, Dentists, Veterinarians & Nurses*, which stipulated in the section "Criteria of Essentiality for Nurses," that private duty nurses be used only for acutely ill patients. The 1943 report also recommended that nurses not necessary for acute care should work on other types of essential nursing service such as general staff nursing, public health nursing, or work in industrial health services or physicians' offices.[13]

Private duty registries took the primacy of private duty nurses seriously. Brooklyn's NB14 asked physicians to elicit patients' cooperation in hiring nurses only when necessary and reminded nurses that they must care solely for the critically ill.[14] The guidelines, which did not carry the force of law, were confusing. Patients often interpreted the guidelines as prohibiting all private duty nursing, which the council lumped into the category of "luxury nursing," that it defined as using private duty nurses during periods of convalescence.[15] In letters to the *American Journal of Nursing*, nurses debated the issue. One nurse challenged private duty nurses to give up their independent practices and take hospital positions to preserve the country's sovereignty and liberties.[16] Another nurse defended private duty as providing essential services, listing the types of patients she cared for as including asthmatics with coexisting pneumonia and surgical patients receiving postoperative procedures requiring continuous monitoring, as well as patients with skull fractures, peritonitis, and severe burns.[17]

The national inventory found that private duty nurses comprised 27 percent of actively employed nurses, a significant percentage responsible for care delivery.[18] A 1943 study carried out by the War Manpower Commission's Procurement and Assignment Service calculated that private duty nurses provided more than 30 percent of bedside care delivered by graduate nurses; in some hospitals private duty service almost equaled the hours of nursing service given by general staff nurses. Removing them would only increase the work of general staff nurses. The study also noted that many nurses unable to work as general staff nurses due to age or physical status could still care for patients that required close monitoring in an era before the introduction of intensive and cardiac care units.[19]

Hospitals also continued using private duty nurses as temporary per diem nurses to supplement small staffs.[20] The ANA monthly reports on professional registries reported a 19 percent increase in calls for private duty nurses for per diem hospital positions from 1940 to 1941, a measure that stabilized between 1942 and 1944 and remained a vital service provided by professional nurse registries as part of the effort to maintain hospital nurse staffing.[21] Private duty nurses also did their part by volunteering for military service; an estimated 14.4 percent of returning veterans were previous private duty nurses, a percentage similar to that of public health, industrial, and office nurses.[22]

As the nation struggled to supply enough nurses, two groups of nurses remained grossly underutilized—African American women and men of all races. Historian Charissa Threat eloquently chronicles how gender and race prevented full use of a vital portion of the professional nurse workforce, noting that even before Pearl Harbor African American female nurses "rushed to the nearest Red Cross recruiting location to join the nurse corps."[23] Once they arrived they were rebuffed and refused acceptance into the Army Nurse Corps, a situation not reversed until the final years of the war. Men of all races who were nurses received similar if slightly different treatment. Denied admittance as nurses into the all-female Army Nurse Corps, men who were nurses served either as less-skilled medical technicians or orderlies, or as frontline soldiers.[24]

Those charged with addressing the shortage problem, the National Nursing Council, the Subcommittee on Nursing, and federal legislators, reached a consensus that the nation faced a nursing crisis requiring significant measures and developed a focused approach. Referred to as "the three-point program," the plan consisted of increasing student nurses and auxiliary nonprofessional nurse workers while distributing graduate nurses in an equitable manner, such as moving private duty nurses into general staff nurse positions where they could care for more than one patient, to meet war needs.[25] Despite limited evidence of their effectiveness, these strategies remained the mainstay of approaches to nurse shortages throughout the later twentieth century. The first, increasing the supply of student nurses, was the most successful at achieving its objectives and represented the first massive federal program for nursing education, the United States Cadet Nurse Corps.

Underlying all approaches to wartime nurse shortages was the reasoning that military requirements for nurses took precedence over civilian needs. Encouraging young women through financial incentives to enter nursing education programs became the main means of staffing hospitals. Two appropriations, in 1941 and 1942, represented the initial foray of the federal government into supporting nursing education but the paltry amounts, a little over five million dollars, failed to appreciably increase the numbers of students. By 1943, concerns over the lack of nurses created a public health crisis that laid the groundwork for a much larger program.[26]

The Cadet Nurse Corps

The 1943 Nurse Training Act, known as the Bolton Act in honor of its congressional sponsor, Ohio Representative Frances Payne Bolton, was designed to remedy shortages through the creation of the Cadet Nurse Corps (CNC) program. The act further provided massive amounts of federal aid, approximately $180 million by the act's end, to nursing schools and students for educational purposes. The financial support to students attracted entrants who augmented understaffed hospitals, freeing up graduate nurses to serve in the military. It provided monies to students either directly or on their behalf for tuition, uniforms, instructional materials, and a monthly stipend over the course of their studies, with schools receiving funds for student maintenance costs.[27]

The enormously popular CNC received credit for averting a complete wartime breakdown of hospital nursing service and successfully increased the number of nursing students delivering hospital care from 99,952 in 1943 to 125,677 in 1945.[28] Analyses of the CNC emphasize improvements in the state of nursing education and the precedent-setting role of federal government support for nursing education.[29] Approximately 90 percent of existing nursing schools participated in the CNC. It stabilized nursing education by requiring adherence to a set of regulations promulgated by the surgeon general and the program's administrator, the U.S. Public Health Service's Division of Nurse Education, not heretofore required of nursing education, such as state accreditation and connection with a hospital approved by the American College of Surgeons.[30] Consultative services offered to those schools requiring improvement aided inferior programs. The program included a nondiscrimination clause opening it up to all schools of nursing and providing typically underfunded African American schools of nursing (both in historically black colleges and universities and hospitals) with welcome financial assistance.

The CNC's commitment to and implementation of nursing education reform is considered the program's major contribution, yet the CNC's influence on nursing practice, although less recognized, was considerable. First and foremost, the CNC model situated student nurses as the main providers of hospital nursing service. Although this was a traditional model used by hospitals, use at this time validated the practice of using partially educated nurses as primary patient caregivers in times of shortage. Reliance on student nurses also contributed to the dominance of hospital-controlled nurse education programs, at least in the immediate postwar era. Perhaps most critically, CNC graduates favored hospital employment over the private duty market, which changed the pattern of nurses' postwar careers. This shift, the direct result of the way in which the CNC program organized the program of studies, intensified and accelerated the transformation of the nurse labor market begun in the 1930s.

The key to the CNC's aims was the requirement that educational programs reduce study time from thirty-six to thirty months. Students spent the first twenty-four months in course work and practical experience, with the last six months, identified as the "senior cadet" period, working full time under supervision in a federal or nonfederal hospital in a role similar to that of the graduate nurse.[31] In theory, senior cadets replaced fully educated nurses destined to serve in the military. Estimates on how that worked in practice do not exist. In 1944, the first year senior cadets were available, only 12,000 students qualified, an insignificant amount. A year later, a more robust pool of 25,000 senior cadets entered hospital practice as the war was winding down.[32] Most senior cadets (73 percent) stayed in their home hospitals; the remaining 27 percent worked in the army, navy, Veterans Administration, Public Health Service, and Indian Service.[33]

The senior cadet period, considered innovative because it changed traditional ways of educating nurses, exerted more influence on the types of jobs nurses sought after graduation.[34] Working as staff nurses for the last six months of their education normalized hospital employment for graduate nurses who typically stayed at their home hospitals. Hospitals reaped the benefits of having available a steady stream of new staff nurses who did not require extensive and expensive orientations and the practice prolonged the time a hospital could depend on their services.

The transition to hospital employment caused a drop in the percentage of nurses working as private duty nurses. Between 1941 and 1949, the number of active private duty nurses actually rose from 46,793 to 65,032, yet the percentage of working nurses who engaged in private duty fell from 27 percent to 21.6 percent.[35] Multiple factors drove the decrease in private duty nurses, but the impact of the CNC on nurses' professional decisions was noteworthy and long-lasting. The assumption that new graduates would seek out the private sector for work disappeared as hospitals became the employer of choice.

All Who Nurse for Hire

For many, the quickest way to produce the massive number of caregivers required for the war effort was to create a group of assistive personnel who could carry out non-essential nursing tasks not requiring the expertise and knowledge of a professional nurse. This approach, which divided nursing work into different levels based on education and skills, was an important facet of the three-point program laid out at the beginning of the war. The program recommended expanding the use of auxiliary, nonprofessional nurse workers through the training of nurse aides and licensed practical nurses (LPNs). However, introducing large numbers of assistive personnel, previously known as subsidiary workers, was controversial for private duty nurses who traditionally viewed such workers as competitors. The roots of the LPN movement lay in Depression-era attempts to alleviate an overcrowded nurse labor market, but took on a far different purpose during the 1940s when LPNs received support as the answer to nurse shortages.

During the Great Depression New York State passed a mandatory nurse practice act that included a provision addressing LPNs. New York was a prime location for the start of the LPN movement; it was the most populous state and the largest home state of nurses, with an estimated seventy thousand individuals hiring out as nurses.[36] In 1933, anxious to deal with an overcrowded labor market and firmly establish the status of legitimate registered nurses, the NYSNA set out on a course to improve and replace the standing 1920 Nurse Registration Act.[37]

The push for new legislation received significant support in 1934 when the State Education Department released the results of the Horner Report, a survey of the nurse labor market that provided data and statistics validating assumptions that the private duty nurse market was overcrowded and underpaid. An estimated 32,404 licensed registered nurses and 36,579 unlicensed individuals, most of whom worked in the private duty field, competed for patients and jobs in an unregulated market with a declining number of job opportunities that was the result of the financial crisis.[38]

The Horner Report recommended passage of a mandatory nurse practice act with the inclusion of a new nurse classification, the LPN.[39] Building on the report's conclusions and recommendations, the NYSNA drafted a bill for a new nurse practice act requiring licensing for "all who nurse for hire," creating a second-level practical nurse category, and providing definitions of both professional and practical nursing that distinguished between the two fields of nursing practice.[40] These three provisions reflected the legislative requirements professional leaders had developed over the years to create "a real" nurse practice act.[41] The most important aspect of the act required anyone who nursed to secure a license to work as a nurse, with penalties imposed on those who did not. For years, professional nurse associations had hoped to strengthen existing nurse registration acts with mandatory licensure provisions; the situation in New York presented the best opportunity to achieve this aim, with acceptance of an LPN category considered worth the price.

On a national level, organized nursing faced increasing pressure to create a category of less-trained nurses and welcomed New York State's efforts to license LPNs. At the same time that New York State nurses lobbied for a new nurse practice act, a joint committee of the three major nursing associations, the ANA, the National League for Nursing Education (NLNE), and the National Organization for Public Health Nursing (NOPHN), also addressed the issue. The culmination of the joint committee's work was the 1940 release of *Subsidiary Workers in the Care of the Sick*, which outlined the major, pre–World War II positions of organized nursing regarding subsidiary workers.[42]

Opposition to the practical nurse provision came primarily from working private duty nurses, who worried about increased competition and believed licensing practical nurses legitimized such employees in the eyes of the public, further encouraging their use. Proponents argued that the bill would eliminate competition by controlling unlicensed nurses, pointing out that patients often hired nurses based purely on financial considerations; they employed a registered nurse if they could afford one, and resorted to an unlicensed practical nurse if they could not. Two levels of practice would guide families and physicians when choosing nursing personnel based on patient need and eliminate nurses who were unable to meet the licensing requirements.[43] The act's proponents also held out hope that a second regulating device would work to control LPN practice and create acceptance from the private duty group. Nursing leaders believed that LPNs would seek work through the professional registry system, ensuring their appropriate assignment to patients, such as homebound individuals with chronic conditions, and that their fees would be lower than those of registered nurses.

The act, known as the Todd-Fell Act, passed in 1938 but an overwhelming number of applications from both registered and practical nurses led to a delay in enacting the mandatory provisions until 1941. Nurses could continue to register under the two levels of the act, but registration would not be obligatory for practice as a nurse.[44] In December 1941 the state hospital association requested a further delay, claiming that the wartime nurse shortage would cause a hardship for hospitals if they were required to adhere to the mandatory provisions. A 1942 amendment to the act delayed implementation of the mandatory provisions until six months after hostilities ended; this delay was extended beyond the war years based on reports of persistent nurse shortages.[45] Postponement of the act at the request of hospital authorities continued until 1948 when the NYSNA successfully promoted an amendment to require enforcement. In 1949, New York State finally achieved a mandatory nursing practice law when the "all who nurse for hire" provision became obligatory.[46]

The Modern Licensed Practical Nurse Emerges

As only the mandatory provisions of the Todd-Fell Act were delayed, practical nurse licensing proceeded once the law was passed in 1938. Licensed practical nurse educational programs grew, and by 1940 the New York State Education Department approved nine schools of practical nursing.[47] Nursing leaders cooperated in the establishment of LPN programs and exerted as much control as they could over the type and use of graduates emerging from such programs. Between 1942 and 1943, decisions made by the joint committee promoted the training and use of practical nurses as an effective measure to increase the supply of nurse workers available to the civilian population.[48] In 1945 the National

Nursing Planning Committee, a committee charged with outlining a postwar program for nursing, included full recognition of practical nurses.[49] By the end of the war, seven states had joined New York in licensing either practical nurses or trained attendants, bringing the total number of states with such provisions to twenty.[50] Forty-eight state-approved schools opened in those states with licensing laws for LPNs.[51]

While leaders participated fully in the integration of LPNs into health care, private duty nurses continued to be suspicious of them. Janet Geister, still a champion of working nurses, gave voice to their concerns in a 1944 article in *Trained Nurse and Hospital Review*.[52] Acknowledging that some private duty nurses felt betrayed by the professional associations for promoting practical nurses, Geister warned that the LPN movement was vigorous and unstoppable, endorsing the approach adopted by national groups for "safe" practical nursing via licensing. She revived the idea that the private duty registry system could control LPN practice and proclaimed that expansion and better financial support of the registry system were the best means of supervising and distributing LPNs. Geister maintained her belief that nurse-run agencies could and should exert tight control over LPNs. However, events within the nurse labor market dictated a different path for practical nurses. Examination of how professional nurse registries adjusted to licensed practical nurses illustrates World War II–era changes in the nurse labor market that directly influenced private duty and practical nurse practice.

The presence of a nursing shortage shortly after passage of the New York State nurse practice act licensing practical nurses provided the testing ground for the two-level nursing system. The experience of Brooklyn's NB14 failed to show the validity of the system. Although the NB14 enrolled practical nurses from the beginning, a decline in practical nurse registrants occurred during the war years, dropping from a pre–World War II level of 35 percent to 19 percent of registrants in 1943, with a further decline to 13 percent in the postwar years.[53] The registry received many calls appropriate for practical nurses and seriously considered the shortage of registrants.[54] Registry officials blamed the lower number of practical nurse registrants on commercial agencies, which permitted practical nurses to charge patients higher fees than allowed by the NB14.[55] The NB14 maintained a comparatively lower rate of practical nurse fees until 1943, when it raised fees to $5 for an eight-hour shift to attract more registrants.[56] As LPN fees became more uniform throughout the city, the NB14 agreed to set practical nurse charges at 75 percent of the registered nurse rate.[57] Despite these efforts designed to draw in more registrants, membership of practical nurses remained flat. NB14 director Emma Collins predicted that the registry, unable to fill calls, would see its market for LPNs diminish.[58] However, Collins's forecast did not account for the considerable change in the nurse labor market. Employment patterns of LPNs in the initial years after the passage of the mandatory nurse practice act illustrates why the NB14 failed to capture more of the practical nurse market.

Analysis of available statistics on LPNs indicates that they sought hospital jobs, with a clear national trend demonstrating hospitals' expanded employment of ancillary staff in all categories, including LPNs. In New York State, over a five-year period from 1945 to 1949, the number of auxiliary workers employed in hospitals more than doubled, from 17,573 to 38,735 workers.[59] Because LPNs were counted together with all auxiliary workers, the actual number of practical nurses employed by hospitals is unknown, yet studies completed during the 1940s suggest that anywhere from 30 to 70 percent of practical nurse graduates entered hospital employment.[60]

Considering the educational system developed for practical nurses, it was not surprising that graduate LPNs sought work in acute care institutions. Regulations for clinical experience for student LPNs prescribed a system different from that of earlier programs, which emphasized the home care of patients. The schools that educated LPNs in the 1940s required at least six months' clinical experience in a general hospital, and graduates logically sought hospital employment after graduation.[61] Given the prolonged nursing shortage, it was reasonable that hospitals would take advantage of this new group of licensed personnel.[62]

National figures indicated that professional registries placed only small numbers of nonprofessional workers, despite a 1944 call from ANA urging registries to list nonprofessionals and a steady increase in requests for nonprofessional services received by registries.[63] In 1948, the total number of practical nurse registrants listed in 101 professional nurse registries was under 2,000.[64]

Conflicted Relationships

The war years posed the same problems for the NBMB that were encountered by the NB14. By early 1942, registry reports indicated tremendous difficulties in filling private duty calls, especially for night cases.[65] To relieve the shortage situation, registry officials implemented plans such as requiring nurses to rotate to night shifts for a specified period and adopting special nurse insignia indicating willingness to work in an emergency. These solutions were not enough to address the enormous demand.[66] Unlike the NB14, where stable financial circumstances lessened the economic threat to the agency, wartime membership in the NBMB declined as private duty nurses either entered the military or sought hospital positions, resulting in a loss of operating income. In July 1943, an emergency occurred: monthly expenses doubled expected income. The NBMB faced potential bankruptcy.[67] Reorganizing registry operations, increasing registrant fees, and cutting staff, including the executive director and her assistant, reduced expenses and saved the agency from financial ruin.[68] One year later, profits increased and registry staff received salary increases. By December 1944, income received from membership receipts was so high that the board of directors voted to rebate a portion of the fees back to registrants.[69]

The good fortunes of the registry did extend to its practical nurse registrants. The NBMB enrolled practical nurses from its inception, and, until the mid-1940s, issues surrounding less-trained nurses did not receive much notice, with few discussions in meetings centering on practical nurse issues. Practical nurse registrants campaigned for and obtained higher fees around the same time the NB14 debated the subject, indicating acceptance of LPN concerns.[70] Despite seemingly peaceful relations, a major battle over the new nurse group erupted in 1944 and resulted in the expulsion of LPNs from the registry.

A new NBMB executive director, Anne Reilly, encouraged the focus on LPNs with her extreme antagonism towards LPN registrants.[71] Once named NBMB's director, Reilly lost no time in removing LPNs from registry membership. She complained to the registry's board of directors that placing LPNs cost more and required extra work, and she questioned whether the registry should continue LPN enrollment.[72] Reilly's attitude toward practical nurses is especially notable for the personal nature of her attacks. At one New York State Nurses Association meeting, Reilly publicly argued that LPNs had innumerable moral problems, such as excessive drinking while on duty. She also accused LPNs of overcharging patients and doubling up on cases to earn more income.[73] Reilly's remarks often used either explicit or coded racial terms. At registry meetings, Reilly identified nurses who were causing problems for the registry as "Negro," reported such nurses as having psychiatric illnesses or emotional difficulties, and accused them of having been employed previously as "kitchen workers." Other registrants followed Reilly's lead, referring to LPNs as former "domestic girls."[74]

Reilly used her position as director to galvanize NBMB registrants against LPNs. At a 1944 NBMB meeting convened to discuss registrant issues, members revived common complaints against LPNs. Members voiced disapproval of LPNs wearing the same uniforms as registered nurses, making it difficult for patients to differentiate between the professional and practical group. The adoption of nurses' caps worn by LPNs was irksome, as were rumors that LPNs charged more than professional nurses. One registrant recounted a case in which she shared the care of a patient with an LPN. She charged the LPN with implying to the family that practical nurses received training comparable to registered nurses. At an NBMB registrants' meeting called to discuss LPN issues, registrants voted unanimously to remove LPNs from the registry.[75]

The elimination of LPNs had little effect on registry operations and seemed to have none on LPNs, who could easily sign up with another area registry eager to place them. Four years later, by which time Reilly had resigned and a new regime was in charge, the Practical Nurses of New York, Inc., requested the NBMB reconsider the placement of LPNs.[76] NBMB membership voted to return LPNs to registry enrollment, although some registrants continued to express resentment against LPNs.[77]

On one level, viewing the vote to exclude LPNs as an emotional response from a group with very long memories of past injustices makes sense. Private duty nurses continued to perceive the new LPNs as major competitors in a full labor market. Fears persisted that the newly licensed group would take away jobs from professional nursing despite the growing reality that it was nurses, not jobs, that were in short supply. The racial overtones of the discussion most likely reflected not just overt racism but underlying resistance to more robust efforts taken to integrate the profession underway during World War II and the postwar era.[78] The anger of private duty nurses toward their new colleagues also reflected genuine concerns over the proposed shape of the postwar nurse labor market. The popularity and promotion of LPNs as a solution to nurse shortage problems concerned private duty nurses directly. Private duty nurses did not have to look far to find plenty of support for the position that LPNs were the future of bedside nursing.

Two major postwar studies of the nursing profession encouraged and advanced the use of LPNs. *Nursing for the Future*, also known as the Brown Report, and *A Program for the Nursing Profession*, authored by economist Eli Ginzberg under the auspices of the Committee on the Function of Nursing, advocated the use of a differentiated nursing staff composed of professional and practical nurses. The Brown Report recommended a two-level nursing system with each worker assigned to functions based on background, training, and experience.[79] The Committee on the Function of Nursing endorsed increasing the number of LPNs and the scope of their duties as the best way to close the gap between supply of and demand for nursing services.[80]

Physician groups saw LPNs as a quick solution to nursing shortages. In 1946, the American College of Surgeons urged adoption of practical nurse licensure by every state and advised hospitals to admit, utilize, and provide short courses for training vocational nurses (which were different from LPNs and had attained a lower skill level).[81] Two years later, the American Medical Association's

Committee on Nursing Problems strongly recommended the use of LPNs to deliver much of hospital bedside nursing care.[82]

These reports reflected the continuing shift in emphasis from using LPNs for the care of home-based, chronically ill patients to employing them chiefly in acute care institutions. Different groups offered varying reasons why hospitals should employ LPNs. The American College of Surgeons and the American Medical Association were interested in having LPNs supplement and extend the work of professional nurses. The Brown Report focused on competent home care by recommending that LPNs engage in a year of fully paid, supervised experience in a hospital before entering private practice.[83] The result of all the recommendations regarding the proper role and placement of LPNs was that their practice would take place primarily in acute care hospitals. Private duty nurses, who believed they were the group uniquely qualified to deliver close, personal bedside care in acute care settings, received a clear and unwelcome message: private duty nursing was not part of the postwar nursing movement.

Ironically, while the introduction of LPNs was changing the nature of the nursing workforce, NBMB professional nurse registrants had little to fear by admitting the practical nurse group back to the registry. In the years after the vote to re-admit LPNs, the NBMB attracted few LPN registrants. In 1949, only sixty LPNs enrolled with the NBMB, representing a mere 6 percent of the total number of NBMB registrants.[84] Although the NBMB rate of calls filled improved from the mid-1940s, when the rate of calls filled for 1945–1946 was a mere 38 percent, the registry still filled only 59 percent of calls received in 1949.[85] It was not a shortage of jobs that confronted the private duty field in the late 1940s, but, rather, a lack of nurses.

The First Great Nursing Shortage

The increased demand for nurses taxed the country's professional private duty registries, which experienced decreasing ability to meet patient calls. On a national level, in 1940, registries filled 99 percent of all calls received for private duty service; by 1944, the rate of calls filled plummeted to 65 percent.[86] A corresponding decline in the number of nurse registrants available for calls accompanied the decrease in the percentage of calls filled, with 10 percent fewer nurses registered for work from 1942 to 1943. By 1944, registries recorded 22 percent fewer registrants from 1943 levels.[87] As noted previously, the percentage of active nurses working in the field dropped from 27 to 21 percent.[88]

The professional nurse registries in New York City mirrored national trends. The NB14 radically cut delivery of services as the rate of calls filled by the agency dropped precipitously over a six-year period from a high of 95 percent in 1940 to a low of 33 percent in 1945.[89] The lower percentage rate of filled calls reflected not just the registry's difficulty in finding nurses to take cases but also a tremendous increase in requests for nurses, which the NB14 was unable to meet. Calls received doubled between 1940 and 1945, rising from 9,826 to 20,108.[90] Although NB14 membership totals remained stable during this period, the registry reported frequent shortages of nurses available to accept calls, reflecting the general nurse shortage.

Registry officials attributed the poor rate of calls filled to several factors beyond high demand. Nurses continued to avoid accepting cases for the unpopular evening and night shifts, which represented most of the calls received; 80 percent of NB14 calls by 1944 were for these shifts.[91] Nurses also registered at multiple registries, some of which promised higher patient fees than the NB14. In the early 1940s, NB14 fees stalled at a Depression-level rate of $5 for an eight-hour shift until 1942 when the fee increased to $6.[92] Private duty nurses dissatisfied with this growth agitated for and received an increase to $7 for eight hours in 1944.[93] Not until 1946 did nurses win a more reasonable increase to $8 for eight hours of work.[94] Finally, NB14 Director Collins noted a troubling trend in which hospitals bypassed the registry and contacted nurses directly for work. Nurse-poor hospitals hiring nurses directly for private duty or staff nurse positions on a per diem basis depleted the reserve of nurses from which the NB14 could answer calls.[95]

The national shortage of nurses worsened by the end of the war even as military nurses returned home. Scores of investigations filled professional journals chronicling the causes and extent of the shortage and the means to alleviate it.[96] The main catalyst for nursing shortages was increasing demand in proportion to higher hospital utilization. A host of factors contributed to increased nursing needs. There were continued increases in hospital insurance plans as well as new, complex medical treatments that required hospitalization and close attention from professional nurses for safe delivery. An expanded Veterans Administration system to care for returning military personnel, a higher birth rate, and increased hospital construction secondary to the passage of the 1946 Hospital Survey and Construction Act (Hill-Burton Act) also occurred. At the same time, the supply of potential nurses continued to decline because fewer students entered nursing programs as young women settled into postwar marriages and raised families. Many nurses also took advantage of the 1944 GI Bill to return to school and earn advanced degrees. An anticipated flow of military nurses back to the civilian sector failed to take place.[97]

A decline in the proportion of the population made up of young, single women, the typical sector on which schools of nursing relied for prospective students, added to nursing recruitment problems. The percentage of single women between the ages of 16 and 24 years dropped from 15 percent of all women in 1940 to 11 percent in 1950.[98] Declining enrollment at schools of nursing reflected the seriousness of the shortage situation. Admissions to schools of nursing fell from a high of 67,051 in 1944 (during the Cadet Nurse Corps program) to a low of 38,210 in 1947, with a slight rebound to 43,373 in 1948.[99]

The solutions advocated for the postwar shortage mirrored those used during the war years—recruiting more students into the profession and implementing greater utilization of assistive personnel. However, as student recruitment lagged, hospitals, faced with increasing numbers of patients who required caregivers immediately, turned to hiring more and more assistive personnel. Hospitals looked to personnel below the skill level of LPNs, generally referred to as nurse aides, to handle the daily flow of patients. Hospitals found the nurse aide an ideal type of worker. An aide, trained for a specific set of duties, required minimal instruction and could be moved from department to department or from job to job as patient requests demanded. As the lowest worker in the now three-level hierarchy, the nurse aide received a minimum rate of pay. After World War II, personnel-starved hospitals increasingly relied on a variety of assistive personnel to care for patients. By 1949, an estimated two hundred thousand individuals worked as nurse aides nationwide.[100]

Support for nurse aides was widespread. The American College of Surgeons advised hospitals in 1946 to admit and utilize the assistance of auxiliary nurses (typically referring to untrained volunteer and paid personnel under various names), sending a letter to all college-approved hospitals urging them to begin nurse aide programs.[101] Ginzberg emphasized a two-level, professional/practical nursing system of care delivery, but saw a major role for assistive personnel who would take on numerous housekeeping and patient-related services of a nonprofessional nature.[102] The Brown Report recognized that historically attendants were a fixture in many hospitals, particularly those specializing in the care of the mentally ill and long-term patients, highlighting the importance of health aides in modern hospitals to relieve the professional nurse of routine tasks.[103] These reports focused on well-thought-out rationales for using nurse aides. Others more bluntly stated the reasons why aides were a preferred solution. One hospital director hypothesized that even if hospitals could find enough nurses to hire, the salaries would be unaffordable. Hiring more assistive personnel would provide nurse workers at a lower cost.[104]

Left obscured in the discussions over the structure of the post–World War II nurse labor market was the role nurse salary and benefits played in alleviating the shortage. Many nurses identified inadequate compensation and employee

benefits as contributing to nurse shortages, yet few suggested concrete proposals for improving the economic situation for nurses or using improved pay
and benefit scales as inducements for nurses to work.[105] A 1947 U.S. Bureau of
Labor Statistics study, *The Economic Status of Registered Professional Nurses,
1946–47*, laid out nurse economic problems in stark terms. The study, with its
extensive data and observations of nurses, provided a compelling and dismal
picture of nurses' compensation, benefits, and work environment.

The study indicated the average nurse earned about $2,100 per year, with a
range of from $2,484 per year for nurse educators to $1,836 per year for private
duty nurses.[106] Comparing nurses' earnings with those of workers in various
occupations, both those that did not require specialized training and those that
did, resulted in mixed findings; nurses' earnings were equal to those of low-
skilled employees such as assemblers and office workers but lower than those
of sewing machine operators. Stenographers, bookkeepers, and clerk-typists
earned higher salaries than nurses. Teachers, deemed most comparable in educational preparation and professional status, earned salaries considerably higher
than did nurses. An average salary for teachers employed in city school systems
was about $2,500 but dropped to $2,100 if the entire population of teachers in
both city and rural areas was included. On a wider level, in 1949 women engaged
in professional and related services earned on average $1,824 a year, with the
average yearly salary for both women and men being around $2,017. This placed
nurses within the range of other professional workers.[107] Nurses failed to view
their wages as sufficient. One nurse survey participant summed up the general
perspective of many nurses: "As it stands today, nursing offers only enough to
cover the essentials of living with no chance to save for the future or for emer-
gencies . . . it is obvious that a nurse cannot live on the gratitude of patients;
she must have sufficient income."[108]

Nurses also expressed great concern over the lack of retirement pension
plans offered by hospitals, rating it the most substandard aspect of their work.
Hospitals were exempt from the original provisions of the Social Security Act,
which did not change until 1950, when amendments to the act allowed private
duty nurses coverage with an additional mechanism in which religious, charitable, educational, and similar institutions could waive their exemption to allow
employee coverage.[109] All nonprofit hospitals were not required to participate
until 1983.[110] For nurses, this presented a double bind. Not only did they receive
low salaries and few benefits during their working years, but they also had little to
no financial security to look forward to in retirement.

The major reason nurses left the profession was to marry, according to the
1947 study, with 79 percent of inactive nurses indicating marriage or household

responsibilities as the cause of their inactivity. Family obligations presented obvious impediments to work, but as the study noted the case was not so clear with many nurses, indicating that better pay and working conditions might serve to attract them back to work despite their family obligations. For many, child care costs, travel expenses, laundry (of uniforms and caps), and other professional expenditures lessened earnings to the point where it was not profitable to work.

The study concluded that two main factors contributed to the nurse shortage: the drain of nurses leaving the profession to marry and the attraction of women to other fields with better pay, benefits, and working conditions. Shortages were not caused by nurses leaving the field, but, rather, nurses' working conditions. These factors deflected young women from entering the field primarily at the point of entry into the profession. One nurse eloquently summed up the problem: "Young girls soon learn that the work is long and arduous hours are most unattractive, and the net take-home pay pitifully inadequate. They soon learn that, in comparison with outside situations, there is smaller chance of promotion that is paid promotion, though for the most part the outside situations required less time and money spent on education and preparation."[111]

The study uncovered valuable data on the private duty field, shedding light on why private duty persisted as a viable occupational field. It seems the private duty field still offered nurses choices not available in other fields. Private duty nurses earned the lowest monthly salaries, yet their hourly earnings, at $1 an hour, were the highest. Higher hourly earnings reflected the lower number of hours worked per month, thirty-nine hours for private duty nurses versus forty-four hours on average for staff nurses, whose work frequently required uncompensated overtime. Many private duty nurses worked short work weeks. Twenty-two percent worked less than eighty-five hours a month, approximately twenty-one hours a week, which the study noted to be a personal preference on the part of the nurse.

Private duty nursing continued to offer nurses freedom to work when they wanted, an advantage for married nurses or for those who had family responsibilities. In an age when full-time employment was the norm for most working nurses, private duty offered alternative part-time jobs welcomed by many. Comments provided by nurses who completed the study's survey testify to the value nurses placed on both higher hourly earnings and the freedom to blend work with family responsibilities.[112] Moreover, in a comment reminiscent of nineteenth-century nurse Chloe Cudsworth Littlefield, one nurse highlighted how private duty permitted her to do work and help out her family at home. The respondent stated, "Am a housewife on a farm. Because of shortage of help on the farm I cannot leave my husband much as his work is much harder with me away. However, at night when I am wanted badly I do night duty—last year doing 82 nights and 18 this year to date."[113]

The study uncovered another critical aspect of private duty work. Nursing work, a twenty-four-hour-a-day occupation, is typically divided into three eight-hour shifts. In the late 1940s, 74 percent of staff nurses worked only one shift; for the majority, 55 percent, this was the day shift. Unlike today's staff nurses, nurses in the late 1940s did not rotate shifts with any frequency. Private duty nurses, on the other hand, worked different shifts more frequently and with greater variation. Although a similar percentage of private duty nurses, 75 percent, worked only one shift, the shifts worked varied over the twenty-four-hour day. Only 36 percent of private duty nurses worked the day shift, while 15 and 24 percent worked the evening and night shifts, respectively. Registries noted this as a major problem over many decades. Private duty nurses were the unsung heroes, called upon to deliver a greater portion of care during the evening and night hours when fewer medical personnel were present and unstable patients required close monitoring.

Unsung heroes or not, private duty nursing continued its decline as an occupational choice for nurses. The shortage of nurses left private duty registries with fewer and fewer nurses to send to patients, and professional private duty registries, once viewed as the go-to resource for nurses, lost their ability to deliver on their main service: sending a nurse to a patient whenever needed. As registries' reliability declined, hospitals, now caught up in structuring a nurse workforce of differently skilled workers, turned their back on the private duty market and took on the responsibility for hiring their staff on their terms. These terms may or may not have been acceptable or appreciated by nurses. Private duty nursing would continue as an identifiable occupational field for nurses for several more decades, but it lost its prominence, its dependability, and its aura as the field best able to deliver safe, individualized, personal care of patients. As the country entered the second half of the twentieth century, a far different practice of nursing and way of staffing hospitals emerged.

Conclusion

Demand for nurses reached insatiable proportions during the 1940s. The threat posed by World War II, the rapid growth of highly sophisticated and complex therapies and technologically driven medical care, and the tremendous increase in the number and variety of hospital services both elevated the status of the profession and emphasized the critical importance of a reliable, stable nurse workforce. Hospitals' dependence on temporary, itinerant workers in the form of private duty nurses and partially trained student workers became untenable in the face of an immediate need for larger and larger numbers of caregivers. The decade created an opportunity for more focused nurse shortage solutions while at the same time exposing difficulties in relying on traditional solutions or finding new workable ones in a rapidly changing labor market.

Solutions utilized were both progressive and expedient. During World War II, the CNC emphasized not just numbers of nurses but the value of well-educated professional nurses. The various postwar studies on the status and future of the nursing profession were unanimous in advancing better prepared and educated professional nurses. The proliferation and acceptance of differently skilled hospital-employed assistive personnel became the quickest means through which hospitals could conveniently and cheaply staff their units. These two approaches—improve the quality of nursing and continue to use more workers and less-skilled workers—were exemplars of both forward thinking and backward glances. Health-care leaders and hospitals were in agreement that they wanted better nurses, but when facing patients lying in beds requiring immediate care, they were forced to fall back on past strategies: cheaper, less-trained workers.

For private duty nurses, the decade was cataclysmic. The emphasis on better-educated nurses, preferably graduates of college or university programs (that were growing in number and popularity), and the hiring of more and more assistive personnel, marginalized private duty nurses to the outskirts of the profession and devalued their role as providers of close, personal, individualized patient care. As most nurses sought hospital employment, private duty nurses' status as independent contractors determining their terms of employment ceased. At the same time, the power of professional nurse registries to control nurse employment diminished. Hospitals, as nurse employers, became the standard. Hospitals then had the power to establish pay rates, hours of work, benefits, and other employment conditions. As the postwar nurse shortage continued into the second half of the twentieth century, hospitals failed to question whether improving the working lives of nurses could make a positive impact on nurses' decisions to enter and stay in the workforce. In the absence of a strong third party, a role often taken by professional nurse registries, nurses were left to their own devices to receive the treatment and compensation they deserved as professionals.

Conclusion

For almost fifty years, the private duty market existed as the main supplier of professional graduate nursing services for hospitals and patients and provided nurses with their primary source of work. By the mid-twentieth century, significantly diminished in influence, private duty occupied an isolated and marginalized position in the nurse labor market. A host of interrelated factors occurring as part of the changing patterns of nursing and health-care delivery in the United States in the early part of the twentieth century led to both the dominance of private duty as a professional field and its subsequent decline.

Early twentieth-century nurse leaders believed the registry system would become an influential agent meeting the full nursing needs of the public. They envisioned the private duty field as providing regular work opportunities for the legions of graduate nurses pouring out of schools of nursing, anticipating that it would supply nurses to the public at a reliable and sufficient rate. Private duty nursing both succeeded and failed to accomplish those goals and in the process became an anachronous system of nurse distribution.

Distributing Nurses

For early practitioners of nursing, private one-to-one services on a cash basis made sense. The traditional source of caregivers, patients' families, did not possess the specialized knowledge needed for modern medical care. Furthermore, hospitals at the turn of the twentieth century were not yet interested in hiring and paying for the nursing staff necessary to deliver the specialized care required by advances in modern medicine. Offering private nursing services to individual patients both at home and in the hospital met the immediate needs of some of the ill and provided graduate nurses a livelihood. The private nursing services era was at its peak when the idea that citizens had a "right to health care" was a foreign concept unaligned with American ideas about individualism and free-market enterprises. Most ill individuals did not possess the financial resources to afford a product—in this case, nursing services. Not providing every patient with a nurse was troubling to the profession but not limiting.

Nurses reaped major advantages from the system. The private duty field offered professional nurses one, and in many cases the only, opportunity for work. Although private nursing was by no means an ideal occupational field, the ability to pick when and where to work bolstered nurses' sense of independence and may have assisted nurses to plan working days while meeting familial responsibilities. The alternative to private duty, employment as staff nurses in hospitals, was unpalatable for most private duty nurses. Unlike nurses employed by institutions, private duty nurses did not have to manage many of the regulations, obligations, and burdens imposed by hospitals. The third-party system, in which registries served as a brokerage point for nurses and patients, simplified the process of securing cases. Nurses were active participants when registries determined fees and hours of work, and had a sense of control over their careers. Professional registries sustained nurses in other less tangible ways. Associating with a professional group increased the status enjoyed by nurses. Registries provided a means of differentiating professional nurses from untrained nurse workers, offering a small measure of control over the competition. Nurse registrants demonstrated vigorous and enduring loyalty to both private duty and the registry system.

Hospitals used the private duty system to their full advantage. Throughout the first half of the twentieth century, hospitals remained committed to student-centered nursing care. Although professing happiness with students as workers, hospitals recognized that some patients either preferred or required more expert care. Hospitals relied on the private duty market as a fallback system, a way of obtaining a graduate nursing staff for patients willing and able to afford private care without the hospital incurring the expense and bother of employing nurses. Providing these services gave hospitals better reputations and marketing power. Hospitals exerted effective control over the working lives of private nurses by requiring the approval of fee schedules and working hours by institutional boards of directors. This institutional stranglehold maintained traditional patterns of authority considered essential to effective hospital operations. Hospitals themselves became savvy consumers of the registry system and used registries as a source of temporary staff nurses. In the late 1930s and early 1940s, many nurses considered to be staff nurses most likely were private duty nurses working on a per diem basis. This arrangement allowed hospitals to continue to avoid employing permanent staff and sustaining associated expenses, such as pensions. Registries also verified that nurses possessed the necessary educational preparation and work background for safe care, sparing hospitals the necessity to do so.

Physicians actively supported the private duty system. For their hospitalized patients, private duty nurses provided more expert care than that given by students. The availability of a group of graduate nurses who could closely monitor patients' conditions and proficiently and safely carry out treatments permitted physicians to apply more complex patient therapeutics and procedures demanded by advances in medical care. The inclusion of doctors in decisions regarding nurses' fees and working conditions allowed them to influence nurses' work and was a source of physician power. Even so, physicians expressed ambivalence toward private practice nurses. The high expense of private nursing limited such care to those with the means to pay the fees. Many patients deemed by doctors to need nurses went without close nursing observation. Difficulties in securing nurses for patients strained physician-nurse relationships. Physicians, frustrated that not all patients could afford or obtain graduate nurses, sought to establish a cheaper solution. Less-trained nurses promised to both lower the cost to patients and be potentially easier to control than the professional nurse group.

The lack of an alternative or substitute system that would both ensure care for patients and jobs for graduate nurses assured private duty's survival, at least for the first half of the twentieth century. Even so, private duty nursing was a field with significant liabilities. The inherently high cost of delivering a personal, intensive, professional service limited the patients served to the wealthy few. Most patients were untouched by private duty nurses. Professional nursing recognized this problem and worked hard to invent strategies to overcome financial barriers to private nursing care. Diversifying the delivery of private duty care as a means of opening up the field to more customers held promise for private duty growth. However, alternative schemes to broaden access to traditional private duty failed to capture a larger share of the market or much support from professional groups. The main method through which demand for nurse services increased resulted from the campaign for shorter working hours. The standardized schedule spread work among more nurses, and it succeeded in lowering the unit cost of services rendered, which led to a significant increase in requests for private nursing services.

Shorter work hours did not represent the sole factor driving up demand for professional nurse services. By the 1930s, hospitals, reconciled to hiring greater numbers of nursing staff, became major consumers of nursing services. An increase in hospital utilization, the result of hospital insurance plans, added to the need for a stable staff. The health care needs of the armed forces during World War II further heightened demand. By the early 1940s, professional nursing entered into a lengthy period in which cries of nurse shortages drowned out previous complaints that too many nurses existed. Registries failed to keep pace with higher demand for services. Rates of unfilled requests for nurses soared.

The inability to supply sufficient nurses to meet demand was the most prominent and abysmal failure of the private duty system and spelled doom for it as a permanent system for nurse distribution. The nurse educational system, instead, proved to be a prolific supplier of professional nurses. The increase in the number of nurses over the first half of the twentieth century was the most remarkable characteristic of the profession. Even so, increasing the number of nurses failed to make a dent in repeated nurse shortages and created the ironic situation wherein no matter how many nurses the system produced, the nation never had enough.

Unable to depend on the private duty field for an adequate supply of graduate nurses, nurse-poor hospitals resorted to other means of obtaining staff. Hospitals discovered they could easily hire nurses on either a temporary or permanent basis without registry help. They found that using a differentiated nursing staff composed of several different types of nurse workers met the need for employees and decreased their reliance on private practitioners. Hospital success in doing so allowed them to employ many less-trained, cheaper workers and fewer, more expensive, registered nurses. A decreased reliance on private practitioners gave the illusion that hospitals had finally adopted a permanent nurse staffing model able to meet post–World War II health-care needs.

The passage of mandatory nursing practice acts during the middle of the century eased the way for hospitals to vary their employee base and reduce competition between unlicensed and professional nurses. However, hospitals, not nurses, used the new licensing system to the best advantage. Mandatory licensing acts both strengthened regulations governing registered nurse practice and created a new type of licensed worker, the licensed practical nurse. The acts also provided hospitals with greater options in whom they could hire and how they could hire them. The state-sponsored system of nurse credentialing for not one but two levels of nurses provided institutions with a minimum standard with which to evaluate safe practitioners. Moreover, as the licensing system did not affect categories of workers below the practical nurse level, hospitals were free to increase employment of unlicensed assistive personnel who were frequently substituted for professional nurse care.

The practice of staffing hospitals with large proportions of auxiliary workers and a smaller number of registered nurses strained the system and threatened patient safety. The increasingly complex care given to post–World War II patients required practitioners that were more educated and skilled than licensed practical nurses and nurse aides. High demand for private duty nurses, charged with caring for very sick patients unable to receive care from a differentiated staff, continued into the 1950s. At the same time, the ability of registries to serve as a dependable source of nurses declined. Although the number of private duty nurses actively working in the field remained relatively stable throughout the 1950s, too many requests for nurses went unfilled.[1] Between 1948 and 1960, the rate of calls filled by professional nurse registries on a national level averaged 70 percent.[2] During the same time, the Chicago Nurses Professional Registry was filling calls at a dismal rate of 50 percent.[3] The Nursing Bureau of District 14's rate was not much higher, averaging 54 percent.[4] The Nursing Bureau of Manhattan and Bronx's rate of filled calls plummeted from 59 percent in 1949 to 45 percent in 1960.[5] Historians Julie Fairman and Joan Lynaugh identified the extreme difficulty that physicians at Philadelphia's Hospital of the University of Pennsylvania had in obtaining private duty nurses, causing them to devise other methods of care delivery, such as intensive care units.[6] While professional registries struggled with an unprecedented demand for nurses, hospitals experimented with care models other than private duty to supply nursing care. The introduction of intensive care units in the 1950s revolutionized acute health care delivery and helped meet hospitals' obligation for the provision of care. All care required by patients, whether routine or highly specialized, became an institutional responsibility.[7]

The employment of a permanent hospital nursing staff solved many problems the private duty system failed to address. Permanent staff members, assigned at a hospital's convenience, were more reliable than intermittently hired private workers. Hospital prerogative in assigning staff as needed by institutional demand eliminated nurses' tendency to avoid unpopular shifts and cases. Dependable reimbursement rates from hospital insurance plans provided the financial base necessary for salaries, managing the cost issue. By becoming their employer, hospitals solidified their control over nurses' conditions of work.

Post–World War II nurses tended to more readily accept hospital employment than did prewar graduates. Smaller percentages of nurses sought work in the private duty field. New graduates did not see the private duty field as the proper venue in which to practice. The uncontested substitution of licensed practical nurses for registered nurses, which enabled hospitals to solve staffing problems, blurred the distinction between the two groups and lessened the value attached to private professional nursing care. By the 1960s, private duty nursing faded as a job choice for nurses.

Organizing Nurses' Work

The private duty system served the dual function of distributing nurses and serving as a labor market in which nurses established and solidified patterns of work. The registry system allowed nurses to negotiate with hospitals over fees, working hours, employment conditions, and a miscellany of other factors relevant to their working lives. Nurses were active, if not always successful, participants in negotiations regarding employment. The loss of this aspect of the private duty market is one that had a profound influence on nursing and is key to understanding the way and conditions under which contemporary nurses work.

The involvement of local professional nurses' associations in determining conditions of work for private duty nurses was tremendous. Local districts, through the sponsorship of professional registries, closely engaged in activities that regulated the day-to-day working lives of professional nurses. Participation from member nurses varied, but was always in some degree present. Neither professional leaders nor working nurses were passive victims in determining conditions of work. At times they were less powerful and failed to achieve their aims. At other times conflict over goals led to defeat. In several cases, nurses succeeded in winning better conditions.

The early work of professional nurse associations in negotiating employment matters, particularly in setting fees and hours of work, resembled activities later engaged in by the profession's bargaining units as nurses sought economic security. Registry work served as a training ground for nurses who subsequently assumed a greater role in bargaining over conditions of work. Although professional participation in collective bargaining activities has remained controversial for nurses, negotiating employment matters was an early and prominent part of local district association programs.

The success nurses achieved in improving working conditions requires balancing the result against a private system of nurse employment. District associations assumed responsibility for getting nurses to patients and took this on as an essential mission of the professional association. By maintaining the registry system, district associations unwittingly allowed hospitals to avoid hiring and paying directly for a permanent nursing staff. A large number of nurses, rejected by hospitals as too expensive and left to compete for the small number of patients able to afford nursing services, flooded the market and drove down nurses' incomes.

When hospitals finally did employ nurses in large numbers, they effectively hid the nursing costs in patient room-and-board costs they charged to insurers. Earlier generations were well aware of the high cost of private nursing care and engaged in vigorous debate over ways to lower such costs. Once nursing became a part of hospital service, the actual cost to patients was unknown, which obscured and devalued a service considered to be essential to modern health care.

As a system of nursing care delivery, private duty was expensive, inefficient, and wasteful of nursing resources. Despite these disadvantages, private duty nursing provides a compelling example of a unique relationship between nurse and patient. Private duty nursing was the first and most enduring form of nursing, in which nurses assumed independent responsibility for the total nursing care of their patients. Although other patterns of nursing care delivery have attempted to duplicate it, none have succeeded in recapturing the intimate one-to-one nurse-patient relationship provided by private duty nursing. Private duty was a form of nursing for which patients were willing to reach into their own pockets and pay cash for care. The willingness of patients to do so for so many years stands as a testament to the essential nature of nursing as a critical service to modern societies.

Studies on nurses' work often concentrate on the subordinate position the profession has assumed in the health care field. This book recognizes that status but offers a perspective of the private duty registry system as a nurse-run, women-run business enterprise. This book does not romanticize or aggrandize the role taken by those who operated registries. They remained accountable to and too frequently constrained by other groups of men as part of their daily work. However, it does acknowledge a little-known episode in nursing history: nurses operated viable business organizations that sold nursing services to the public and experienced a degree of success. The professional nurse registry system continued to supply nurses for private care well after private duty nursing went into eclipse. The registries investigated in this book remained in operation until the early 1980s, when dwindling membership and financial problems led to their closure. For over seventy years professional registries were a major distribution center of registered nurses. Their story is an intriguing part of American nursing history and demands attention as an example of women-run enterprise in the business of employing or seeking employment for large numbers of predominantly women workers.

This book is concerned with a field in which the vast majority of workers are women. Unraveling the evolution of nurses' work contributes to a better understanding of the larger labor history of women's work; it expands our knowledge of how nurses shaped their work in general by exploring nurse employment on a local, micro level. It discloses the workings of the labor market in which earlier generations of nurses began to practice.

The premise of this book is that supplying sufficient professional nurses to meet American health-care needs remained a persistent problem throughout the twentieth century to the present day. Investigating the reasons why nurse distribution proved to be so unpredictable and undependable for previous generations suggests areas of interest for those involved in delivering contemporary nursing care. In particular, today's policy makers need to be well aware of the critical influence two characteristics of nursing have on the supply of nurses: First, nurses require satisfactory working conditions. Second, nursing care is a very expensive commodity.

Both these statements should appear to be obvious. Yet, there has simultaneously existed a history of inattention and denial of these factors. Those involved in obtaining nursing services seemed to give little recognition to the relationship between working conditions and nurse employment. Hospitals, physicians, and registry officials acknowledged that when nurses did not like a job, they did not work. Nurses refused cases when the patient was inconveniently located, when the hours were too long or unpopular, or when the demands of the case or position were too high. Hospitals, by virtue of their authority over nurses' work situation, were in a powerful position to help institute strategies that gave nurses less choice while motivating them to take undesirable cases or work. Better compensation, more flexible scheduling, fringe benefits, and institutional support of nurses' work might have served as motivating factors. There seems to be little evidence that institutions considered this to be a valuable course of action. Instead, hospitals used more manipulative and forceful techniques to make nurses work. And when those failed, hospitals resorted to hiring less-trained, easier-to-control workers.

This history presents a cautionary tale for those involved in present-day nurse distribution. Relying on less-trained workers is no longer a viable option for the medically complicated patients cared for in contemporary health-care settings. The supply of registered nurses available for and willing to work continues to vary considerably. Rumors are surfacing that a new nurse shortage may be soon approaching. As a large number of baby-boomer nurses age and begin retiring, hospitals and other health-care agencies may find themselves unprepared to meet future nursing demand. Meeting the nursing needs of the population requires reconsideration of how to immeasurably improve nursing as an occupation. Nursing has always been a satisfying, ennobling career that provides numerous intangible benefits. Nurses need to receive equally satisfying concrete rewards.

How to pay for those tangible rewards continues to perplex the American health-care system. The individualistic, cash-based private duty system highlighted the cost issue. However, private duty nursing resisted efforts at cost reduction. Focusing on lower costs missed an important point. Professional nursing care has been, is now, and most likely always will be expensive. The critical problem to be solved may not be how to reduce costs but rather how to arrange the financing of nursing care in the first place.

When private duty nursing originated, health care in the United States existed as a predominantly private effort of voluntary agencies. Financial responsibility for care rested with the individual patient, who either paid cash for services or relied on the charitable instincts of others. Private duty nursing fit neatly into this scheme. Private nurses served those who had disposable income to spend on health care. Despite efforts to expand services and claims by professional organizations that all ill individuals deserved professional nursing care, registered nurses strictly divided their work between those who could pay and those who could not; this was not dissimilar to how hospitals and other health-care agencies divided patients.

By the 1930s, cracks in the pay/nonpay patients categories appeared. The expansion of health insurance plans opened up private hospital care to a larger patient population. Former ward patients suddenly found that as paying customers they were welcome in semiprivate rooms. The increased demand for nurses caused by the surge in insurance plans eliminated underemployment problems and changed the nurse distribution model to address the needs of the sick public. Allocating nurses based on financial status no longer seemed logical. Government entry into the health-care field through the Medicare and Medicaid programs continued the process. As health care became more and more a public responsibility, private nursing became less and less credible as a model of distribution and work.

In 1963 the surgeon general's report on nursing, *Toward Quality in Nursing*, called for greater government involvement in meeting the nursing needs of the country. The report recommended increased government funding for nursing education, practice, and research to meet future needs.[8] It downplayed the role private duty nursing would play in future health-care systems. Noting that the number of private practitioners had decreased over the years, the report anticipated little growth in the private duty labor market, forecasting instead an immense need for nurses employed in acute care institutions.[9]

This stand was consistent with trends in health care evident by the 1960s. Using the patient's ability to pay as a criterion for care delivery became unacceptable when medical need, not income, was deemed a worthier factor. This perspective assumed cost sharing throughout the larger population and expected the government to be a willing partner in meeting those costs. It did not, of course, allow for the growing reluctance of the government to pay for the runaway health-care expenses of the 1970s and 1980s and could not foresee the more recent drive to rein in those costs. The American health-care system has vacillated between providing more and more expensive health services and recognizing that unlimited care carries a staggering price. Paying the price of nursing services contributes to this tension and remains an issue in search of a solution.

I am completing this book after the 2016 presidential election and seven years after the passage of the revolutionary Affordable Care Act (ACA). As of this writing, it remains unclear how the ACA will survive, as the Republican Party remains committed to a repeal plan with a murky strategy for replacement. Much of the discussion on replacement of the ACA revolves around the greater involvement of the free market in deciding who should pay for health insurance. There are also questions about how much and for what type of coverage consumers should pay. With these issues are continued concerns about the diminishing expectations of the care patients will receive because of reduced regulatory processes intended to standardize care and ensure that all patients receive some bare minimum of services. The unraveling of the health-care system as we know it opens discussions on privatization schemes aimed at Medicare and the Veterans Administration. Proponents of such ideas believe firmly, with scant evidence to back up their claims, that a private free-market system of health-care delivery is the answer to the nation's health-care ills. As no double-blind study exists that would provide the evidence base to select one system over another, proponents of free-market solutions ask for blind trust with no proof.

History offers, and in fact becomes, a critical form of inquiry to use in planning future policy initiatives. The private duty nurse system delivers a prime and clear example of how the delivery of care took place in an entirely free-market approach. When the system reigned, patients who wanted a nurse and could afford to pay for one received a nurse; those who could not afford a nurse did not. As this book demonstrates, such a system carried with it serious liabilities and more often than not failed to deliver on either of its promises: a nurse for every patient and a job for every nurse. Moreover, when national crises hit, such as during World War II, the free market barely managed to avoid a complete breakdown of hospital services until the federal government stepped in with financial support. Free-market principles work exceedingly well in many instances, but their utility in health care has garnered mixed results. The question I began this book with was "Why does the United States never seem to have enough nurses?" I now contend that Americans should contemplate and consider the history of the nurse labor force as one example of how privatization can go wrong. My hope is that our next question is not "Why does the nation never seem to have a health-care system that can deliver enough care to its citizens?" Rather, we should be asking how we can effectively provide care and how much care is enough.

Appendix

Table A.1.
Membership of the Committee on the Grading of Nursing Schools

William Darrach, MD, chair
May Ayres Burgess, director
Mary M. Roberts, RN, consultant

Members:
National League of Nursing Education
American Nurses' Association
National Organization for Public Health Nursing
American Medical Association
American College of Surgeons
American Hospital Association
American Public Health Association

Members at large:
Frances Payne Bolton, prominent citizen of Cleveland, Ohio
Sister Domitilla, director, St. Mary's Training School
Henry Suzzallo, PhD, trustee, Carnegie Foundation
Samuel Capen, PhD, chancellor, University of Buffalo
Edward A. Fitzpatrick, PhD, dean, graduate school, Marquette University
W. W. Charters, PhD, professor, University of Chicago
Nathan B. Van Etten, MD, general practitioner

Source: May Ayres Burgess, ed. *Nurses, Patients, and Pocketbooks* (New York: Committee on the Grading of Nursing Schools, 1928).

Acknowledgments

As this was written after Jean's death, there will be some who will be missed here, and apologies are offered. Without her guidance, it is difficult to reconstruct an outstanding scholar's life, her love of research, and her work on this book, which was a major enlargement of her dissertation. Elisa Stroh and Amanda Mahoney worked diligently to bring this book to press. But in the end, this was all Jean's work.

This book could not have been possible without the support of many people, as well as the faculty of the Barbara Bates Center for the Study of the History of Nursing. Jean always prized the sage advice of her friend and mentor Joan Lynaugh, director emerita of the center, as well as colleagues Karen Buhler Wilkerson (her dissertation chair) and Neville Strumpf. Jessica Clark, archivist of the center, was a true friend. Tiffany Hope Collier and Elisa Stroh supported Jean through their editing skills and friendship. Friend and mentee Amanda Mahoney always responded frankly to her ideas. Hafeeza Anchrum shared an office and highly valued Jean's mentorship.

Jean was also proud of her work with the American Association for the History of Nursing, and served as its president from 2012 to 2016. She also served as the associate director of the Barbara Bates Center for the Study of the History of Nursing, School of Nursing, University of Pennsylvania, for many years, as she supported the center's work. One of her most valued accomplishments was the luncheon reunion for the alumnae of the Mercy- Douglass Training School. She brought together these women, some of them in their 90s and from as far away as California, and their families, to celebrate their school, their heritage, and their decades-long friendships.

Jean also found friends and colleagues in the many archives and libraries she visited. She frequently mentioned how much she appreciated the staff at the archives at the Pennsylvania Hospital Historical Collections, the Historical Society of Pennsylvania, Women's Hospital of Pennsylvania Collections, the New York Hospital Archives, the Foundation of the New York State Nurses Association Collections, the Bellevue Alumni Center for Nursing History, the Howard Gotlieb Archival Research Center, the Medical Center Archives of New York-Presbyterian/Weill Center, and the College of Physicians of Philadelphia.

Above all, Jean would want to especially acknowledge her husband Mark Gilbert and son Paul Gilbert, who were her main supports throughout the process of writing this book. Her family was with her in this project and in so much more to the very end.

Julie Fairman

Notes

Introduction

1. Mary Elizabeth Carnegie, *The Path We Tread: Blacks in Nursing Worldwide, 1854–1994* (Sudbury, MA: Jones and Bartlett, 2000); Darlene Clark Hine, *Black Women in White: Racial Conflict and Cooperation in the Nursing Profession, 1890–1950* (Bloomington: Indiana University Press, 1989).
2. Carnegie, *The Path We Tread*; Hine, *Black Women in White*.
3. Mabel Keaton Staupers, *No Time for Prejudice: A Story of the Integration of Negroes in Nursing in the United States* (New York: Macmillan, 1961), 22; Adah Thoms, *Pathfinders: A History of the Progress of Colored Graduate Nurses* (New York: Kay, 1929), 87–88, 214–215.
4. Linda Aiken, "The Hospital Nursing Shortage. A Paradox of Increasing Supply and Increasing Vacancy Rates," *Western Journal of Medicine* 15 (1989): 87–92; Peter I. Buerhaus, "Is Another RN Shortage Looming?," *Nursing Outlook* 46, no.3 (1998): 103–108; Kevin Grumbach et al., "Measuring Shortages of Hospital Nurses: How Do You Know a Hospital with a Nursing Shortage When You See One?," *Medical Care Research and Review* 58 (2001): 387–403.
5. Stuart H. Altman, *Present and Future Supply of Registered Nurses* (Bethesda: U.S. Department of Health, Education and Welfare, 1971); Julie Fairman and Joan E. Lynaugh, *Critical Care Nursing: A History* (Philadelphia: University of Pennsylvania Press, 1998); Joan Lynaugh and Barbara Brush, *American Nursing: From Hospitals to Health Systems* (Cambridge, MA: Blackwell, 1996); Frank A. Sloan, *The Geographic Distribution of Nurses and Public Policy* (Bethesda: U.S. Department of Health, Education and Welfare, 1975).
6. Lois Friss, "Nursing Studies Laid End to End Form a Circle," *Journal of Health Politics, Policy and Law* 19 (1994): 597–631; Joan Lynaugh, "Riding the Yo-Yo: The Worth and Work of Nursing in the 20th Century," *Transactions and Studies of the College of Physicians of Philadelphia* 11, no. 5 (1989): 201–217; Donald E. Yett, *An Economic Analysis of the Nurse Shortage* (Lexington, MA: D. C. Heath, 1975).
7. Linda Aiken, "Nurses' Reports on Hospital Care in Five Countries," *Health Affairs* 20 (2001): 43–53; Julie Sochalski, "Nursing Shortage Redux: Turning the Corner on an Enduring Problem," *Health Affairs* 21 (2002): 157–164; Dana Weinberg, *Code Green: Money-driven Hospitals and the Dismantling of Nursing* (Ithaca, NY: Cornell University Press, 2003).
8. Institute of Medicine, *The Future of Nursing: Leading Change, Advancing Health* (Washington, DC: National Academies Press, 2011).
9. Barbara Melosh, *"The Physician's Hand": Work Culture and Conflict in American Nursing* (Philadelphia: Temple University Press, 1982); Susan Reverby, *Ordered to Care: The Dilemma of American Nursing, 1850–1945* (Cambridge: Cambridge University Press, 1987).
10. Joan E. Lynaugh, "Riding the Yo-Yo," 201–217; Reverby, *Ordered to Care*; Charles Rosenberg, *The Care of Strangers: The Rise of America's Hospital System* (New York: Basic Books, 1987), 212–235; Rosemary Stevens, *In Sickness and in Wealth: American Hospitals in the Twentieth Century* (New York: Basic Books, 1989), 95–98.

11. Wendell W. Oderkirk, "Setting the Record Straight: A Recount of Late Nineteenth-Century Training Schools," *Journal of Nursing History* 1 (November 1985): 30–37.

12. Joan Lynaugh, "Riding the Yo-Yo," 202–205; Reverby, *Ordered to Care*, 60–94.

13. For a contemporary description of early twentieth-century private duty nursing see Katherine De Witt, *Private Duty Nursing* (Philadelphia: J. B. Lippincott, 1913).

14. Variations on the one-to-one nurse/patient model include primary nursing (see Sue Hegyvary, *The Change to Primary Nursing: A Cross-Cultural View of Professional Nursing Practice* [St. Louis: C. V. Mosby, 1982]; Marie Manthey, "Primary Nursing Is Alive and Well in the Hospital," *American Journal of Nursing* [January 1973]: 83–87 [hereafter cited as *AJN*]), patients assigned to one nurse in intensive care units (see Fairman and Lynaugh, *Critical Care Nursing*, 3), and home care nursing.

15. Josephine Goldmark, *Nursing and Nursing Education in the United States* (New York: Macmillan, 1923), 13.

16. See *Facts about Nursing 1941* (New York: American Nurses Association, 1941), 11; *1951 Facts about Nursing* (New York: American Nurses Association, 1951), 12; *Facts about Nursing 1962–1963* (New York: American Nurses Association, 1963), 12.

17. "Nursing at Recent Hospital Conventions," *AJN* 36 (1936): 1156–1162; "The Nursing Situation in New York State," *Trained Nurse and Hospital Review* 96 (1935): 253.

18. *The United States Cadet Nurse Corps and Other Federal Training Programs* (Washington, DC: Government Printing Office, 1950).

19. *The United States Cadet Nurse Corps*, 80; U.S. Department of Labor, Bureau of Labor Statistics, *The Economic Status of Registered Professional Nurses 1946–47* (Washington, DC: Government Printing Office, 1947), 4.

20. See Lynaugh and Brush, *American Nursing*, 1–25. See also *The Economic Status of Registered Professional Nurses 1946–47*, 4.

21. C. J. Considine, "The Private Duty Market: Operational and Staffing Considerations," *Home Healthcare Nurse* 21 (2003): 454–459; Rebecca Friedman Zuber and Terry Cichon, "Adding Private Duty Services: Organizational and Regulatory Issues to Consider," *Home Healthcare Nurse* 21 (2003): 461–465.

22. Ginia Bellafante, "Enhanced Medical Care for an Annual Fee," *New York Times*, December 6, 2012; Pauline W. Chen, "Can Concierge Medicine for the Few Benefit the Many," *New York Times*, August 6, 2010; Paul Sullivan, "Dealing with Doctors Who Take Only Cash," *New York Times*, November 23, 2012.

23. Reverby, *Ordered to Care*, 180.

1. Have Cap Will Travel

1. See Eric Larrabee, *The Benevolent and Necessary Institution* (Garden City, NY: Doubleday, 1971), 114–115.

2. "Board of Managers Meeting Minutes, 1844–1863," 4 November 1844, vol. 1, Records of Philadelphia Lying-In Charity Hospital, Philadelphia Lying-In Charity Hospital Collection, Pennsylvania Hospital Historic Collections (hereafter cited as PLCHC).

3. "Report of the Executive Committee to the Managers and Lady Visitors," Report of the Several Branches of the Philadelphia Lying-In Charity and Nurse Society, 1852, box 1, 15–16, Philadelphia Medicine, Historical Society of Pennsylvania (hereafter cited as PMHSP).

4. "Annual Report, 1882," Fifty-Second Annual Report of the Board of Managers of the Philadelphia Lying-In Charity and Nurse School, box 1, 7–8, PMHSP.

5. "Annual Report," January 1863; Annual Report," January 1865, Minutes of the Governing Board, MC 89, 1863–1881, box 1, folder 11, Woman's Hospital of Philadelphia

Collection, Barbara Bates Center for the Study of the History of Nursing. See also Patricia O'Brien, "All a Woman's Life Can Bring: The Domestic Roots of Nursing in Philadelphia, 1830–1885," *Nursing Research* 36, no. 1 (1987): 12–19; Victor Robinson, *White Caps: The Story of Nursing* (Philadelphia: J. B. Lippincott, 1946), 236–238.

6. See Joan E. Lynaugh, "Riding the Yo-Yo: The Worth and Work of Nursing in the 20th Century," *Transactions & Studies of the College of Physicians of Philadelphia* 11, no. 3 (1989): 201–217; Susan Reverby, *Ordered to Care: The Dilemma of American Nursing, 1850–1945* (Cambridge: Cambridge University Press, 1987); Robinson, *White Caps.*

7. See Patricia D'Antonio, *Founding Friends: Families, Staff, and Patients at the Friend's Asylum in Early Nineteenth-Century Philadelphia* (Bethlehem, PA: Lehigh University Press, 2006); Barbra Mann Wall, *Unlikely Entrepreneurs: Catholic Sisters and the Hospital Marketplace, 1865–1925* (Columbus: Ohio State University Press, 2005).

8. Reverby, *Ordered to Care,* 11–21.

9. Chloe Cudsworth Littlefield to Elizabeth Littlefield, 5 January 1882, transcription, MC 144, box 3, Chloe Cudsworth Littlefield Papers, viewed at Barbara Bates Center for the Study of the History of Nursing (hereafter cited as CCLP). Original found at Rensselaer County Historical Society (hereafter cited as RCHS).

10. Between 1870 and 1900, the largest and second-largest employment fields for women were domestic and personal service and manufacturing, respectively. See Helen L. Sumner, *Report on the Condition of Women and Child Wage-Earners in the United States* (Washington, DC: Government Printing Office, 1910), 246.

11. Chloe Cudsworth Littlefield to Ellen Hubbard, 22 August 1883, transcription, box 3, CCLP. Original found at RCHS.

12. Chloe Cudsworth Littlefield diary, 18 August 1884, box 1, CCLP.

13. Chloe Cudsworth Littlefield to Elizabeth Littlefield, 3 December 1884, box 3, CCLP. Original found at RCHS.

14. United States Bureau of Education, "Schools for Nurses," in *Education Report 1902* (Washington, DC: Government Printing Office, 1903), 2051.

15. Chloe Cudsworth Littlefield to Abijah Daniel Littlefield, 20 May 1884, transcription, box 3, CCLP. Original found at RCHS.

16. Chloe Cudsworth Littlefield diary, 3 June 1884, box 1, CCLP.

17. Chloe Cudsworth Littlefield to Elizabeth Littlefield, 15 January 1885, transcription, box 3, CCLP. Original found at RCHS.

18. Chloe Cudsworth Littlefield to Elizabeth Littlefield, 1 February 1885, box 4, CCLP.

19. Chloe Cudsworth Littlefield to Elizabeth Littlefield, 1 February 1885, box 4, CCLP.

20. Chloe Cudsworth Littlefield to Ellen Hubbard, 30 June 1885, transcription, box 3, CCLP. Original found at RCHS.

21. Chloe Cudsworth Littlefield diary, 26 January 1885, box 1, CCLP.

22. Chloe Cudsworth Littlefield diary, 22 June 1885, box 1, CCLP.

23. Ellen Hubbard to Chloe Cudsworth Littlefield, 14 March 1887, box 4, CCLP.

24. Ellen Hubbard to Chloe Cudsworth Littlefield, 24 March 1887, box 4, CCLP.

25. Chloe Cudsworth Littlefield to Ellen Hubbard, 23 March 1887, box 4, CCLP.

26. Chloe Cudsworth Littlefield to Ellen Hubbard, 23 March 1887, box 4, CCLP.

27. Chloe Cudsworth Littlefield to Ellen Hubbard, 3 September 1884, box 3, CCLP. Original found at RCHS.

28. Chloe Cudsworth Littlefield to Ellen Hubbard, 23 September 1884, box 4, CCLP.

29. Chloe Cudsworth Littlefield diary, 5 August 1892, box 2, CCLP.

30. Reverby, *Ordered to Care*, 129.
31. Oderkirk provides the most accurate estimate of 549 schools of nursing existing at the turn of the twentieth century. See Wendell W. Oderkirk, "Setting the Record Straight: A Recount of Late Nineteenth-Century Training Schools," *Journal of Nursing History* 1, no.1 (November 1985): 30–37. Government estimates place the number higher, at approximately 867 schools. See U.S. Department of Commerce and Labor, Bureau of the Census, *Special Report: Benevolent Institutions 1904* (Washington, DC: Government Printing Office, 1904), 34.
32. U.S. Department of the Interior, *Population of the United States in 1860; Compiled from the Original Returns of the Eighth Census under the Direction of the Secretary of the Interior* (Washington, DC: Government Printing Office, 1864), 670–671.
33. For U.S. Census enumerations of nurses for the years 1870–1900, see U.S. Department of the Interior, *Ninth Census of the United States: 1870*, vol. 1, *The Statistics of the Population of the United States* (Washington, DC: Government Printing Office, 1870); U.S. Department of the Interior, *Tenth Census of the United States: 1880, Statistics of the Population of the United States* (Washington, DC: Government Printing Office, 1880); U.S. Department of the Interior, *Eleventh Census of the United States: 1890, Statistics of the Population of the United States, Part II* (Washington, DC: Government Printing Office, 1890); U.S. Department of Commerce and Labor, *Twelfth Census of the United States: 1900—Occupations the Twelfth Census* (Washington, DC: Government Printing Office, 1904).
34. See U.S. Department of Commerce and Labor, *Twelfth Census of the United States*, xxvi.
35. See U.S. Department of Health, Education, and Welfare, *Source Book: Nursing Personnel* (Bethesda, MD: U.S. Department of Health, Education, and Welfare, Public Health Service, Division of Nursing, December 1974). For consistency, this chapter uses numbers of nurses as listed in the U.S. Census reports.
36. See U.S. Department of Commerce and Labor, *Twelfth Census of the United States*, xxvi.
37. Anita Newcomb McGee, "The Growth of the Nursing Profession in the United States," *Trained Nurse and Hospital Review* 24 (June 1900): 441–445 (hereafter cited as *TNHR*).
38. J. M. Toner, "Statistics of Regular Medical Associations and Hospitals of the United States: Section II, Statistics of the Hospitals in the United States, 1872–1873," *Transactions of the American Medical Association* 24 (1873): 314.
39. U.S. Department of Commerce and Labor, *Benevolent Institutions 1904*, 32.
40. "Hospital Service in the United States," *Journal of the American Medical Association* 96 (March 28, 1931): 1012.
41. See Sumner, *Report on the Condition of Women*, 233–242.
42. Bureau of Education, *The Inception, Organization, and Management of Training Schools of Nursing* (Washington, DC: Government Printing Office, 1882), 13–14.
43. M. Adelaide Nutting, *Educational Status of Nursing* (Washington, DC: Government Printing Office, 1912), 25–26.
44. Committee on Nursing and Nursing Education in the United States, *Nursing and Nursing Education in the United States* (New York: Macmillan, 1923), 219.
45. Committee on the Grading of Nursing Schools, *The Second Grading of Nursing Schools* (New York: Committee on the Grading of Nursing Schools, 1932), 18.
46. "Editorially Speaking," *TNHR* 16 (February 1896): 101–103; Marie L. Cuthbertson, "The Advisability of a Club Life for Nurses," *AJN* 2 (July 1902): 781; Mary Riddle, "The President's Address," *AJN* 3 (August 1903): 841.

47. Darlene Clark Hine, *Black Women in White: Racial Conflict and Cooperation in the Nursing Profession 1890–1950* (Bloomington: Indiana University Press, 1989), 9.

48. The Provident Hospital offered physicians as well as nurses a place in which to practice their profession. Although many of the black hospitals and nurse training schools were established in response to discriminatory practices aimed at African Americans, Vanessa Northington Gamble cautions against viewing black-controlled hospitals solely as a reaction to segregation. A long-standing tradition in the African American community of providing for its members as well as an emphasis on black self-reliance and development of black institutions was also instrumental in the founding of black-controlled hospitals and schools of nursing. For the history of black hospitals see Vanessa Northington Gamble, *Making a Place for Ourselves: The Black Hospital Movement, 1920–1945* (New York: Oxford University Press, 1995). For the establishment of the Provident Hospital Training School see Richard M. Krieg and Judith A. Cooksey, *Provident Hospital: A Living Legacy* (Chicago: Provident Foundation, 1998).

49. See *My Oath: Fiftieth Anniversary of the Mills School of Nursing* (New York: Mills School of Nursing, Bellevue Hospital, 1937).

50. See Patricia D'Antonio and Jean Whelan, "Counting Nurses: The Power of Historical Census Data," *Journal of Clinical Nursing* 18 (2009): 2714–2724.

51. See Florence C. Carmen, "Some of the Differences between a Trained Nurse and an Untrained Nurse," *TNHR* 16 (August 1896): 409–410; "The Quack Nurse," editorial, *TNHR* 10 (November 1893): 226–227; "Nurses and Nursing on the Pacific Coast," *TNHR* 13 (October 1894): 207.

52. Janet N. Hooks, "Women's Occupations through Seven Decades," *Women's Bureau Bulletin*, no. 218 (Washington, DC: Government Printing Office, 1947), 39.

2. Starting Out

1. See Minnie Ahearns, "Discussion, 18th Annual Convention, ANA," *AJN* 15 (August 1915): 1036; "Commercial Directories," *AJN* 9 (July 1909): 723–724; "The Commercial Registry," *AJN* 14 (February 1914): 329–330; Martha Russell, "Clubhouses, Hostelries, and Directories for Nurses," *AJN* 5 (August 1905): 803; Mary Thorton, letter to the editor, "Commercial Directories," *AJN* 3 (December 1903): 243–244.

2. See *The Alumni Association of the Bellevue School of Nursing* (New York: Alumni Association of the Bellevue School of Nursing, 1989); Dorothy Giles, *A Candle in Her Hand* (New York: G. P. Putnam's Sons, 1949); Elizabeth Christophers Hobson, *Recollections of a Happy Life* (New York: G. P. Putnam's Sons, 1916): 77–114; Jane E. Mottus, *New York Nightingales: The Emergence of the Nursing Profession at Bellevue and New York Hospital 1850–1920* (Ann Arbor, MI: UMI Research Press, 1980).

3. See *The Alumni Association of the Bellevue School of Nursing*, 25.

4. Giles, *A Candle in Her Hand*, 126; Mottus, *New York Nightingales*, 53–54.

5. Giles, *A Candle in Her Hand*, 129–132.

6. Giles, *A Candle in Her Hand*, 154–155.

7. Giles, *A Candle in Her Hand*, 154–155; Mottus, *New York Nightingales*, 74–75.

8. See Mary M. Roberts, *American Nursing: History and Interpretation* (New York: Macmillan, 1954), 26.

9. See Ella Best, "Nursing Supply—How to Balance Supply and Demand," *The Modern Hospital* 39 (August 1932): 97–102.

10. "Special Meeting," Alumni Association Minutes, 10 November 1896, Alumni Association of the New York Hospital, box 1, New York Hospital School of Nursing Collection, New York Hospital Archives (hereafter cited as NYHSON).

11. "Annual Meeting," Alumni Association Minutes, 10 March 1897, Alumni Association of the New York Hospital, box 1, NYHSON.

12. Mottus, *New York Nightingales*, 181–182; "In the Nursing World: Bellevue Graduates Association," *Trained Nurse and Hospital Review* 15 (May 1897): 275–276.

13. See "History, of the Directory for Nurses of the College of Physicians," 1936, Series 4: Miscellaneous (History of the Directory), CPP10/0001-01, College of Physicians of Philadelphia (hereafter cited as CPP).

14. Dr. W. W. Keen (per Dora Keen Handy) to Dr. Frederick Fraley, 29 April 1932, Series 1: Correspondence (Establishment of Directory), CPP.

15. See "To the Fellows of the College of Physicians of Philadelphia," 1890, Series 2: Committee Reports & Recommendations (Committee on the Directory for Nurses) 1882–1890, CPP.

16. S. D. Gross, "Report of the Committee on the Training of Nurses," *Transactions of the American Medical Association* 20 (1869): 172, 173.

17. See Dr. Keen from E. H. Hollaway, secretary, 11 March 1882, Series 1: Correspondence (Establishment of Directory) (Committee on the Directory for Nurses), 1882–1890, CPP.

18. See "Report of Committee to the College of Physicians," 20 February 1882, Series 2: Committee Reports and Recommendations (Committee on the Directory for Nurses), 1882–1890, CPP.

19. See Giles, *A Candle in Her Hand*, 92, 94; Hobson, *Recollections*, 98–99.

20. See Ethel Johns and Blanche Pfefferkorn, *The Johns Hopkins Hospital School of Nursing, 1889–1949* (Baltimore: Johns Hopkins Press, 1954), 40; "The Superintendents' Convention, The Superintendents in Council," *Trained Nurse and Hospital Review* 13 (February 1894): 95–96.

21. See Sara E. Parsons, *History of the Massachusetts General Hospital Training School for Nurses* (Boston: Whitcomb & Barrows, 1922), 28–33.

22. See "Nurses' Club Houses and Central Directories," *AJN* 8 (March 1908): 423–424; Reba Thelin Foster, "The Organization of Nurses Clubs and Directories under State Association," *AJN* 9 (January 1909): 247–252; [Mrs.] Phillpotts, "A Central Directory for Nurses and How Best to Manage It," *AJN* 4 (July 1904): 794–796.

23. See "The Educational Value of a Central Directory," editorial, *AJN* 13 (January 1913): 251–252; Sophia Rutley, "Private Duty Nurses and Their Relationship to the Directory," *AJN* 15 (August 1915): 939–943.

24. See Julia Mellichampe, "The Development and Value of a Nurses Registry," *AJN* 16 (October 1916): 24–28; Rutley, "Private Duty Nurses," 939–943.

25. "Sixth Annual Convention of the Nurses' Associated Alumnae of the United States, Minutes of the Proceedings," *AJN* 3, no. 11 (July 1903): 881.

26. See Theresa Ericksen, "A Graded Registry," *AJN* 8 (September 1908): 964–966; Mellichampe, "The Development and Value of a Nurses Registry," 24–28.

27. For discussion of the state network of registries, see "Central Registries and the Idle Nurse," editorial, *AJN* 9 (December 1909): 145–147.

28. See Katherine De Witt, "The County Association and Its Relation to the State," *AJN* 9 (August 1909): 809–815; Foster, "The Organization of Nurses Clubs," 247–252; Sarah F. Martin, "Central Directories," *AJN* 10 (December 1909): 162–167.

29. See "Central Registries," *AJN* 12 (January 1912): 281–282; Foster, "The Organization of Nurses Clubs," 247–252; Grace Holmes, "An Ideal Central Directory," *AJN* 6 (June 1906): 606–608; Susan Bard Johnson, "The Boston Nurses Club," *AJN* 9 (June 1909): 662–663; Lily Kanely, "A Successful Central Registry," *AJN* 9 (April 1909):

496–498; Martin, "Central Directories," 162–167; Marian Mead, "Registry System of the Hennepin County Graduate Nurses' Association, Minneapolis, Minn.," *AJN* 10 (August 1910): 819–824.

30. See *The Alumnae Association of the Bellevue School of Nursing*, 30; "2nd Annual Meeting, American Society of Superintendents of Training Schools for Nurses," 13 February 1895, MS c 274, box 2, National League for Nursing Collection, courtesy of the National Library of Medicine (hereafter cited as NLN).

31. See "Nurses' Club of Brooklyn," *TNHR* 9 (May 1893): 236–237; "Nurses' Clubs," *TNHR* 12 (February 1894): 90; "A Club for Nurses," *TNHR* 13 (December 1894): 363; Sophia Palmer, "Alumnae Associations," *TNHR* 14 (April 1895): 203–204; Member, "The Graduate Nurses' Association," letter to the editor, *TNHR* 16 (January 1896): 41; "Nurses Seek Protection," *TNHR* 16 (April 1896): 200; "Nurses' Clubs," editorial, *TNHR* 16 (December 1896): 675.

32. "Nurses' Club of Brooklyn," *TNHR* 9 (May 1893): 236–237; "Nurses' Clubs," *TNHR* 13 (February 1894): 90; "Nurses Seek Protection," *TNHR* 16 (April 1896): 186; "Nurses' Club," *TNHR* 16 (December 1896): 675; "Protective Association," *TNHR* 18 (December 1897): 275.

33. The term *directory* was also used interchangeably with *registry*.

34. "Nurses' Protective Association," *TNHR* 22 (January 1899): 36–37.

35. See Alice Kessler-Harris, *Out to Work: A History of Wage-Earning Women in the United States*, 20th anniversary ed. (New York: Oxford University Press, 2003), 81–86.

36. Despite her notoriety and influence on early professional nursing, no biography exists of Robb. The following section is culled predominantly from three works that address Robb's career in detail: Lavinia L. Dock, *A History of Nursing: From the Earliest Times to the Present Day with Special Reference to the Work of the Past Thirty Years*, vol. 3 (New York: G. P. Putnam's Sons, 1912), 122–134; Ethel Johns and Blanche Pfefferkorn, *The Johns Hopkins School of Nursing 1889–1949* (Baltimore: Johns Hopkins Press, 1954); and Meta Rutter Pennock, ed., *Makers of Nursing History Portraits and Pen Sketches of Fifty-Nine Prominent Women* (New York: Lakeside, 1928).

37. "Discussion on the Benefits of Alumnae Associations," *Hospitals, Dispensaries and Nursing, Papers and Discussions in the International Congress of Charities, Correction and Philanthropy Section III, Chicago, June 12th to 17th, 1893* (1894; repr., New York: Garland, 1984), 577.

38. Isabel Hampton Robb, "The Aims, Methods and Spirit of the Associated Alumnae of Trained Nurses of the United States and Canada," *TNHR* 21 (June 1898): 307.

39. See Lyndia Flanagan, *One Strong Voice: the Story of the American Nurses' Association* (Kansas City: American Nurses Association, 1976), 32–33.

40. "Discussion on the Benefits of Alumnae Associations," 578.

41. Associated Alumnae of Trained Nurses of the United States and Canada, *Minutes of the Proceedings of the Second Annual Meeting of the Associated Alumnae of Trained Nurses of the United States and Canada* (n.p.: Associated Alumnae of Trained Nurses of the United States and Canada, 1899), 18; "Constitution and By-Laws of the Nurses' Associated Alumnae of the United States," *AJN* 4 (July 1904): 812.

42. Sylveen V. Nye, "The Proposed New York State Nurses Association," *TNHR* 25 (December 1900): 397.

43. See Ethel Gordon Fenwick, "The Organization and Registration of Nurses," in *The Transactions of the Third International Congress of Nurses Held in Buffalo 18–21 September 1901*, ed. Committee on Publication (Cleveland: J. B. Savage, 1901), 337.

44. See Sylveen Nye, "The Organization and Registration of Nurses," in *The Transactions of the Third International Congress of Nurses Held in Buffalo 18–21 September 1901*, ed. Committee on Publication (Cleveland: J. B. Savage, 1901), 346–347.

45. I. C. Rose, "The Necessity for Low Standards in the Beginning," *AJN* 4 (July 1904): 778.

46. Celia R. Heller, "A Word to Graduates," *TNHR* 24 (January 1900): 310–334; "In the Nursing World," *TNHR* 31 (October 1903): 241.

47. Associated Alumnae Trained Nurses of the United States and Canada, *Minutes of the Proceedings of the Associated Alumnae Trained Nurses of the United States and Canada*, n.d., microfilm, 5, courtesy of the National Library of Medicine (hereafter cited as NLM).

48. "Third Annual Convention of the Associated Alumnae of Trained Nurses of the United States: Minutes of the Proceedings," *AJN* 1, no. 1 (October 1900): 67–95; "In the Nursing World, Protective Association," *TNHR* 18 (May 1897): 274–275.

49. L. L. Dock, letter to the editor, *TNHR* 18 (May 1897): 274–275.

50. "Protective Association," *TNHR* 18 (June 1897): 332–333; Celia R. Heller, letter to the editor, *TNHR* 18 (June 1897): 337–340; "Nurses Clubs and Associations," *TNHR* 19 (August 1897): 104; "Protective Association," *TNHR* 19 (November 1897): 273–274; M. Flower Dayon, letter to the editor, *TNHR* 19 (November 1897): 275; L. L. Dock, letter to the editor, *TNHR* 20 (January 1898): 42–43; Olivia A. Grafstrom, letter to the editor, *TNHR* 20 (January 1898): 43–44.

51. See "Fifth Annual Convention of the Nurses' Associated Alumnae of the United States, Minutes of Proceedings, May 1–3, 1902," *AJN* 10 (July 1902): 766.

52. See "Sixth Annual Convention of the Nurses' Associated Alumnae of the United States, Minutes of the Proceedings," *AJN* 3, no. 11 (August 1903): 859.

53. "Constitution and By-Laws of the Nurses' Associated Alumnae of the United States," *AJN* 4 (July 1904): 812–815.

54. "The Biennial," *AJN* 44, no. 7 (July 1944): 627.

55. "Report of the Sixth Annual Convention of the Nurses Associated Alumnae of the United States, Minutes of Proceedings, June 10–12, 1903," *AJN* 3, no. 11 (July 1903): 848; "Seventh Annual Convention of the Nurses' Associated Alumnae of the United States, Minutes of the Proceedings, May 12–14, 1904," *AJN* 4 (July 1904): 752.

56. See Adah Thoms, *Pathfinders: A History of the Progress of Colored Graduate Nurses* (New York: Kay, 1929), 87. For New York Counties Registered Nurses Association membership, see "Minutes, Regular Meeting, NYCRNA," 4 February 1919, box 19, New York Counties Registered Nurses Association Papers, Foundation of NYS Nurses, Bellevue Alumni Center for Nursing History (hereafter cited as NYCRNAP).

57. See "Minutes, Regular Meeting, NYCRNA," 2 October 1928, box 6, NYCRNAP. For a history of the establishment of professional schools of nursing for African Americans see Darlene Clark Hine, *Black Women in White: Racial Conflict and Cooperation in the Nursing Profession, 1890–1950* (Bloomington: Indiana University Press, 1989), 26–84.

58. Hine, *Black Women in White*, 94–95.

59. For Freedman's Hospital status in the ANA, see "Meeting of the Board of Directors of the American Nurses Association," 11 May 1918, folder Executive Committee meetings beginning January 12, 1912–1923, box 33, American Nurses Association Collection, Howard Gotlieb Archival Research Center at Boston University.

60. Susan Reverby, *Ordered to Care: The Dilemma of American Nursing, 1850–1945* (Cambridge: Cambridge University Press, 1987), 142.

3. Supplying Nurses

Epigraph: Elizabeth Burgess, "The Future of the Central Registry," *AJN* 15 (August 1915): 1034.

1. See American Nurses Association, *Facts about Nursing* (New York: American Nurses Association, 1939), 43; American Nurses Association, *Facts about Nursing* (New York: American Nurses Association, 1953), 80; American Nurses Association, *Facts about Nursing* (New York: American Nurses Association, 1957), 109; American Nurses Association, *Facts about Nursing* (New York: American Nurses Association, 1966), 116.
2. United States Bureau of Education, "Schools for Nurses," in *The Report of the Commissioner of Education for 1902* (Washington, DC: Government Printing Office, 1903), 2044, 2053–2055.
3. U.S. Department of Commerce, *Thirteenth Census of the Unites States*, vol. 1, *Population* (Washington, DC: Government Printing Office, 1913).
4. See Historical Committee, "Manuscript of History of New York Counties Registered Nurse Association, January 1904–May 1939," box 18, 21, 23, NYCRNAP; "Certificate of Incorporation of the New York County Nurses' Association," 2 April 1904, amended 18 July 1910, amended 23 March 1920, box 18, NYCRNAP.
5. See E. H. Lewinski-Corwin, *The Hospital Situation in Greater New York* (New York: G. P. Putnam's Sons, 1924), iii.
6. See Historical Committee, "Manuscript of History of New York Counties Registered Nurse Association."
7. "Minutes, Annual Meeting, NYCRNA," 6 June 1907, box 19, NYCRNAP; "Central Registries," editorial, *AJN* 9 (June 1909): 639.
8. County Registry Committee, "Conditions in New York Calling for a Registry under Professional Control," 22 May 1909, box 8, NYCRNAP; Committee on Registry, "Registry under the Control of the New York County Nurse's Association Report for 1 June 1909," box 19, NYCRNAP.
9. "Minutes, Committee on Registry, NYCRNA," 28 April 1910, box 8, NYCRNAP.
10. "Minutes, Committee on Registry, NYCRNA," 28 January 1910, box 8, NYCRNAP.
11. "Prospectus of the Central Registry for Nurses," 1910, box 8, NYCRNAP.
12. "Report of the Proceedings of the Governing Board of the Central Registry," 28 July 1910, box 15, NYCRNAP.
13. See Helen Macmillan, "Central Registration," *AJN* 4 (July 1904): 793.
14. See NYCRNA, "Organization of the Central Registry," box 15, NYCRNAP.
15. For the qualifications of an ideal registrar see Nellie Chapman, "Discussion on Registry Problems," *AJN* 14, no.10 (1914): 834; Katherine Hyde, "Business Women as Registrar," *AJN* 15 (August 1915): 943; Julia Mellichampe, "The Development and Value of a Nurses Registry," *AJN* 16 (1916): 28.
16. See "Massachusetts General Hospital Nurses' Alumnae, Boston," *AJN* 1 (September 1901): 890.
17. See "Minutes, Governing Board, Central Registry," 7 June 1910, box 8, NYCRNAP.
18. See Sara Parsons, "Why Private Nurses Should Organize," *AJN* 16 (January 1916): 297–230; Ruth Brewster Sherman, "Some Aspects of Private Nursing," *AJN* 10 (August 1910): 829–830.
19. See "Why Nurses Refuse Tuberculosis Cases," *AJN* 6 (June 1906): 772–773; Julia Reed, "Are Nurses Refusing Contagious Cases?," *AJN* 6 (June 1906): 773–775.
20. See "Prospectus of the Central Registry for Nurses, Rules for Nurses," 1910, box 8, NYCRNAP.

21. For the differences between the two methods of assignment see "Discussion, 18th Annual Convention," *AJN* 15 (August 1915): 947; Frances Stone, "The Management of a Registry for Nurses," *AJN* 3 (August 1903): 885–886.

22. See "Prospectus of the Central Registry for Nurses, Rules for Nurses."

23. See Veronica Driscoll, *Legitimizing the Profession of Nursing: The Distinct Mission of the New York State Nurses Association* (Guilderland, NY: Foundation of the New York State Nurses Association, 1976), 5, 18.

24. See Nancy Tomes, "The Silent Battle: Nurse Registration in New York State, 1903–1920," in *Nursing History, New Perspectives, New Possibilities,* ed. Ellen Condliffe Lagermann (New York: Teachers College Press, 1983), 110.

25. See Tomes, "The Silent Battle," 119.

26. See Shirley Fondiller, "Licensing and Titling in Nursing and Society: An Historical Perspective," in *Looking Beyond the Entry Issue: Implications for Education and Service,* ed. National League for Nursing (New York: The League, 1986), 3–9; Tomes, "The Silent Battle," 114; and William White, "The Introduction of Professional Regulation and Labor Market Conditions; Occupational Licensure of Registered Nurses," *Policy Science* 20, no. 1 (April 1987): 34.

27. See Tomes, "The Silent Battle," 119.

28. "Minutes, Annual Meeting, NYCRNA," 7 June 1914, box 19, NYCRNAP.

29. See Committee on Registry, "Registry under the Control of the New York County Nurse's Association Report for 1 June, 1909."

30. For the number of schools in 1900 see Wendell Oderkirk, "Setting the Record Straight: A Recount of Late Nineteenth-Century Training Schools," *Journal of Nursing History* 1 (November 1985): 30–37. For the years 1910–1930, see U.S. Department of Health, Education and Welfare, *Sourcebook Nursing Personnel* (Bethesda, MD: Government Printing Office, 1974).

31. See "Prospectus of the Central Registry for Nurses."

32. See Committee on Registry, "Registry under the Control of the New York County Nurses Association Report for 1 June 1909."

33. See "Minutes, Governing Board, Central Registry, November 1910–January 1915," box 15, NYCRNAP.

34. "Minutes, Executive Committee, NYCRNA," 30 December 1915, 28 January 1916, box 15, NYCRNAP.

35. See "Minutes, Executive Committee, NYCRNA," 30 December 1921, box 15, NYCRNAP.

36. See L. L. Dock, "Central Directories and Sliding Scales," *AJN* 7 (October 1906): 12.

37. See, for example, Shirley Titus, "Meeting the Cost of Nursing Service," *AJN* 27 (March 1927): 166.

38. "April 14, 1920, Regular Meeting," Alumnae Association Minutes, 1902–1910, Alumnae Association New York Hospital Training School for Nurses Reports from Meetings 1893–1902, Cornell University New York Hospital School of Nursing Alumnae Records, box 1, Medical Center Archives of New York-Presbyterian/Weill Center (hereafter cited as CUNYHSON).

39. "May 10, 1920, Regular Meeting," Alumnae Association Minutes, 1902–1910, Alumnae Association New York Hospital Training School for Nurses Reports from Meetings 1893–1902, box 1, CUNYHSON.

40. See Christine Kefauver, "What Is the Matter with the Training Schools," *TNHR* 59 (August 1920): 113–114.

41. Donald E. Yett, "The Chronic 'Shortage' of Nurses: A Public Policy Dilemma," in *Empirical Studies in Health Economics*, ed. H. E. Klarman (Baltimore: Johns Hopkins Press, 1970), 375–376.

42. For discussion on the oligopsonistic nurse labor market and its connection to nurse shortages see Stuart H. Altman, "The Structure of Nursing Education and Its Impact on Supply," in *Empirical Studies in Health Economics*, ed. H. E. Klarman (Baltimore: Johns Hopkins Press, 1970), 339; Donald E. Yett, "The Chronic 'Shortage' of Nurses," 379–381.

43. See Joann Ashley, *Hospitals, Paternalism, and the Role of the Nurse* (New York: Teachers College Press, 1976); Barbara Melosh, *"The Physician's Hand": Work Culture and Conflict in American Nursing* (Philadelphia: Temple University Press, 1982), 82–83.

44. See "Prospectus of the Central Registry for Nurses."

45. See "Minutes, Regular Meeting, NYCRNA," 3 October 1911, box 19, NYCRNAP.

46. See "Minutes, Executive Committee, NYCRNA," 31 May 1912, box 15, NYCRNAP.

47. See "Minutes, Governing Board, Central Registry, NYCRNA, 27 November, 1912," box 15, NYCRNAP.

48. See "Nurses Form Trust to Get Higher Pay," *New York Times*, 22 February 1912.

49. New York Physician, "Physician Says Higher Salaries Give the Nurses Lofty Notions," letter to the editor, *New York Times*, 2 March 1912.

50. RN, "The Nurses' Trust," letter to the editor, *New York Times*, 24 February 1912.

51. A Nurse Who Knows, "The Nurse's Salary," letter to the editor, *New York Times*, 5 March 1912.

52. See "Minutes, Executive Committee, NYCRNA," 1 March 1918, box 15, NYCRNAP.

53. See "Minutes, Annual Meeting, NYCRNA," 4 March 1919, box 19, NYCRNAP.

54. See S. S. Goldwater, "The Nursing Crisis: Efforts to Satisfy the Nursing Requirements of the War. A Way Out of the Difficulty," *AJN* 18 (August 1918): 1032.

55. See "Minutes, Executive Committee, NYCRNA," 30 January 1920, box 15, NYCRNAP.

56. See Frank Allport, "The Graduate Nurse versus the Patient of Moderate Income," *Chicago Medical Recorder* 31 (1909): 465–473; "The Question of Compensation," editorial, *AJN* 5 (November 1904): 76; Lina Lightbourn, "How Can We Provide Skilled Nursing for People of Moderate Means," *AJN* 9 (September 1909): 977–983.

57. See Richard Bradley, "Household Nursing in Relation to Other Similar Work," *AJN* 15 (August 1915): 969; Charles Stover, "The Relation of the Nurse to the Total Sickness of the Community," *TNHR* 59 (December 1917): 327.

58. See Richard Beard, "The Trained Nurse of the Future," *JAMA* 61 (13 December 1913): 2151; A. S. Kavanagh, "Report of the Sub-Committee on the Training of Nurses," in *Transactions of the 10th Annual Conference of the American Hospital Association Held in Detroit 1908*, ed. American Hospital Association (Chicago: American Hospital Association, 1908), 155–176; Jennie Walters, "A Plan Suggested for Providing Skilled Nursing for Those of Moderate Means," *AJN* 8 (April 1908): 527–529.

59. See Isabel McIsaac, "Discussion," *AJN* 6 (August 1906): 768; Grace Fay Schryver, *A History of the Illinois Training School for Nurses, 1880–1929* (Chicago: Board of Directors of the Illinois Training School, 1930), 64–66.

60. See Wilma Weller, "How Shall We Provide for Families with Moderate Incomes," *AJN* 13 (September 1913): 1009–1010.

61. See "How the Toronto Nurses Are Meeting It," editorial, *AJN* 6 (April 1906): 415–416.

62. See "Prospectus of the Central Registry for Nurses."
63. See Allport, "The Graduate Nurse," 467; "Skilled Nursing Care for the Great Middl Class," editorial, *AJN* 6 (April 1906): 414; C. May Hollister, "How Can Skilled Nurs ing Service Be Procured by the Family of Moderate Means," *AJN* 6 (August 1906] 763–766.
64. See "Central Registries and the Idle Nurse," editorial, *AJN* 9 (1909): 145–147. Se also Hollister, "How Can Skilled Nursing," 763–766; Sara Parsons, "The Sliding Scal of Charges for Private Nurses," *AJN* 11 (June 1911): 694–696.
65. See "Central Registries and the Idle Nurse," 145–147; Hollister, "How Can Skille Nursing," 763–766; Parsons, "The Sliding Scale of Charges for Private Nurses, 694–696.
66. See Hollister, "How Can Skilled Nursing," 764; Lightbourn, "How Can We Provid Skilled Nursing," 978; L. W. Quintard, "Provisions Already Existing for the Care c the Sick of Moderate Means," *AJN* 7 (July 1907): 780.
67. See Sister Ignatius Feeny, "How May a Nurse Charge Below Her Price withou Lowering Her Standard," *AJN* 6 (August 1906): 766–767; Lightbourn, "How Can W Provide Skilled Nursing," 977–983.
68. Allport, "The Graduate Nurse," 466.
69. See "Central Registries and the Idle Nurse," 145–147; Reba Thelin Foster, "The Organ ization of Nurses Clubs and Directories under State Association," *AJN* 9 (Janu ary 1909): 250.
70. See Dock, "Central Directories and Sliding Scales," 10–14.
71. See "Minutes, Regular Meeting, NYCRNA," 2 April 1907, box 19, NYCRNAP; "Min utes, Annual Meeting, NYCRNA," 6 June 1907.
72. See Allport, "The Graduate Nurse," 466; Kavanagh, "Report of the Sub-Committe on the Training of Nurses," 167–168.
73. See Theresa Ericksen, "A Graded Registry," *AJN* 8 (1908): 964–966.
74. See Grace Holmes, "Working for Our Living," *AJN* 9 (1909) 252–256.
75. See Kavanagh, "Report of the Sub-Committee on the Training of Nurses," 169.
76. See "Report of Special Committee on Grading and Classification of Nurses," in *Trans actions of the 16th Annual Conference of the American Hospital Association i Kingston 1914*, ed. American Hospital Association (Chicago: American Hospita Association, 1914), 163–188.
77. See "The Grading of Nurses," editorial, *AJN* 14 (April 1914): 503; Mary Riddle, "Th Grading of Nurses," in *Transactions of the 15th Annual Conference of the America Hospital Association in Ontario 1913*, ed. American Hospital Association (Chicagc American Hospital Association, 1913), 130–140.
78. See Beard, "The Trained Nurse of the Future," 2152.
79. See "Minutes, Executive Committee, NYCRNA," 29 April 1920, box 15, NYCRNAP "Minutes, Regular Meeting, NYCRNA," 1 June 1920, box 19, NYCRNAP.
80. See "Minutes, Governing Board, Central Registry," 1913–1914, box 8, NYCRNAP "Minutes, Executive Committee, NYCRNA," 1918, box 15, NYCRNAP; "Minutes Registry Committee, NYCRNA," 2 November 1923," box 8, NYCRNAP.
81. See "Minutes, Governing Board, Central Registry," 27 November 1911, 22 April 1914 box 15, NYCRNAP; "Minutes, Executive Committee, NYCRNA," 28 March 1913 box 15, NYCRNAP; "Minutes, Governing Board, Central Registry," 25 January 1911 28 March 1913, box 8, NYCRNAP.
82. "Minutes, Governing Board, Central Registry," 25 January 1911, 28 March 1913, box 8 NYCRNAP.

83. See Mary M. Roberts, *American Nursing: History and Interpretation* (New York: Macmillan, 1954), 110.

84. See Louis, "Report of Nursing Resources," 439.

85. See "Minutes, Regular Meeting, NYCRNA," 4 February 1919, box 19, NYCRNAP.

86. See "Minutes, Governing Board, Central Registry," 27 November 1911, 22 April 1914, box 15, NYCRNAP; "Minutes, Executive Committee, NYCRNA," 28 March 1913," box 15, NYCRNAP; "Minutes, Governing Board, Central Registry," 25 January 1911, 28 March, 1913, box 8, NYCRNAP.

87. See Philip Kalisch and Beatrice Kalisch, *The Advance of American Nursing* (Boston: Little, Brown, 1978), 360–362; Arlene Keeling, "'Alert to the Necessities of the Emergency': U.S. Nursing during the 1918 Influenza Pandemic," *Public Health Reports* 125, suppl. 3 (2010): 105.

88. The best contemporary description of how the nation met the demand for nurses during World War I is Lavinia L. Dock et al., *History of American Red Cross Nursing* (New York: Macmillan, 1922), 239–309.

89. See "Minutes, Executive Committee, NYCRNA," 30 October 1913, box 15, NYCRNAP.

90. See "Minutes, Regular Meeting, NYCRNA," 1 October 1918, box 19, NYCRNAP.

91. See "Minutes, Regular Meeting, NYCRNA," 2 December 1919, box 19, NYCRNAP.

4. Surpluses, Shortages, and Segregation

1. For contemporary discussion on nursing educational reform see M. Adelaide Nutting, "How Can We Attract Suitable Applicants to Our Training Schools for Nurses," in *A Sound Economic Basis for Schools of Nursing and Other Addresses* (New York: G. P. Putnam's Sons, 1926), 154–170; M. Adelaide Nutting, "A Sound Economic Basis for Schools of Nursing," in *A Sound Economic Basis for Schools of Nursing and Other Addresses*, 3–17. For an extensive historical analysis of the reform movement in nursing education see Susan Reverby, *Ordered to Care: The Dilemma of American Nursing, 1850–1945* (Cambridge: Cambridge University Press, 1987), 121–179; Sr. Dorothy Sheahan, "The Social Origins of American Nursing and Its Movement into the University: A Microscopic Approach" (PhD diss., New York University, 1980), 201–223.

2. "Meeting of the Executive Committee," 1 December 1924, Nursing Education, 1924–1926, Public Health Committee Archives, New York Academy of Medicine.

3. "Meeting of the Executive Committee."

4. "Meeting of the Executive Committee."

5. U.S. Department of Commerce, *Fourteenth Census of the United States*, vol. 4, *Population* (Washington, DC: Government Printing Office, 1923), 42–43.

6. See Josephine Goldmark, *Nursing and Nursing Education in the United States* (New York: Macmillan, 1923), 15.

7. See Goldmark, *Nursing and Nursing Education*, 13.

8. See E. H. Lewinski-Corwin, *The Hospital Situation in Greater New York* (New York: G. P. Putnam's Sons, 1924), 212–213.

9. See Lucy Van Frank, "The Problems of a Registrar" (paper presented at the annual meeting of the Illinois State Nurses' Association, Peoria, IL, 10–12 October 1923), box 2, folder 1, Illinois Nurses Association Papers, Illinois State Historical Library (hereafter cited as INAP.)

10. See Janet Geister, "Hearsay and Facts in Private Duty," *AJN* 26 (July 1926): 517; Goldmark, *Nursing and Nursing Education*, 166.

11. Terminology differentiating nurses who cared for patients in the home from those who cared for them in the hospital varied regionally and at different points in time.

Private duty referred specifically to a nurse caring for a private patient in the home. *Special duty* was sometimes adopted by hospitals to indicate a nurse privately hired to care for a patient in a hospital. This book uses *private duty* for the most part. However, the two terms are considered synonymous.

12. May Ayres Burgess, ed., *Nurses, Patients, and Pocketbooks* (New York: Committee on the Grading of Nursing Schools, 1928), 74.

13. See "Hospital Service in the United States," *JAMA* 82 (12 January 1924): 124–125.

14. Lewinski-Corwin, *The Hospital Situation*, 212.

15. See "The Viewpoint of the Nurse," *TNHR* 67 (November 1921): 427–432; Carolyn Grey, "What Are the Aims of Nursing Education," *AJN* 21 (February 1921): 308–313; Cora Nifer, "The Universal Shortage of Nurses and What Is Possible for the Training School to Do to Help the Situation," *Hospital Progress* 3 (April 1922): 155–157; Clara Noyes, "Response, and President's Address," *AJN* 20 (July 1920): 782.

16. For the post–World War I nurse shortage, see May Ayres Burgess, "The Nursing Shortage," *JAMA* 90 (24 March 1928): 898–890.

17. See Joseph Doughty, "The Present Status of Nursing Service as Viewed by the Hospital Superintendent," *Bulletin of the American College of Surgeons* 11 (January 1927): 12–13; Grey, "What Are the Aims of Nursing Education," 308–313; Joseph Howland, "How Can the Shortage of Nurses Be Met?," *Boston Medical and Surgical Journal* 183 (25 November 1920): 628–632; Lewinski-Corwin, *The Hospital Situation in Greater New York*, 222–228.

18. See Richard Beard, "The Social, Economic, and Educational Status of the Nurse," *AJN* 20 (September 1923): 957; Sally Johnson, "How Are the Sick to Be Provided with Nursing Care," *AJN* 22 (February 1922): 353–356; Lewinski-Corwin, *The Hospital Situation in Greater New York*, 222–223; Adelaide Nutting, "How Can We Care for Our Patients and Educate the Nurse?," *Modern Hospital* 21 (September 1923): 305–310.

19. "Hospital Service in the United States," *JAMA* 92 (30 March 1929): 1054.

20. See Goldmark, *Nursing and Nursing Education*, 347–352; Lewinski-Corwin, *The Hospital Situation in Greater New York*, 222–224.

21. Committee on Education of the National League for Nursing Education, *Standard Curriculum for Schools of Nursing* (Baltimore: Waverly, 1917).

22. See Johnson, "How Are the Sick," 354.

23. See Lyman Allen, "The Nursing Problem," *Boston Medical and Surgical Journal* 189 (25 October 1923): 62–63; "The Supply of Nurses," editorial, *JAMA* 72 (25 January 1919): 276–277; F. A. Washbourne, "Discussion on 'How Can the Shortage of Nurses Be Met,'" *Boston Medical and Surgical Journal* 183 (25 November 1920): 631–632.

24. See Elizabeth Burgess, "The Subsidiary Worker in Nursing Services from the Point of View of the Committee on Subsidiary Workers in Nursing Services," in *Proceedings, 40th Annual Convention of the National League for Nursing Education, in Washington, D.C., April 25, 1934*, ed. National League for Nursing Education (New York: National League for Nursing Education, 1934), 163–170. See also "The Subsidiary Worker," editorial, *AJN* 37 (March 1937): 284.

25. See Martin Fischer, "Nursing Education," *Modern Hospital* 17 (December 1921): 503–504; Goldmark, *Nursing and Nursing Education*, 14–16.

26. See "Appeals to Nurses to Lessen Demands," *New York Times*, 1 May 1925.

27. See "Minutes, Board of Directors, NYCRNA," 30 June 1925, box 6, NYCRNAP.

28. See Thew Wright, "The Nurses' Official Registry of Buffalo," *AJN* 28 (April 1928): 321.

29. See "Meeting of Sub-committee on Nursing of Medical Society of New York State," 1926, 22, box 37, folder 309, series 100: International, record group 1, Rockefeller Foundation Archives, Rockefeller Archive Center (hereafter cited as RFA).

30. See Janet Geister, "Report of a Survey of Private Duty Nursing," in *Proceedings, Official Meeting, New York State Nurses Association, 24th Annual Meeting, 1925*, ed. New York State Nurses Association, New York State Nurses Association Papers, AC-2, box 5, Foundation of NYS Nurses, Bellevue Alumni Center for Nursing History (hereafter cited as NYSNAP).

31. This section's subheading "Your Money and Your Life" was taken from the study questionnaire title sent to private duty nurses in New York State 1925–1926. See "Your Money and Your Life for One Week of Private Duty Nursing," *AJN* 25 (December 1925): 992.

32. See "Central Registry Rules for Nurses," 1920, box 8, NYCRNAP.

33. See Geoffrey Moore and Janice Hedges, "Trends in Labor and Leisure," *Monthly Labor Review* 94 (February 1971): 5.

34. See Geister, "Hearsay and Facts," 524.

35. Geister, "Hearsay and Facts," 519.

36. All comments taken from Geister, "Report of a Survey."

37. See "Meeting of Sub-committee on Nursing of the Medical Society of New York State."

38. See "The Nursing Situation Tentative Suggestions of the Sub-committee," 18 May 1925, Nursing Education, 1924–1926, Public Health Committee Archives, New York Academy of Medicine; "Conference on the Nursing Situation," 17 December 1925, Nursing Education, 1924–1926, Public Health Committee Archives, New York Academy of Medicine.

39. See "Study of Private Duty Nursing (the Grading Committee)," 1926, 19–23, folder 309, box 37, series 100: International, record group 1, RFA.

40. See Helen W. Munson, *The Story of the National League of Nursing Education* (Philadelphia: W. B. Saunders, 1934), 53–54; Helen Marshall, *Mary Adelaide Nutting: Pioneer of Modern Nursing* (Baltimore: Johns Hopkins University Press, 1972), 192–193.

41. See Elizabeth Burgess, "Eight Years of the Grading Committee," *AJN* 34 (October 1934): 937–945; Laura Logan, "A Program for the Grading of Schools of Nursing," *AJN* 25 (December 1925): 1005–1012; C.-E.A. Winslow, "Program and Preliminary Results of the Committee on the Grading of Nursing Schools," *American Journal of Public Health* 18 (April 1928): 449.

42. See "Grading Schools of Nursing," *AJN* 26 (May 1926): 401.

43. See "Grading Committee Adopts Official Program," *Modern Hospital* 28 (January 1927): 103–104; William Darrach, "Report on Committee on the Grading of Nursing Schools," 16 April 1926, box 121, folder 1492, series 200: United States, record group 1.1, RFA.

44. See Burgess, *Nurses, Patients, and Pocketbooks*.

45. Burgess, *Nurses, Patients, and Pocketbooks*, 304–309.

46. Burgess, *Nurses, Patients, and Pocketbooks*, 66–89.

47. See "Nurses, Patients, and Pocketbooks, Some Highlights from Dr. Burgess' Presentation of the Book to the National Nursing Association at Louisville," *AJN* 28 (July 1928): 674.

48. See Burgess, *Nurses, Patients, and Pocketbooks*, 148–149.

49. Carrie Hall, "Effect of the Grading Committee Report on Schools of Nursing," *AJN* 29 (February 1929): 133.

50. See "Nurses, Patients, and Pocketbooks—A Symposium," *Modern Hospital* 31 (December 1928): 73–78.

51. See "Conference Opens Program for Grading Nursing Schools," *Modern Hospital* 24 (May 1925): 471; Joseph Doane, "Reviewing the Objectives of the Five-Year Grading Program," *Modern Hospital* 28 (March 1927): 130–132; Charles Lockwood, "The Doctor Gives His Opinion," *Pacific Coast Journal of Nursing* 24 (October 1928): 505–506, 611 (hereafter cited as *PCJN*); Laura Logan, "Conference on the Grading of Nursing Schools," *AJN* 25 (April 1925): 306.

52. The two publications were Ethel Johns and Blanche Pfefferkorn, *An Activity Analysis of Nursing* (New York: Committee on the Grading of Nursing Schools, 1934) and Committee on the Grading of Nursing Schools, *Nursing Schools Today and Tomorrow* (New York: Committee on the Grading of Nursing Schools, 1934).

53. Darlene Clark Hine, *Black Women in White: Racial Conflict and Cooperation in the Nursing Profession, 1890–1950* (Bloomington: Indiana University Press, 1989), 100.

54. Hine, *Black Women in White*, 62.

55. See Ethel Johns, "A Study of the Present Status of the Negro Woman in Nursing, 1925," unpublished report, exhibit A-21, box 122, folder 1507, series 200: United States, record group 1.1: Projects, RFA.

56. Johns, "A Study of the Present Status of the Negro Woman in Nursing," exhibit B-2.

57. "Minutes, Third Annual Convention of the National Association of Colored Graduate Nurses, New York," 18 August 1910, microfilm, National Association of Colored Graduate Nurses Records, Manuscripts, Archives and Rare Books Division, Schomburg Center for Research in Black Culture, New York Public Library (hereafter cited as NACGNR); "Minutes, Fourth Annual Convention of the National Association of Colored Graduate Nurses, Washington, DC," 18 August 1911, NACGNR.

58. "Minutes, Executive Board Meeting per Correspondence, National Association of Colored Graduate Nurses," February 1917, NACGNR.

59. "Minutes, Tenth Annual Convention of the National Association of Colored Graduate Nurses, Louisville, KY," 23 August 1917, NACGNR.

60. "Minutes, Eleventh Annual Convention of the National Association of Colored Graduate Nurses, St. Louis," 20 August 1918, NACGNR.

61. "Adah B. Thoms to Membership, National Association of Colored Graduate Nurses," 29 October 1920, NACGNR.

62. "Minutes, Executive Board Meeting per Correspondence, National Association of Colored Graduate Nurses," 3 December 1918, NACGNR.

63. For a general description of the registry as told by Thoms to Ethel Johns, see Johns, "A Study of the Present Status of the Negro Woman in Nursing, 1925."

64. Johns, "A Study of the Present Status of the Negro Woman in Nursing, 1925," 1.

65. See Hospital Library and Service Bureau, "Report on an Informal Study of the Educational Facilities for Colored Nurses, 1924–1925, Part II Colored Nurses in Public Health Work," box 122, folder 1505, series 200: United States, record group 1.1: Project, RFA.

66. Johns, "A Study of the Present Status of the Negro Woman in Nursing, 1925," tables, p. 8.

67. See Committee on the Grading of Nursing Schools, *Nursing Schools Today and Tomorrow*, 40–41.

68. Committee on the Grading of Nursing Schools, *Nursing Schools Today and Tomorrow*, 40.

5. Private Duty's Golden Age

1. The Chicago registry was known by various names throughout its life, including Central Directory, Registry, and Official Registry. In the 1940s the name was changed to Nurses Professional Registry; this name remained until the organization was disbanded in the early 1980s. To avoid confusion with different names, First District's registry is referred to as the Nurses Professional Registry (NPR) throughout this book.

2. Lucy Van Frank, "The Problems of a Registrar" (paper presented at the annual meeting of the Illinois State Nurses Association, Peoria, IL, 10–12 October 1923), box 2, folder 1, INAP. The original name for the organization was the Illinois Graduate Nurses' Association. The name was changed in 1902 to the Illinois State Association of Graduate Nurses and later in 1929 to the Illinois State Nurses Association (ISNA). See Mary Dunwiddie, *A History of the Illinois State Nurses' Association 1901–1935* (Chicago: Illinois State Nurses' Association, 1937), 4. The present name of the association is Illinois Nurses Association.

3. See "Nurses Professional Registry, Average Number of Registrants and Average Monthly Number of Private Duty Assignments, 1917–1948," box 1, Chicago Nurses Registry Collection, Midwest Nursing History Resource Center, College of Nursing, University of Illinois (hereafter cited as CNRC).

4. See Lucy Van Frank, "Problems of the Registry," *AJN* 27 (December 1927): 1013–1014.

5. See Dunwiddie, *A History*.

6. See "Illinois State Nurses' Association," *AJN* 1 (1901): 925–927.

7. See Dunwiddie, *A History*, 93.

8. See Dunwiddie, *A History*, 94; Minnie Ahrens, "Discussion, 18th Annual Convention, American Nurses Association," *AJN* 15 (August 1915): 946–947, 1035–1036.

9. See Dunwiddie, *A History*, 163–165.

10. See Dinwiddie, *A History*, 94; "Annual Report Club and Registry, 1926," *First District Bulletin* 24 (February 1927): 10–11, box 3, folder 10, INAP.

11. See Dunwiddie, *A History*, 96; Ahrens, "Discussion," 946–947.

12. For examples of Van Frank's writings see Van Frank, "The Problems of a Registrar"; Van Frank, "Problems of the Registry"; Van Frank, "The Private Duty Nurse" (paper presented at the annual meeting of the Illinois State Nurses Association, Moline, IL, 10 October 1929), box 4, folder 12, INAP.

13. Van Frank, "The Problems of a Registrar."

14. Van Frank, "Problems of the Registry," 3–10.

15. Van Frank, "The Private Duty Nurse."

16. NPR statistics for the years prior to 1942 contain only the number of calls assigned to nurses. How many calls were received and filled or unfilled for that time is not known.

17. For the number of graduate nurses in Illinois and Chicago, see Department of Commerce, *Fifteenth Census of the United States: 1930, Population*, vol. 4 (Washington, DC: Government Printing Office, 1930), 428. For number of nurses enrolled on the NPR, see "Nurses Professional Registry, Average Number of Registrants and Average Monthly Number of Private Duty Assignments, 1917–1946," 26 July 1947, box 1, CNRC. The census figures for 1930 included student nurses in the same category with graduate nurses, which makes the estimates of percentages of NPR registrants of total number of city and state nurses conservative.

18. See "Nurses Fees, 1913–1980," 7 April 1976, box 1, CNRC; "Annual Report, Private Duty Section, Illinois State Nurses Association, 1926–1927," box 3, folder 10, INAP.

19. See "Income over Expenses," n.d., most likely 1947, box 1, CNRC.
20. See "Annual Report, First District, 1924," box 2, folder 2, INAP; "Annual Report Club and Registry Committee, 1926," 11.
21. See "Report of the Registry Committee," 7 June 1930, box 4, folder 13, INAP.
22. See "The Registry as Placement Bureau," *First District Bulletin* 24 (August 1927): 4, box 3, folder 10, INAP.
23. See "Registry," *First District Bulletin* 23 (March 1926): 3, box 3, folder 8, INAP.
24. Van Frank, "The Problems of a Registrar."
25. See Van Frank, "The Problems of a Registrar"; Van Frank, "The Private Duty Nurse."
26. For nurses' complaints see Van Frank, "The Problems of a Registrar"; Van Frank, "The Private Duty Nurse."
27. For excessive hours of work, see Mary Anne Goode, "Working Hours for Nurses," *TNHR* 51 (August 1913): 77–79. For student hours of work see Josephine Goldmark, *Nursing and Nursing Education* (New York: Macmillan, 1923), 413–414; M. Adelaide Nutting, *Educational Status of Nursing*, bulletin no. 7, whole number 475 (Washington, DC: U.S. Bureau of Education, 1912), 30.
28. See "Twelve-Hour Day for Specials?," *TNHR* 70 (June 1923): 516–518.
29. See Ruth Brown, "Twelve-Hour Duty," *AJN* 24 (March 1924): 435–440; Alice Gilman, "The Twelve Hour Day for Graduate Nurses on Special Duty in the Hospital," *AJN* 21 (June 1921): 639–641; M. Kingston Kelley, "Nurses vs. Twelve-Hour Duty," *PCJN* 16 (February 1920): 81–82; Anna Maxwell, "The Private Nurse and Twenty-Four Hour Hospital Duty," *AJN* 17 (December 1916): 191–194; Josephine Vandergon, "Should the Private Duty Nurse Work Longer than Twelve Hours?," *PCJN* 16 (August 1920): 494–496.
30. See "Twelve-Hour Special Duty in Hospitals," editorial, *AJN* 26 (August 1926): 623–624.
31. See Brown, "Twelve-Hour Duty"; Gilman, "The Twelve Hour Day for Graduate Nurses on Special Duty"; Helen Hanson, "The Private Duty Nurse," *AJN* 23 (March, 1923): 448–450; Kelley, "Nurses vs. Twelve-Hour Duty"; Maxwell, "The Private Nurse and Twenty-Four Hour Hospital Duty"; Vandergon, "Should the Private Duty Nurse Work Longer?"
32. See "Report of the Registry Committee," 7 June 1930.
33. See "Symposium, Private Duty Section, Illinois State Nurses Association Annual Meeting," 23 October 1923, box 2, folder 1, INAP.
34. See "Status of Twelve-Hour Duty," *AJN* 25 (August 1925): 660–661.
35. See May Ayres Burgess, ed., *Nurses, Patients, and Pocketbooks* (New York: Committee on the Grading of Nursing Schools, 1928), 322–329; M. S., letter to the editor, *AJN* 26 (November 1926): 888; Merle Duncan, "Twelve-Hour Duty: Another View," *AJN* 24 (March 1924): 441; Annette Fiske, "Twelve-Hour Day for Specials? Individual Adaptation," *TNHR* 70 (June 1923): 519; Esther O'Dowd, "Twenty-Four Hour Duty from the Standpoint of the Nurse," *AJN* 24 (March 1924): 442.
36. See "Some Administrative Aspects of Special Nursing," *AJN* 31 (October 1931): 1166.
37. "Private Duty Nursing," *First District Bulletin* 20 (May 1923), box 2, folder 1, INAP.
38. "Symposium, Private Duty Section, Illinois State Nurses Association Annual Meeting."
39. See Dunwiddie, *A History*, 106–107; "Annual Report, Private Duty Nurses Section, Illinois State Nurses Association, 1926–1927," box 3, folder 8, INAP.
40. "Private Duty Section, First District, Annual Report, 1926," box 3, folder 8, INAP.
41. See Van Frank, "The Private Duty Nurse."

42. "Nurses Professional Registry, Average Number of Registrants and Average Monthly Number of Private Duty Assignments, 1917–1946," 26 July 1948, box 1, CNRC.
43. See Janet Geister, "Hearsay and Facts," *AJN* 26 (July 1926): 515–528. District 14, officially known as the Nurses' Association of the Counties of Long Island, included Kings, Queens, Nassau, and Suffolk Counties.
44. The registry was originally called the Official Registry of the Nurses Association of Counties of Long Island. See "Minutes, Special Meeting Registry Committee, NB14," 6 April 1926, Nurses Association of the Counties of Long Island, Papers, Foundation of the NYS Nurse, Bellevue Alumni Center for Nursing History (hereafter cited as NACLIP). For the area served by the registry see "Survey of the Nursing Bureau of Brooklyn, Inc.," 1939, box 20, folder 22, 5, NACLIP.
45. See "Minutes, Registry Committee, NB14," 14 April 1926, box 4, folder 25, NACLIP. Geister commented favorably on the cooperation between District 14 and the Medical Society in the published results of her studies on private duty nursing. See Geister, "Hearsay and Facts," 515.
46. See "Minutes, Registry Committee, NB14," 2 March 1926, box 4, folder 25, NACLIP.
47. See "Annual Report, Registry Committee, NB14," 25 January 1927, box 4, folder 25, NACLIP. By 1939, seven alumnae associations belonged to the NB14. See "Survey of Nursing Bureau of Brooklyn, Inc.," 12–13.
48. See "Report of the Registry Committee at the Annual Meeting," 25 January 1927, box 4, folder 25, NACLIP; "Minutes, Registry Committee, NB14," 23 January, 6 April, 14 April 1926, box 4, folder 25,NACLIP; Emma Collins, "What the Registry Means to the Private Duty Nurse," *AJN* 28 (July 1928): 679.
49. See Emma Collins, "What the Registry Means to the Private Duty Nurse," 677–680; Emma Collins, "Economics and Private Duty," *AJN* 32 (July 1932): 734–738; Emma Collins, "Registry Goals," *TNHR* 100 (April 1938): 432–437. For examples of Collins's presentations see Emma Collins, "The Co-operative Movement among Nurses Which Is Called the Official Registry," in *Proceedings, Official Meetings, New York State Nurses Association, 27th Convention, 1928,* ed. New York State Nurses Association, AC-2, box 6, folder 6–1, NYSNAP; Emma Collins, "The Employment Situation in the Private Duty Field in New York State," in *Proceedings, Official Meetings, New York State Nurses Association, 29th Convention, 1930,* ed. New York State Nurses Association, AC-2, box 6, NYSNAP; Emma Collins, "Registries and Their Problems," in *Proceedings, Official Meetings, New York State Nurses Association, 30th Convention, 1931,* ed. New York State Nurses Association, AC-2, box 7, NYSNAP.
50. See "By-Laws of the Nursing Bureau of Brooklyn, Inc.," 28 May 1931, box 19, folder 24, NACLIP.
51. See "Minutes, Registry Committee, NB14," 23 January 1926; "Annual Report, Registry Committee, NB14," 25 January 1927, box 4, folder 25, NACLIP.
52. See "Minutes, Special Meeting, AGNMB," 11 April 1933, box 1, Nursing Bureau of Manhattan and Bronx (NBMB).
53. See "Answers to Questions Frequently Asked," *Nursing News,* bulletin no. 4, May 1939, box 20, folder 15, NACLIP; "Survey of Home Nursing, NB14," October 1940, box 20, folder 15, NACLIP.
54. See "What Registries Did: A Summary 1934–1935," *AJN* 35 (August 1935): 784; "What Registries Did: A Summary 1935–1936," *AJN* 37 (July 1937): 734; "What Registries Did in 1937," *AJN* 38 (October 1938): 1118; "What Registries Did in 1938," *AJN* 39 (September 1939): 1001; "What Registries Are Doing," *AJN* 41 (August 1941): 907.

55. See "Minutes, Registry Committee, NB14," 23 January 1926, 25 February 1927, 26 April 1927, 19 September 1928, 21 November 1928, and 18 June 1930, box 4, folder 25, NACLIP.

56. See "Minutes, Registry Committee, NB14," 21 March 1934, 17 April 1935, box 4, folder 25, NACLIP; "Minutes, Registry Committee, NB14," 17 March 1937, 22 April 1937, 16 February 1938, 24 October 1938, and 15 November 1939, box 4, folder 26, NACLIP; "Annual Report of the Nursing Bureau of District 14," 24 January 1939, box 20, folder 16, NACLIP.

57. See "Minutes, Registry Committee, NB14," 15 April 1936, 20 May 1936, box 4, folder 25, NACLIP; "Minutes, Registry Committee, NB14," 20 January 1937, 17 March 1937, and 22 April 1937, box 4, folder 26, NACLIP.

58. See "Minutes, Registry Committee," 15 March 1929, box 4, folder 26, NACLIP; "Report on the Study of Home Nursing for the Month of March 1940," box 4, folder 26, NACLIP; "Nursing Bureau of District 14 to Medical Profession," 26 December 1939, box 20, folder 11, NACLIP.

59. See "Nursing Bureau of District 14 to Medical Profession."

60. See Collins, "The Employment Situation in the Private Duty Field in New York State."

61. See Collins, "The Employment Situation in the Private Duty Field in New York State"; Collins, "The Co-operative Movement among Nurses Which Is Called the Official Registry"; "Minutes, Registry Committee," 16 December 1929, box 4, folder 25, NACLIP.

62. See Collins, "The Co-operative Movement among Nurses Which Is Called the Official Registry."

63. See "Annual Report of the Nursing Bureau of Brooklyn, Inc.," 24 January 1939.

64. For comments and quotes see "Night Nurses Fees," *Nursing News*, bulletin no. 4, March 1939, 1, box 20, folder 11, NACLIP.

65. See "On Collection of Night Nurses' Fees," *Nursing News*, bulletin no. 4, May 1939, 2, box 20, folder 11, NACLIP.

66. See "Minutes, Registry Committee," 13 October 1939, box 4, folder 26, NACLIP.

67. See "Answers to Questions Frequently Asked," *Nursing News*, bulletin no. 4, May 1939, 2, box 20, folder 11, NACLIP.

68. See Emma Collins, "Progress Notes on Eight-Hour Duty from Brooklyn, New York," *AJN* 34 (May 1934): 455.

69. See "Report of Nursing Demonstrations for Registrants of Nursing Bureau of Brooklyn," 19 December 1938, box 4, folder 26, NACLIP.

70. See "Minutes, Registry Committee, NB14," 21 February 1940, box 20, folder 15, NACLIP.

71. See "Secretary's Report, NB14, Registry Meeting," 16 December 1929, box 4, folder 25, NACLIP.

72. See "Minutes, Registry Committee, NB14," 16 September 1931, 15 January 1937, box 4, folder 25, NACLIP.

73. See "Minutes, Registry Committee, NB14," 15 December 1937, box 4, folder 26, NACLIP.

74. See "Minutes, Registry Committee, NB14," 16 September 1931.

75. See "Report of Registry Committee Meeting, NB14," 28 October 1931, box 4, folder 25, NACLIP.

76. See Emma Collins, executive director, NB14, to Margaret Bentley, secretary, Nurses Association of the Counties of Long Island, 21 November 1936, box 20, folder 11, NACLIP.

77. See "Minutes, Registry Committee, NB14," 17 February 1937, box 4, folder 26, NACLIP.
78. See "Minutes, Registry Committee, NB14," 29 October 1941, box 20, folder 15, NACLIP.
79. See "Minutes, Registry Committee, NB14," 29 October 1941.
80. See "Minutes, Registry Committee, NB14," 15 January 1937.
81. See "Minutes, Registry Committee, NB14," 19 January 1938, 17 May 1939, box 4, folder 26, NACLIP.
82. See "By-Laws of the Nursing Bureau of Brooklyn, Inc.," 28 May 1931. See also Collins, "The Co-operative Movement among Nurses Which Is Called the Official Registry."
83. See "Minutes, Special Meeting, Registry Committee, NB14," 6 April 1926; "Minutes, Registry Committee," 26 April 1927.
84. See "Minutes, Annual Meeting, Registry Committee," 16 January 1935, box 4, folder 25, NACLIP. For other advice and support given by physicians, see "Minutes, Registry Committee," 10 February 1926, 23 April 1930, 16 December 1931, 16 May 1934, and 15 May 1935, box 4, folder 25, NACLIP.
85. See "Minutes, Registry Committee," 19 March 1930, box 4, folder 25, NACLIP.
86. See "Minutes, Registry Committee and Board of Directors, NB14," 15 February 1939, box 4, folder 26, NACLIP.

6. The Great Depression

1. See "Receipts and Disbursements," 1 January 1932 to 28 April 28 1932, box 8, NYCRNAP; "Minutes, Board of Director, NYCRNA," 29 April 1932," box 4, NYCRNAP.
2. See "Minutes, Board of Directors, NYCRNA," 12 September 1932, box 4, NYCRNAP; Ernestine Wiedenbach, secretary, District 13, "Notification of Special Meeting," 21 October 1932, 5 October 1932, box 8, NYCRNAP.
3. See "Minutes, Board of Directors, NYCRNA," 19 December 1932, box 4, NYCRNAP.
4. See "Minutes, Special Committee," 29 November 1932, box 1, Nursing Bureau of Manhattan and Bronx, Papers, Archives of the Foundation of the New York State Nurses Association, Bellevue Alumni Center for Nursing History (hereafter NBMBP); "Minutes, Special Committee," 29 November 1932, box 1, NBMBP; Ernestine Wiedenbach, president, Association of Graduate Nurses of Manhattan and Bronx, to Marguerite Gelatt, chair, Registry Committee, New York Hospital Graduate Nurses Club, 6 December 1932, box 2, NBMBP; Margaret Gelatt to Ernestine Wiedenbach, 19 December 1932, box 2, NBMBP.
5. See "Minutes, Membership, NYCRNA," 20 September 1932, box 4, NYCRNAP; "Minutes, Special Membership, NYCRNA," 21 October 1932, box 4, NYCRNAP; "Minutes, Special Meeting," 11 April 1933, box 1, NBMBP.
6. See "Minutes, Special Committee," 29 November 1932, box 1, NBMBP; "Minutes, Special Registry Committee, AGNMB," 2 December 1932, 8 December 1932, box 1, NBMBP; "Minutes, Special Meeting, AGNMB," 12 December 1932, box 1, NBMBP; "Minutes, Finance Committee, Registrants of NBMB," 28 December 1932, box 1, NBMBP; "Minutes, Special Meeting," 11 April, 1933, box 1, NBMBP.
7. See "Minutes, Special Registry Committee," 2 December 1932, box 1, NBMBP; "Minutes, Registrants," 14 December 1932, box 1, NBMBP.
8. See Committee on the Grading of Nursing Schools, *Nursing Schools Today and Tomorrow* (New York: Committee on the Grading of Nursing Schools, 1934), 237–246.

9. See "Minutes, Registrants, District 13," 12 December 1932, box 1, NBMBP; "Minutes, Finance Committee of the Registrants," 3 January 1933, box 1, NBMBP; "Contributions," n.d., box 1, NBMBP. The AGNMB remained the sponsor of the NBMB until 1942, when the AGNMB dissolved. For the dissolution of the AGNMB see "'Manhattan and Bronx' Dissolves," *AJN* 42 (December 1942): 1460.
10. See "Annual Report, Director, NBMB," 1934, box 1, NBMBP; "Minutes, Board of Directors, NBMB," 17 January 1936, box 1, NBMBP.
11. See "Annual Report, Director, NBMB," 1934; "Minutes, Finance Committee, NBMB," 1 April 1935, box 1, NBMBP; "Minutes, Special Meeting, Board of Directors, NBMB," 29 April 1935, box 1, NBMBP.
12. See "Report to the State Private Duty Section, Annual Business Session, ISNA," 16 October 1930, box 4, folder 13, INAP.
13. See "Report of the State Private Duty Section, Regular Meeting, Board of Directors, ISNA," 13 October 1931, box 4, folder 14, INAP.
14. See "Registry," *ISNA Bulletin* 31 (April 1933): 6, box 5, folder 16, INAP.
15. For NPR finances, see "Income over Expenses," n.d., most likely 1947, box 1, CNRC.
16. See Lenore Tobins, president, First District, ISNA, and Millie Brown, chair, Private Duty Section, First District, ISNA to members, First District, ISNA, 23 December 1932, box 1, CNRC.
17. See "Private Duty Section," *ISNA Bulletin* 30 (April 1933): 7, box 5, folder 16, INAP.
18. See "Annual Report, First District, ISNA," 1933, box 5, folder 20, INAP.
19. See "Unemployment and Relief," *ISNA Bulletin* 30 (April 1933): 7–8, box 5, folder 16, INAP.
20. See "Annual Report, Private Duty Section, First District," 1933, box 5, folder 20, INAP.
21. See "Registry," *ISNA Bulletin* 30 (April 1933), box 5, folder 16, INAP.
22. Lenore Tobins and Millie Brown to members, First District, ISNA, 23 December 1932.
23. See "Objectives of the Private Duty Section for the Coming Year," *ISNA Bulletin* 29 (March 1932): 7–8, box 5, folder 16, INAP.
24. See "Annual Report, Private Duty Section, ISNA," 1933, INAP.
25. See "Minutes, Annual Meeting, Private Duty Section, ISNA," 13 October 1933, box 5, folder 20, INAP.
26. See "Annual Report, First District," 14 October 1931, box 4, folder 14, INAP; "Education and Distribution of Nursing Service," *ISNA Bulletin* 29 (December 1932): 6, box 5, folder 16, INAP. See also Margaret Ashmun, "The Cause and Cure of Unemployment in the Nursing Profession," *AJN* 33 (July 1933): 656–658.
27. See "Education and Distribution of Nursing Services," *ISNA Bulletin* 29 (December 1932).
28. See "Annual Report, First District, ISNA," 1933.
29. See "Annual Report, First District, ISNA," 1933. For free service see Lenore Tobins and Millie Brown to superintendents of hospitals and chief of medical staff, 23 December 1932, box 1, CNRC. For number of patients receiving free care see "Registry," *ISNA Bulletin* 30 (April 1933); "Brief Comparative Report of a Three Months' Period Including May, June, and July, 1933 and 1934," *ISNA Bulletin* 31 (September 1934): 6, box 6, folder 21, INAP.
30. See "Report of Committee on Distribution of Nursing Service, ISNA," 11 October 1933, box 5, folder 20, INAP; "Report of Illinois Committee on the Distribution of Nursing Service, Questionnaire, No. II," 1933, box 5, folder 20, INAP.

31. See Matilda Blewitt, "Eight-Hour Duty," *PCJN* 28 (December 1932): 728; Hazel Grant Kershaw, "Eight-Hour Duty for Specials: It Can Be Done," *AJN* 32 (March 1932): 259–261; Cora Belle Rhodes, "Eight-Hour Duty," *PCJN* 28 (September 1931): 583–584; Ethel Swope, "The Eight-Hour Day Makes Progress," *AJN* 33 (December 1933): 1151.

32. See Mary Bliss, "The Eight-Hour Plan Makes Progress in Massachusetts," *AJN* 34 (June 1934): 571–573; Minnie Carlson, "Reasonable Hours for Private Duty Nurses" (paper presented at the annual meeting of the Illinois State Nurses Association, Danville, IL, 26–27 September 1935), box 6, folder 25, INAP; Emma Collins, "Progress Notes on Eight-Hour Day from Brooklyn, New York," *AJN* 34 (May 1934): 455–456; "The Eight-Hour Plan Works," editorial, *TNHR* 91 (November 1933): 459–460; Sally Johnson, "A Trial of the Eight-Hour for Hospital Special Nurses," *Bulletin of the American Hospital Association* 9 (January 1935): 123–130; Mary Lee Mitchell, "The Eight-Hour Day for the Private Duty Nurse," *AJN* 34 (May 1934): 443–445; Helen Moir, "Another Successful Eight-Hour Plan," *AJN* 33 (August 1933): 775–776.

33. See "Can't Afford the Eight-Hour Day? Comparative Income in Twelve-Hour and Eight-Hour Schedule for Private Duty Nurses," *AJN* 35 (May 1935): 423; Swope, "The Eight-Hour Day," 1147; Margaret Tracy, "The Eight-Hour Day for Special Nurses: At the University of California Hospital," *AJN* 35 (January 1935): 31.

34. See Swope, "The Eight-Hour Day," 1147.

35. See "The Eight-Hour Day for Special Nurses," *AJN* 37 (May 1937): 471.

36. See "The Eight-Hour Day," *AJN* 40 (December 1940): 1333.

37. "Board of Directors Meeting, American Nurses Association," 25 August 1933, box 2, folder 3, from the ANA Collection, Howard Gotlieb Archival Research Center at Boston University (hereafter cited as ANAC).

38. See "Report of Private Duty Section, Proceedings, 29th Convention," 1934, 145, box 148, ANAC.

39. "Proceedings of the American Nurses Association (ANA), April 23–27, 1934, Washington, DC, House of Delegates Session," 27 April 1934, box 87, ANAC; see "The American Nurses Association and the Eight-Hour Schedule for Nurses," *AJN* 36 (October 1936): 979.

40. The ANA compiled national monthly reports on professional nurse registry activities beginning in 1934. These reports contain information from most of the professional nurse registries in operation, and are important sources of data on trends in the private duty market. See "What Registries Did: A Summary 1934–1935," *AJN* 35 (August 1935): 779–785.

41. See "What Registries Did: A Summary, 1934–1935"; "What Registries Did: A Summary 1935–1936," *AJN* 37 (July 1937): 729–736; "What Registries Did in 1937," *AJN* 38 (October 1938): 1115–1123; "What Registries Did in 1938," *AJN* 39 (September 1939): 998–1006; "What Registries Are Doing," *AJN* 41 (August 1941): 902–908.

42. American Nurses Association, "The Institution of the Eight-Hour Schedule for Private Duty Nurses," 25 January 1937, box 229, ANAC.

43. See "Annual Report, Private Duty Section, First District, ISNA," 13 February 1934, box 6, folder 21, INAP.

44. See "Annual Report, Committee on the Distribution of Nursing Service, ISNA," 1 October, 1934, box 6, folder 21A, INAP.

45. See "Annual Report, First District, ISNA," 1940, box 7, folder 33, INAP.

46. See "First District Registry Report for May, June, July," *ISNA Bulletin* 31 (September 1934): 6, box 6, folder 21, INAP.

47. See "Annual Report, First District, ISNA," 1936, box 6, folder 26, INAP.

48. See "Annual Report, Private Duty Section, ISNA," 1942, box 246, folder 1, INAP; "What Registries Did in 1941," *AJN* 42 (August 1942): 911–914; "What Registries Did in 1942," *AJN* 43 (June 1943): 563–564.

49. See "Annual Report, Private Duty Section, ISNA," 1942; "Annual Report, Private Duty Section, ISNA," 1945, box 9, folder 1, INAP.

50. See Carlson, "Reasonable Hours"; Sr. M. Hugolina, "Eight-Hour Day for Private Duty Nurses," *Hospital Progress* 19 (March 1938): 95; Johnson, "A Trial of the Eight-Hour," 128; Mitchell, "The Eight-Hour Day for the Private Duty Nurse," 445.

51. See Collins, "Progress Notes," 453–455; Hugolina, "Eight-Hour Day for Private Duty Nurses," 95; Kershaw, "Eight-Hour Duty for Specials," 259–262; Swope, "The Eight-Hour Day," 1147–1152.

52. See "Can't Afford the Eight-Hour Day?," 420–422; Hugolina, "Eight-Hour Day for Private Duty Nurses," 95; Kershaw, "Eight-Hour Duty for Specials," 260–261.

53. See Mitchell, "The Eight-Hour Day for the Private Duty Nurse," 443–445; Rhodes, "Eight-Hour Duty," 583–584; Effie Taylor, "Trends in Nursing Today," *Bulletin of the American Hospital Association* 8 (April 1934): 75; Tracy, "The Eight-Hour Day for Special Nurses," 29–32.

54. See Collins, "Progress Notes," 454.

55. See Kershaw, "Eight-Hour Duty for Specials," 259; Mitchell, "The Eight-Hour Day for the Private Duty Nurse," 444; Swope, "The Eight-Hour Day," 1150; Tracy, "The Eight-Hour Day for Special Nurses," 31.

56. See "Proceedings, Private Duty Section," 25 April, 1938, box 87, American Nurses Collection, ANAC.

57. See "Meetings, Private Duty Section," 24 April 1934, box 148, ANAC; "Meetings, Private Duty Section," 23 June 1936, box 87, ANAC.

58. See American Nurses Association, *Study of Income, Salaries, and Employment Conditions Affecting Nurses* (New York: American Nurses Association, 1938), 500.

59. See "The Eight-Hour Day," *AJN* 40 (December 1940): 1333.

60. See Frances Powell, secretary, First District, ISNA, *Announcement to Alumnae Presidents, First District, ISNA,* 12 November 1945, box 1, CNRC.

61. See "Report of the Private Duty Section, First District, ISNA, to Regional Meeting, ISNA," 26 January 1946, box 1, CNRC.

62. See "Annual Report, First District, ISNA," 1946, box 313, folder 3, INAP.

63. See "The Eight-Hour Day: A Progress Report," *AJN* 34 (February 1934): 163; "Just a Word with You," editorial, *TNHR* 98 (May 1937): 455; Bliss, "The Eight-Hour Plan Makes Progress," 571–573; Mitchell, "The Eight-Hour Day for the Private Duty Nurse," 445; Swope, "The Eight-Hour Day," 1151.

64. See Carlson, "Reasonable Hours"; "Report, Committee on Distribution of Nursing Services, ISNA," 4 May 1935, box 6, folder 23, INAP; "Annual Report, Private Duty Section, ISNA," 1939–1940, box 246, folder 1, INAP; "Minutes, Board of Directors, ISNA," 8 February 1941, box 8, folder 36, INAP.

65. See "Report, Committee on Distribution of Nursing Services, ISNA," 4 May 1935; Carlson, "Reasonable Hours"; "Minutes, Board of Directors, ISNA," 8 February 1941; "Annual Report, Private Duty Section, ISNA," 1939–1940." See also "The Eight-Hour Day: A Progress Report"; Bliss, "The Eight-Hour Plan Makes Progress," 571–573; "Just a Word with You," *TNHR* 98; Mitchell, "The Eight-Hour Day for the Private Duty Nurse," 445; Swope, "The Eight-Hour Day," 1151.

66. See "Common Sense and Sportsmanship," editorial, *TNHR* 104 (March 1940): 241–242; Sr. Celestine, "The Eight-Hour Day for Special Nurses at the Hotel Dieu, New Orleans," *AJN* 35 (January 1935): 34.

67. See Bliss, "The Eight-Hour Plan Makes Progress," 572–573; Mary Roberts, "Private Duty Nurses," *AJN* 34 (July 1934): 664–665; Swope, "The Eight-Hour Day," 1148–1152.

68. See "The American Nurses Association and the Eight-Hour Schedule for Nurses," 980–981; "What Patients Think of the Eight-Hour Schedule," *AJN* 33 (December 1933): 1153; Swope, "The Eight-Hour Day," 1150–1151; Tracy, "The Eight-Hour Day for Special Nurses," 30.

69. See "Can't Afford the Eight-Hour Day?"; "Progress Notes on Eight-Hour Duty from the Jersey City Medical Center," *AJN* 34 (May 1934): 456; Kershaw, "Eight-Hour Duty for Specials," 260.

70. See Margaret Klem, "Who Purchase Private Duty Nursing Services?," *AJN* 39 (October 1939): 1069–1077.

71. See Rosemary Stevens, *In Sickness and in Wealth: American Hospitals in the Twentieth Century* (New York: Basic Books, 1989), 172–199.

72. See Collins, "Progress Notes," 455; Moir, "Another Successful Eight-Hour," 775–776.

73. See "The Eight-Hour Day: A Progress Report," 162–163; Janet Geister, "Private Duty Nursing Then—and Now," *TNHR* 100 (April 1938): 386; Moir, "Another Successful Eight-Hour," 776; Swope, "The Eight-Hour Day," 1151.

74. See May Ayres Burgess, ed., *Nurses, Patients, and Pocketbooks* (New York: Committee on the Grading of Nursing Schools, 1928), 304; Janet Geister, "Report of a Survey of Private Duty Nursing," in *Proceedings, Official Meeting, New York State Nurses Association, 24th Annual Meeting, 1925*, ed. New York State Nurses Association, AC-2, box 5, NYSNAP.

75. See "More Data on Private Duty," *AJN* 34 (May 1934): 458; Bliss, "The Eight-Hour Plan Makes Progress," 573; Johnson, "A Trial of the Eight-Hour," 127–128.

76. See American Nurses Association, *Study of Income, Salaries, and Employment Conditions*.

77. See "Report of the Committee to Improve the Status of the Private Duty Nurse," 6 April 1940, box 304, folder 4, INAP.

78. "Report of the Committee to Improve the Status of the Private Duty Nurse." Some nurses did report increased earnings. See "Annual Report of Secretary, Private Duty Section," 1939–1940, box 246, folder 1, INAP.

79. See Burgess, *Nurses, Patients, and Pocketbooks*, 304–309.

80. See Marilyn Flood, "The Troubling Expedient: General Staff Nursing in United States Hospitals in the 1930s, a Means to Institutional, Educational and Personal Ends" (PhD diss., University of California, Berkeley, 1981), 310–315.

81. See "The Eight-Hour Day: A Progress Report," 162; "Just a Word with You," *TNHR* 98; Rhoda Wickwire, "Forecast for Private Duty Nursing," *AJN* 37 (March 1937): 244–247.

82. See "What Registries Did: A Summary, 1934–1935"; "What Registries Did: A Summary 1935–1936"; "What Registries Did in 1937," 1115–1123; "What Registries Did in 1938," 998–1006; "What Registries Are Doing," *AJN* 41 (August 1941): 904–908.

83. See "Proceedings, ANA Board of Directors," 20 June 1936, box 18, ANAC; 23 June 1936, box 87, ANAC; "Small Hospitals Round Table," *Transactions of the American Hospital Association, 38th Annual Convention* (Chicago: American Hospital Association, 1937), 535–539; "We May Even Run Short of Nurses," *Modern Hospital* 45 (December 1945): 47–48; "Nursing at Recent Hospital Conventions," *AJN* 36 (November 1936): 1156–1162; Peter Ward, "The Eight-Hour Day for Graduate Nurses," *Hospitals* 10 (November 1936): 134.

84. See "Nursing Problems Receive Special Emphasis at Hospital Meetings," *TNHR* 97 (November 1936): 478; "Ties That Bind," *TNHR* 99 (October 1937): 404.

85. See "Hospital Service in the United States," *JAMA* 106 (March 1936): 784; "Hospital Service in the United States," *JAMA* 118 (March 1941): 1056.

86. See Stevens, *In Sickness and in Wealth*, 172–199. See also "Ties That Bind," 404–407; "Recent Hospital Meetings," *AJN* 39 (November 1939): 1263–1264; "Recent Hospital Meetings," *AJN* 40 (November 1940): 1272–1273.

87. See *Facts about Nursing 1939* (New York: American Nurses Association, 1939), 26.

88. See Robin Buerki, "President's Address," *Transactions of the American Hospital Association, 38th Annual Convention* (Chicago: American Hospital Association, 1937), 302; "Small Hospitals Round Table," 538; "American Nurses Convention, 30th Convention, Proceedings, Business Session," 23 June 1936, box 226, ANAC.

89. "Small Hospitals Round Table," 536.

90. See "A Suggested Way to Overcome 'Nurse Shortage' Problem," *TNHR* 100 (January 1938): 70; "Accomplishments at Kansas City," *TNHR* 100 (June 1938): 665–667; "Recent Hospital Meetings," *AJN* 39 (November 1939): 1261; "The Philadelphia Biennial," *AJN* 40 (June 1940): 681; "Just a Word with You," editorial, *TNHR* 106 (February 1940): 93.

91. See "What Registries Did: A Summary 1935–1936," *AJN* 37 (July 1937): 735–736; "What Registries Did in 1937," 1121–1122; "What Registries Did in 1938," 999–1000; "What Registries Are Doing," *AJN* 41 (August 1941): 905–906.

92. See "Brief Comparative Registry Report of a Three Months' Period Including May, June, and July, 1933 and 1934," *ISNA Bulletin* 31 (September 1934): 6, box 6, folder 21, INAP; "Annual Report, Executive Committee, Board of Directors, ISNA," 1936, box 6, folder 26, INAP.

93. See "Annual Report, Private Duty Section, ISNA," 1937, box 7, folder 27, INAP.

94. See "Annual Report, First District, ISNA," 1938, box 7, folder 28, INAP.

95. See "Annual Report, First District, ISNA," 1939, box 7, folder 30, INAP.

96. See "What Registries Did: A Summary 1935–1936," 735–736; "What Registries Did in 1937," 1121–1122; "What Registries Did in 1938," 999–1000; "What Registries Are Doing," 905–906.

97. See "The American Nurses Association and the Eight-Hour Schedule for Nurses," *AJN* 36 (October 1936): 981–982; Barbara Hunter, "An All-Graduate Staff and an Eight-Hour Day," *AJN* 37 (May 1937): 473; Tracy, "The Eight-Hour Day for Special Nurses," 32.

98. See "The American Nurses Association and the Eight-Hour Schedule for Nurses," 981–982.

99. See "What Registries Did: A Summary 1935–1936," 735–736; "What Registries Did in 1937," 1121–1122; "What Registries Did in 1938," 999–1000; "What Registries Are Doing," 905–906.

100. "What Registries Are Doing," 906.

101. See American Nurses Association, *Study of Income, Salaries, and Employment Conditions*, 502.

102. American Nurses Association, *Study of Income, Salaries, and Employment Conditions*, 483.

103. See "Final Report, Committee to Improve the Status of the General Staff Nurse," 1940, box 304, folder 4, INAP. For a full discussion of the inclusion of maintenance in staff nurses' salaries see Flood, "The Troubling Expedient," 304–310.

104. See Flood, "The Troubling Expedient," 502. General duty nurses also objected to discontinuous hours of work. See Flood, "The Troubling Expedient," 310–315.

105. See American Nurses Association, *Study of Income, Salaries, and Employment Conditions*, 509.

106. See American Nurses Association, *Study of Income, Salaries, and Employment Conditions*, 502, 509.

107. For the number of calls the NPR filled for temporary staff nurse positions see "Annual Report, First District, ISNA," 1936, box 6, folder 26, INAP; "Annual Report, First District, ISNA," 1940.

108. See "Annual Report, Private Duty Section, ISNA," 1942.

109. See "Report of Private Duty Round Table," 1940, box 246, folder 1, INAP.

110. See "Report of Private Duty Round Table," 1940. Problems between private duty nurses and hospitals were highlighted in private duty section reports. See "Annual Report, Private Duty Section, ISNA," 1942.

111. See "Annual Report, First District, ISNA," 1940.

112. In 1940 the NPR reported a $1,772.15 profit. See "Income over Expenses."

7. More and More (and Better) Nurses

Epigraph: Lucile Petry Leone, interview by Joan Lynaugh, 11 November 1989, tape 1, side 1, Joan E. Lynaugh Papers, Barbara Bates Center for the Study of the History of Nursing, University of Pennsylvania School of Nursing.

1. See U.S. Department of Health, Education, and Welfare, *Source Book: Nursing Personnel* (Bethesda, MD: U.S. Department of Health, Education, and Welfare, Public Health Service, Division of Nursing, December 1974), 13. Enumerations used are adjusted from census reports, which included student nurses in the total population of nurses until 1950.

2. Discussions on the presence of, causes of, and solutions to the nurse shortage filled reports, professional association meetings and pronouncements, and the professional literature throughout the 1940s. Review of professional journals reveals a voluminous number of articles. A small sample of such articles include, for example, "About the Absent Floor Duty Nurse: Reports from 45 Hospitals Reveal Extent of Graduate Shortage; See Little Hope for Early Relief," *Hospitals* 18 (February 1944): 30–35; "Despite the Release of Nurses in the Armed Forces, Hospitals Still Face Shortage," *Hospitals* 19 (October 1945): 57; "Personnel Shortage Closes Thousands of Hospital Beds," *Southern Hospitals* 15 (May 1947): 44; "See Shortage of Graduate Nurses by 1946 Even If War Is Over," *Hospital Management* 58 (November 1944): 64–65; "The Acute Postwar Shortage Emphasizes Need of 'Help for Hospitals,'" *Hospitals* 20 (March 1946): 60–61; "War Demand for Nurses Is Bound to Be Felt Most by Hospitals," *Hospital Management* 54 (October 1942): 51–52; "The Shortage of Nurses," editorial, *New England Journal of Medicine* 240, no. 25 (June 1949): 1029–1030.

3. Lyndia Flanagan, *One Strong Voice: The Story of the American Nurses Association* (Kansas City: American Nurses Association, 1976), 112–115; "Organization of Nursing in Defense," *AJN* 41 (December 1941): 1415.

4. For a detailed history of the council see Hope Newell, *The History of the National Nursing Council* (New York: National Organization for Public Health Nursing, 1951).

5. Alma C. Haupt, "The Government's Subcommittee on Nursing," *AJN* 42 (March 1942): 257–263.

6. Pearl McIver, "Our Nursing Resources," *Public Health Nursing* 34 (January 1942): 32–33.

7. Pearl McIver, "Registered Nurses in the USA," *AJN* 42 (July 1942): 769.

8. Alma C. Haupt, "National War Nursing Program," *Hospitals* 17 (April 1943): 26. See also "Nurses Balance 1946 Supply against Needs," *Public Health Nursing* 36 (November 1944): 595; "Nursing Needs and Nursing Resources," *AJN* 44 (May 1944): 431; Pearl McIver, "Federal Aid for Nursing Education and Student War Nursing Reserve," *Hospitals* 17 (May 1943): 21.

9. Joseph W. Mountin, "Nursing—A Critical Analysis," *AJN* 43 (January 1943): 31.

10. Ralf Couch, "More Civilian Nurses? Start with Inventory of Needs and Attack from All Angles," *Hospitals* 17 (August 1943): 41; Alma C. Haupt, "Our War Nursing Program," *Southern Hospitals* 11 (January 1943): 13; Newell, *History of the National Nursing Council*, 23; Elmira B. Wickenden, "National Nursing Council for War Services Sums Up Its Efforts to Meet the Need for Nurses," *The Modern Hospital* 30 (March 1943): 76, 78.

11. Mountin, "Nursing—A Critical Analysis," 31.

12. National Nursing Council for War Service, *Distribution of Nursing Service during War* (New York: National Nursing Council for Service, 1942), 8.

13. "Criteria of Essentiality for Nurses," *AJN* 43 (November 1943): 979.

14. See "Minutes, Registry Committee, Board of Directors, NB14," 26 January 1943, box 20, folder 15, NACLIP; "Annual Report, Nursing Bureau of District 14, New York State Nurses Association," 25 January 1944, box 20, folder 16, NACLIP.

15. National Nursing Council for War Service, *Distribution of Nursing*, 22.

16. Zula Shorey, "Private Duty Nurses, We Challenge You!," *AJN* 42 (August 1942): 945–946.

17. Laura Simmons, "When Is Private Duty Nursing a Luxury," *AJN* 43 (February 1943): 211.

18. McIver, "Registered Nurses in the USA," 769.

19. Louise M. Tattershall and Marion E. Alternderfer, "Private Duty Nursing in General Hospitals," *AJN* 44 (July 1944): 651–654.

20. "Criteria of Essentiality for Nurses," 979; National Nursing Council for War Service, *Distribution of Nursing*, 22–23; Mary Bogardus, "Nursing Service at the University of Chicago Clinics Provided by the Graduate Staff," *Hospital Management* 50 (September 1940): 44; "Nurses Contribution," editorial, *Hospitals* 17 (May 1943): 69; Stella M. Freidinger, "Nursing Shortage or Unprecedented Demand?," *PCJN* 38 (June 1942): 350.

21. "What Registries Did in 1941," *AJN* 42 (August 1942): 911; "What Registries Did in 1942," *AJN* 43 (June 1943): 563; "What Registries Did in 1943," *AJN* 44 (November 1944): 1042; "What Registries Did in 1944," *AJN* 45 (September 1945): 697.

22. U.S. Bureau of Labor Statistics, *The Economic Status of Registered Professional Nurses 1946–47*, bulletin no. 931 (Washington, DC: Government Printing Office, 1947).

23. Charissa Threat, *Nursing Civil Rights: Gender and Race in the Army Nurse Corps* (Urbana: University of Illinois Press, 2015), 37.

24. Threat, *Nursing Civil Rights*, 68.

25. Haupt, "National Nurse War Program," 27; "A Three-Point Program for '43," editorial, *AJN* 43 (January 1943): 2.

26. Federal Security Agency Public Health Service, *The United States Cadet Nurse Corps and Other Federal Nurse Training Programs*, PHS publication no. 38 (Washington, DC: Government Printing Office, 1950): 1–6; Philip A. Kalisch and Beatrice J. Kalisch, *The Federal Influence and Impact on Nursing* (Hyattsville, MD: U.S. Department of Health and Human Services, Public Health Service, Health Resources Administration,

Bureau of Health Professions, Division of Nursing, 1980), 82–89, 117, 122; Newell, *History of the National Nursing Council*, 28.

27. Kalisch and Kalisch, *The Federal Influence*, 122.
28. Kalisch and Kalisch, *The Federal Influence*, 138.
29. Kalisch and Kalisch, *The Federal Influence*, 167–169; Newell, *History of the National Nursing Council*, 64–65. See also Joan E. Lynaugh, "Nursing the Great Society: The Impact of the Nurse Training Act of 1964," *Nursing History Review* 16 (2008): 17–18.
30. Kalisch and Kalisch, *The Federal Influence*, 168; Newell, *History of the National Nursing Council*, 39.
31. Kalisch and Kalisch, *The Federal Influence*, 158; Newell, *History of the National Nursing Council*, 39.
32. *The United States Cadet Nurse Corps*, 43–44.
33. *The United States Cadet Nurse Corps*, 45.
34. Kalisch and Kalisch, *The Federal Influence*, 159.
35. American Nurses Association, *Inventory of Professional Registered Nurses 1949* (New York: American Nurses Association, 1949), 17; McIver, "Registered Nurses in the USA," 770.
36. See Harlan Hoyt Horner, *Nursing Education and Practice in New York State with Suggested Remedial Measures* (Albany: University of the State of New York, 1934), 7–8.
37. Veronica Driscoll, *Legitimizing the Profession of Nursing: The Distinct Mission of the New York State Nurses Association* (Guilderland, NY: Foundation of the New York State Nurses Association, 1976), 42–43.
38. Horner, *Nursing Education*, 7–9.
39. Horner, *Nursing Education*, 34–38.
40. See Driscoll, *Legitimizing the Profession*, 42–44; Emily Hicks, "A Crusade for Safer Nursing," *AJN* 38 (May 1938): 563–566.
41. See "Digest of the Nurse Practice Bill Sponsored by the New York State Nurses Association," *AJN* 38 (February 1938): 225–226; Elizabeth Burgess, "A Good Nurse Practice Act: What Are the Essentials?," *AJN* 34 (July 1934): 653–655.
42. Joint Committee (ANA, NLNE, and NOPHN) to Outline Principles and Policies for the Control of Subsidiary Workers in the Care of the Sick, *Subsidiary Workers in the Care of the Sick* (New York: Joint Committee, 1940).
43. See "New York State Nurses Discusses New Legislation," *TNHR* 97 (January 1935): 74–76; "New York's Legislative Struggle," editorial, *AJN* 37 (May 1937): 516.
44. "Legislation," *AJN* 40 (March 1940): 332; "About Registration in New York," *AJN* 40 (May 1940): 548; "A Year of Grace for Nurses in New York State," *TNHR* 104 (February 1940): 168; "Report of the Secretary of the Board of Nurse Examiners, July 1, 1941," *New York State Nurse* 13 (October 1941): 182.
45. Driscoll, *Legitimizing the Profession*, 57.
46. Driscoll, *Legitimizing the Profession*, 57–58.
47. "NY's Attendant Schools," *TNHR* 105 (November 1940): 413.
48. See Dorothy Deming, "Practical Nurses—A Professional Responsibility," *AJN* 44 (January 1944): 40.
49. See "A Comprehensive Program for Nationwide Action," *AJN* 45 (September 1945): 707–713.
50. "Licensed Attendants and Practical Nurses," *AJN* 46 (June 1946): 391–393.
51. "Licensed Attendants and Practical Nurses," 392–393.
52. Janet Geister, "Plain Talk," *TNHR* 112 (March 1944): 202–205.

53. "Annual Reports of the Nursing Bureau of the District 14 of the New York State Nurses Association," 26 January 1943, 17 January 1945, box 20, folder 16, NACLIP; "Annual Reports of the Nursing Bureau of the District 14 of the New York State Nurses Association," 16 January 1946, 28 January 1947, 27 January 1948, and 25 January 1949, box 20, folder 17, NACLIP.

54. See "Minutes, Annual Meeting, Registry Committee, Board of Directors, NB14," 21 January 1942, box 20, folder 15, NACLIP.

55. See "Quarterly Report, Nursing Bureau of District 14," 23 March 1943, 26 September 1944, box 20, folder 16, NACLIP; "Quarterly Report, Nursing Bureau of District 14," 16 January 1946, box 20, folder 16, NACLIP.

56. See "Minutes, Annual Meeting, Registry Committee, Board of Directors, NB14," 21 January 1942; "Minutes, Registry Committee, Board of Directors," 17 March 1943, box 4, folder 27, NACLIP.

57. See "Minutes, Registry Committee, Board of Directors," 16 January 1946, box 20, folder 15, NACLIP.

58. See "Quarterly Report, Nursing Bureau of District 14," 26 September 1944.

59. See *Facts about Nursing 1946* (New York: American Nurses Association, 1946); *Facts about Nursing 1947* (New York: American Nurses Association, 1947); *1948 Facts about Nursing* (New York: American Nurses Association, 1948); *Facts about Nursing 1949* (New York: American Nurses Association, 1949); *1950 Facts about Nursing* (New York: American Nurses Association, 1950).

60. See Lillian V. Inke, *The Outlook for Women as Practical Nurses and Auxiliary Workers on the Nursing Team*, Medical Services Ser., bulletin no. 203–5 (Washington, DC: U.S. Department of Labor, Women's Bureau, 1953), 7–10.

61. See "Recent Hospital Meetings," *AJN* 39 (November 1939): 1261; Ellen Creamer, "Practical Nurses—Their Preparation and Sphere," *Hospitals* 13 (August 1939): 64–67; A. C. Donohue, "Orderlies Today—Practical Nurses Tomorrow," *TNHR* 104 (March 1940): 2331–2333; Josephine Goldsmith, "New York's Practical Nurse Program," *AJN* 42 (September 1942): 1027; Mary Ellen Manley, "The Subsidiary Worker in the Nursing Care of the Sick," *Hospitals* 14 (February 1940): 61–64.

62. See Dorothy Deming, "Practical Nursing and the Changing Professional Attitude," *AJN* 46 (June 1946): 366–370; Stella Hawkins, "Eight Years Experience in New York with Licensed Paid Aides," 111–112, 114–115; John McCormack, "The Practical Nurse," *TNHR* 117 (August 1946): 101–104.

63. See Dorothy Deming, *The Practical Nurse* (New York: Commonwealth Fund, 1947): 314; Deming, "Practical Nurses—A Professional Responsibility," 36–43; Deming, "Practical Nursing and the Changing Professional Attitude," 367.

64. See *Facts about Nursing, 1949*, 65.

65. See "Minutes, Board of Directors, NBMB," 24 February 1942, box 1, NBMBP; "Minutes, Advisory Council, NYCRNA," 9 December 1942, box 4, NYCRNAP.

66. See "Minutes, Board of Directors, NBMB," 13 May 1942, box 1, NBMBP.

67. See "Minutes, Executive Committee, NBMB," 19 April, 1 July, and 8 July 1943, box 1, NBMBP.

68. See "Minutes, Executive Committee, NBMB," 12 July, 25 August, and 9 September 1943, box 1, NBMBP.

69. See "Minutes, Membership, NBMB," 13 July 1944, box 1, NBMBP; "Minutes, Executive Committee, NBMB," 22 September 1944, box 1, NBMBP; "Minutes, Board of Directors, NBMB," 4 December 1944, box 1, NBMBP.

70. See "Minutes, Executive Committee, NBMB," 3 February 1943, box 1, NBMBP.

71. See "Minutes, Executive Committee, NBMB," 25 August 1943, box 1, NBMBP.

72. See "Minutes, Board of Directors, NBMB," 15 February 1944, box 1, NBMBP.

73. See "Minutes, Registry Committee, NYSNA," 18 January 1944, box 12, NYCRNAP.

74. See "Minutes, Executive Committee, NBMB," 5 May 1944, 9 November 1944, box 1, NBMBP.

75. See "Minutes, Membership, NBMB," 13 July 1944," box 1, NBMBP.

76. See "Proceedings, Annual Meeting, NBMB," 25 February 1948, box 1, NBMBP; Mabel Detmold, president, NBMB to Clara Richmond, director, NBMB, 9 July 1945, 20 July 1945, box 2, NBMBP.

77. See "Proceedings, Annual Meeting, NBMB," 25 February 1948.

78. See Darlene Clark Hine, *Black Women in White: Racial Conflict and Cooperation in the Nursing Profession, 1890–1950* (Bloomington: Indiana University Press, 1989); Mabel Keaton Staupers, *No Time for Prejudice: A Story of the Integration of Negroes in Nursing in the United States* (New York: Macmillan, 1961).

79. Esther Lucile Brown, *Nursing for the Future: A Report Prepared for the National Nursing Council* (New York: Russell Sage Foundation, 1948), 59–72.

80. Committee on the Function of Nursing, *A Program for the Nursing Profession* (New York: Macmillan, 1950), 36–43, 100–106.

81. Malcolm MacEachern, "Outlook Brightens for Relief of Nursing Situation," *Bulletin of the American College of Surgeons* 32 (June 1947): 150, 154.

82. "Report of Committee on Nursing Problems," *JAMA* 137 (July 1948): 878–879.

83. Brown, *Nursing for the Future*, 101–105. See also Joan Lynaugh and Barbara Brush, *American Nursing* (Cambridge, MA: Blackwill Publishers, 1996), 12–15.

84. See "Minutes, Executive Committee, NBMB," 19 October 1944, box 1, NBMBP. For the number of LPN registrants see "Proceedings, Annual Meeting, NBMB," 28 February 1950, box 1, NBMBP.

85. See "Report, Executive Director, NBMB," 31 December 1945, box 2, NYCRNAP; "Proceedings, Annual Meeting, NBMB," 27 February 1947, box 1, NBMBP; "Annual Report, President, NBMB," 28 February 1950, box 1, NBMBP.

86. See "What Registries Are Doing," *AJN* 41 (August 1941): 905–906; "What Registries Did in 1944," *AJN* 44 (September 1944): 697.

87. "What Registries Did in 1944," 697.

88. American Nurses Association, *Inventory of Professional Registered Nurses 1949*, 17; McIver, "Registered Nurses in the USA," 770.

89. "Annual Reports of the Nursing Bureau of District 14 of the New York State Nurses Association," 17 January 1940, 17 January 1945, box 20, folder 16, NACLIP.

90. "Annual Reports of the Nursing Bureau of District 14 of the New York State Nurses Association."

91. See "Minutes, Registry Committee and Board of Directors, NB14," 18 October 1944, box 20, folder 15, NACLIP.

92. See "Quarterly Report of the Nursing Bureau of District 14," 23 March 1943.

93. See "Minutes, Private Duty Committee," 31 March 1944, box 4, folder 10, NACLIP.

94. See "Fee Schedule," 1 January 1946, box 4, folder 11, NACLIP.

95. See "Annual Report, Nursing Bureau of District 14," 21 January 1942, box 20, folder 16, NACLIP; "Quarterly Report of the Nursing Bureau of District 14," 28 September 1943, 26 September 1944, box 20, folder 16, NACLIP; "Annual Report, Nursing Bureau of District 14," 17 January 1945, box 20, folder 16, NACLIP; "Quarterly Report of the Nursing Bureau of District 14," 27 March 1945, box 20, folder 17, NACLIP; "Annual Report, Nursing Bureau of District 14," 16 January 1946, box 20, folder 17, NACLIP.

96. The following is a small representative sample of articles addressing the shortage: "What about the Nursing Shortage," *Hospital Topics and Buyer* 25 (February 1947): 18–20; "Supply and Demand for Professional and Practical Nurses," editorial, *AJN* 46 (February 1946): 77–78; Emily Hicks, "Hospital Personnel Shortage New Social Philosophy Is Needed," *TNHR* 116 (March 1946): 179–182; Robert Hudgens, "When Higher Pays Fails," *Hospitals* 20 (November 1946): 37–39; MacEachern, "Outlook Brightens," 150–156; Lucile Petry, "The Adaption of Nursing Education to the Nursing Needs of the Nation," *Hospital Progress* 27 (August 1946): 257–259: Lucile Petry, Margaret Arnstein, and Ruth Gillan, "Survey Measures Nursing Resources," *AJN* 49 (December 1949): 770–772; Elmira Wickenden, "Peace Brings Its Own Serious Problems as Nurses Face Tomorrow," *Hospitals* 20 (February 1946): 42–44.

97. "Few Nurses Plan to Return to Prewar Positions," *Hospitals* 20 (February 1946): 125; "Joint Committee for the Coordination of Medical Activities," *Bulletin of the American College of Surgeons* 32 (September 1947): 280; "What about the Nursing Shortage," 18–20; Brown, *Nursing for the Future*, 9–10, 25–48; "Need for Co-ordinated Planning," editorial, *AJN* 48 (August 1948): 481–482; Edith M. F. Pritchard, "National Nursing Now," *TNHR* 117 (December 1946): 417–420. See also Lynaugh, "Nursing the Great Society," 15.

98. Claudia Goldin, *Understanding the Gender Gap: An Economic History of American Women* (New York: Oxford University Press, 1990), 175–176.

99. American Nurses Association, *Facts about Nursing, 1949*, 40.

100. American Nurses Association, *1950 Facts about Nursing*, 77.

101. MacEachern, "Outlook Brightens," 150.

102. Committee on the Function of Nursing, *A Program for the Nursing Profession*, 30–32, 40–41, 100.

103. Esther Lucile Brown, *Nursing for the Future*, 58–63, 73.

104. Hudgens, "When Higher Pays Fails," 38.

105. "What about the Nursing Shortage," 19; Marjorie Davis, "Comprehensive Program That Offers a Blueprint for the Future," *Hospitals* 20 (February 1946): 45–46; "Supply and Demand for Professional and Practical Nurses," 77–78; Agnes Gelinas, "Professional Nursing; A Look into the Future," *AJN* 46 (January 1946): 129; Hicks, "Hospital Personnel Shortage," 179; Edna Sharritt, "Where Are the Ex-Service Nurses?," *AJN* 46 (December 1946): 849–850.

106. U.S. Bureau of Labor Statistics, *The Economic Status of Registered Professional Nurses 1946-47*, bulletin no. 931 (Washington, DC: Government Printing Office, 1947). Note: unless otherwise noted, all statistics cited included in this discussion are taken from this source.

107. U.S. Department of Commerce, *Current Population Reports Consumer Income*, series P-60, no. 7 (February 1951): 36.

108. U.S. Bureau of Labor Statistics, *Economic Status of Registered Professional Nurses*, 37.

109. William C. Scott and Donald W. Smith, "The New Social Security Law and the Nurse," *AJN* 50 (November 1950): 686.

110. "Nonprofit Hospital Staff Now Covered by Social Security," *AJN* 83 (May 1983): 697, 714.

111. U.S. Bureau of Labor Statistics, *Economic Status of Registered Professional Nurses*, 54.

112. U.S. Bureau of Labor Statistics, *Economic Status of Registered Professional Nurses*, 42.

113. Lily Mary David, "Working Conditions of Private Duty and Staff Nurses," *Monthly Labor Report* 65 (November 1947): 545.

Notes to Pages 147–152   191

Conclusion

1. The number of private duty nurses working in the field between the end of the 1940s and 1963 remained relatively stable, numbering around seventy thousand nurses. The percentage of nurses in the private duty field dropped from 21 percent in 1949 to 12 percent in 1962. This drop in percentage reflected an increase in the overall numbers of nurses. For statistics on nurses see *1951 Facts about Nursing* (New York: American Nurses Association, 1951), 13; *Facts about Nursing 1962–1963* (New York: American Nurses Association, 1963), 9.
2. For the rate of calls filled by professional registries see *Facts about Nursing* (New York: American Nurses Association, 1961), 125.
3. See "Monthly Report of the Nurses Professional Registry," 1948–1960, box 1, CNRC.
4. See "Report of the Work of the Nursing Bureau of District 14," 1948–1960, box 20, folder 17, NACLIP.
5. See "Annual Report, President, NBMB," 28 February 1950, box 1, NBMBP; "Annual Report, President, NBMB," 18 April 1961, box 1, NBMBP.
6. Julie Fairman and Joan Lynaugh, *Critical Care Nursing: A History* (Philadelphia: University of Pennsylvania Press, 1998), 61–62.
7. For a thorough history of the establishment of intensive care units see Julie Fairman, "New Hospitals, New Nurses, New Spaces: The Development of Intensive Care Units, 1950–1965" (PhD diss., University of Pennsylvania, 1992).
8. See U.S. Department of Health, Education and Welfare, *Towards Quality in Nursing*, publication no. 992 (Washington, DC: Public Health Service, 1963).
9. U.S. Department of Health, Education and Welfare, *Towards Quality in Nursing*, 15–17.

Bibliography

"About Registration in New York." *American Journal of Nursing* 40 (May 1940): 548. Hereafter cited as *AJN*.

"About the Absent Floor Duty Nurse: Reports from 45 Hospitals Reveal Extent of Graduate Shortage; See Little Hope for Early Relief." *Hospitals* 18 (February 1944): 30–35.

"Accomplishments at Kansas City." *Trained Nurse and Hospital Review* 100 (June 1938): 665–667. Hereafter cited as *TNHR*.

"The Acute Postwar Shortage Emphasizes Need of 'Help for Hospitals.'" *Hospitals* 20 (March 1946): 60–61.

Ahrens, Minnie. "Discussion, 18th Annual Convention, American Nurses Association." *AJN* 15 (August 1915): 946–1036.

Aiken, Linda. "The Hospital Nursing Shortage. A Paradox of Increasing Supply and Increasing Vacancy Rates." *Western Journal of Medicine* 15 (1989): 87–92.

———. "Nurses' Reports on Hospital Care in Five Countries." *Health Affairs* 20 (2001): 43–53.

Allen, Lyman. "The Nursing Problem." *Boston Medical and Surgical Journal* 189 (25 October 1923): 62–63.

Allport, Frank. "The Graduate Nurse versus the Patient of Moderate Income." *Chicago Medical Recorder* 31 (1909): 465–473.

Altman, Stuart H. *Present and Future Supply of Registered Nurses.* Bethesda, MD: U.S. Department of Health, Education and Welfare, 1971.

———. "The Structure of Nursing Education and Its Impact on Supply." In *Empirical Studies in Health Economics*, edited by H. E. Klarman, 339. Baltimore: Johns Hopkins Press, 1970.

Alumni Association of the Bellevue School of Nursing. New York: Alumni Association of the Bellevue School of Nursing, 1989.

"The American Nurses Association and the Eight-Hour Schedule for Nurses." *AJN* 36 (October 1936): 981–982.

American Nurses Association Collection. Howard Gotlieb Archival Research Center, Boston University.

American Nurses Association. *1948 Facts about Nursing.* New York: American Nurses Association, 1948.

———. *1950 Facts about Nursing.* New York: American Nurses Association, 1950.

———. *1951 Facts about Nursing.* New York: American Nurses Association, 1951.

———. *Facts about Nursing.* New York: American Nurses Association, 1939.

———. *Facts about Nursing.* New York: American Nurses Association, 1953.

———. *Facts about Nursing.* New York: American Nurses Association, 1957.

———. *Facts about Nursing.* New York: American Nurses Association, 1961.

———. *Facts about Nursing.* New York: American Nurses Association, 1966.

———. *Facts about Nursing 1941.* New York: American Nurses Association, 1941.

———. *Facts about Nursing 1946.* New York: American Nurses Association, 1946.

———. *Facts about Nursing 1947.* New York: American Nurses Association, 1947.

———. *Facts about Nursing 1949.* New York: American Nurses Association, 1949.

———. *Facts about Nursing 1962–1963*. New York: American Nurses Association, 1963.

———. *Inventory of Professional Registered Nurses 1949*. New York: American Nurses Association, 1949.

———. *Study of Income, Salaries, and Employment Conditions Affecting Nurses*. New York: American Nurses Association, 1938.

"Appeals to Nurses to Lessen Demands." *New York Times*, 1 May 1925.

Ashley, Joann. *Hospitals, Paternalism, and the Role of the Nurse*. New York: Teachers College Press, 1976.

Ashmun, Margaret. "The Cause and Cure of Unemployment in the Nursing Profession." *AJN* 33 (July 1933): 656–658.

Associated Alumnae Trained Nurses of the United States and Canada. *Minutes of the Proceedings of the Associated Alumnae Trained Nurses of the United States and Canada.* N.p: Associated Alumnae of Trained Nurses of the United States and Canada, n.d.

———. *Minutes of the Proceedings of the Second Annual Meeting of the Associated Alumnae of Trained Nurses of the United States and Canada*. N.p.: Associated Alumnae of Trained Nurses of the United States and Canada, 1899.

Beard, Richard. "The Social, Economic, and Educational Status of the Nurse." *AJN* 20 (September 1923): 957.

———. "The Trained Nurse of the Future." *JAMA* 61 (13 December 1913): 2151.

Bellafante, Ginia. "Enhanced Medical Care for an Annual Fee." *New York Times*, 6 December 2012.

Best, Ella. "Nursing Supply—How to Balance Supply and Demand." *Modern Hospital* 39 (August 1932): 97–102.

"The Biennial." *AJN* 44, no. 7 (July 1944): 627.

Blewitt, Matilda. "Eight-Hour Duty." *Pacific Coast Journal of Nursing* 28 (December 1932): 728. Hereafter cited as *PCJN*.

Bliss, Mary. "The Eight-Hour Plan Makes Progress in Massachusetts." *AJN* 34 (June 1934): 571–573.

Bogardus, Mary. "Nursing Service at the University of Chicago Clinics Provided by the Graduate Staff." *Hospital Management* 50 (September 1940): 44.

Bradley, Richard. "Household Nursing in Relation to Other Similar Work." *AJN* 15 (August 1915): 969.

Brown, Esther Lucile. *Nursing for the Future: A Report Prepared for the National Nursing Council*. New York: Russell Sage Foundation, 1948.

Brown, Ruth. "Twelve-Hour Duty." *AJN* 24 (March 1924): 435–440.

Buerhaus, Peter I. "Is Another RN Shortage Looming?" *Nursing Outlook* 46, no. 3 (1998): 103–108.

Buerki, Robin. "President's Address." *Transactions of the American Hospital Association, 38th Annual Convention*. Chicago: American Hospital Association, 1937.

Burgess, Elizabeth. "Eight Years of the Grading Committee." *AJN* 34 (October 1934): 937–945.

———. "The Future of the Central Registry." *AJN* 15 (August 1915): 1034.

———. "A Good Nurse Practice Act: What Are the Essentials?" *AJN* 34 (July 1934): 653–655.

———. "The Subsidiary Worker in Nursing Services from the Point of View of the Committee on Subsidiary Workers in Nursing Services." In *Proceedings, 40th Annual Convention of the National League for Nursing Education, in Washington, DC, April 25, 1934*, edited by National League for Nursing Education, 163–170. New York: National League for Nursing Education, 1934.

Burgess, May Ayres, ed. *Nurses, Patients, and Pocketbooks.* New York: Committee on the Grading of Nursing Schools, 1928.

———. "The Nursing Shortage." *JAMA* 90 (24 March 1928): 898–890.

"Can't Afford the Eight-Hour Day? Comparative Income in Twelve-Hour and Eight-Hour Schedule for Private Duty Nurses." *AJN* 35 (May 1935): 423.

Carmen, Florence C. "Some of the Differences between a Trained Nurse and an Untrained Nurse." *TNHR* 16 (August 1896): 409–410.

Carnegie, Mary Elizabeth. *The Path We Tread: Blacks in Nursing Worldwide, 1854–1994.* Sudbury, MA: Jones and Bartlett, 2000.

Sr. Celestine. "The Eight-Hour Day for Special Nurses at the Hotel Dieu, New Orleans." *AJN* 35 (January 1935): 34.

"Central Registries." *AJN* 9 (June 1909): 639.

"Central Registries." *AJN* 12 (January 1912): 281–282.

"Central Registries and the Idle Nurse." *AJN* 9 (December 1909): 145–147.

Chapman, Nellie. "Discussion on Registry Problems." *AJN* 14, no.10 (1914): 834.

Chen, Pauline W. "Can Concierge Medicine for the Few Benefit the Many?" *New York Times,* 6 August 2010.

Chicago Nurses Registry Collection. Papers. Midwest Nursing History Resource Center, College of Nursing, University of Illinois.

"A Club for Nurses." *TNHR* 13 (December 1894): 363.

Collins, Emma. "Economics and Private Duty." *AJN* 32 (July 1932): 734–738.

———. "Progress Notes on Eight-Hour Day from Brooklyn, New York." *AJN* 34 (May 1934): 455–456.

———. "Registry Goals." *TNHR* 100 (April 1938): 432–437.

———. "What the Registry Means to the Private Duty Nurse." *AJN* 28 (July 1928): 679.

"Commercial Directories." *AJN* 9 (July 1909): 723–724.

"The Commercial Registry." *AJN* 14 (February 1914): 329–330.

Committee on Education of the National League for Nursing Education. *Standard Curriculum for Schools of Nursing.* Baltimore: Waverly, 1917.

Committee on Nursing and Nursing Education in the United States. *Nursing and Nursing Education in the United States.* New York: Macmillan, 1923.

Committee on the Function of Nursing. *A Program for the Nursing Profession.* New York: Macmillan, 1950.

Committee on the Grading of Nursing Schools. *Nursing Schools Today and Tomorrow.* New York: Committee on the Grading of Nursing Schools, 1934.

———. *The Second Grading of Nursing Schools.* New York: Committee on the Grading of Nursing Schools, 1932.

"Common Sense and Sportsmanship." *TNHR* 104 (March 1940): 241–242.

"A Comprehensive Program for Nationwide Action." *AJN* 45 (September 1945): 707–713.

"Conference Opens Program for Grading Nursing Schools." *Modern Hospital* 24 (May 1925): 471.

Considine, C. J. "The Private Duty Market: Operational and Staffing Considerations." *Home Healthcare Nurse* 21 (2003): 454–459.

"Constitution and By-Laws of the Nurses' Associated Alumnae of the United States." *AJN* 4 (July 1904): 812–815.

Couch, Ralf. "More Civilian Nurses? Start with Inventory of Needs and Attack from All Angles." *Hospitals* 17 (August 1943): 41.

Creamer, Ellen. "Practical Nurses—Their Preparation and Sphere." *Hospitals* 13 (August 1939): 64–67.

"Criteria of Essentiality for Nurses." *AJN* 43 (November 1943): 979.

Cuthbertson, Marie L. "The Advisability of a Club Life for Nurses." *AJN* 2 (July 1902): 781.

D'Antonio, Patricia. *Founding Friends: Families, Staff, and Patients at the Friend's Asylum in Early Nineteenth-Century Philadelphia*. Bethlehem, PA: Lehigh University Press, 2006.

D'Antonio, Patricia, and Jean Whelan. "Counting Nurses: The Power of Historical Census Data." *Journal of Clinical Nursing* 18 (2009): 2714–2724.

David, Lily Mary. "Working Conditions of Private Duty and Staff Nurses." *Monthly Labor Report* 65 (November 1947): 545.

Davis, Marjorie. "Comprehensive Program That Offers a Blueprint for the Future." *Hospitals* 20 (February 1946): 45–46.

Dayon, M. Flower. "Letter to Editor." *TNHR* 19 (November 1897): 275.

Deming, Dorothy. *The Practical Nurse*. New York: Commonwealth Fund, 1947.

———. "Practical Nurses—A Professional Responsibility." *AJN* 44 (January 1944): 40.

———. "Practical Nursing and the Changing Professional Attitude." *AJN* 46 (June 1946): 366–370.

"Despite the Release of Nurses in the Armed Forces, Hospitals Still Face Shortage." *Hospitals* 19 (October 1945): 57.

De Witt, Katherine. "The County Association and Its Relation to the State." *AJN* 9 (August 1909): 809–815.

———. *Private Duty Nursing*. Philadelphia: J. B. Lippincott, 1913.

"Digest of the Nurse Practice Bill Sponsored by the New York State Nurses Association." *AJN* 38 (February 1938): 225–226.

"Discussion, 18th Annual Convention." *AJN* 15 (August 1915): 947.

Doane, Joseph. "Reviewing the Objectives of the Five-Year Grading Program." *Modern Hospital* 28 (March 1927): 130–132.

Dock, Lavinia L. "Central Directories and Sliding Scales." *AJN* 7 (October 1906): 12.

———. *A History of Nursing: From the Earliest Times to the Present Day with Special Reference to the Work of the Past Thirty Years*, vol. 3. New York: G. P. Putnam's Sons, 1912.

———. "Letter to Editor." *TNHR* 18 (May 1897): 274–275.

———. "Letter to Editor." *TNHR* 20 (January 1898): 42–43.

Dock, Lavinia L. et al. *History of American Red Cross Nursing*. New York: Macmillan, 1922.

Donohue, C. "Orderlies Today—Practical Nurses Tomorrow." *TNHR* 104 (March 1940): 2331–2333.

Doughty, Joseph. "The Present Status of Nursing Service as Viewed by the Hospital Superintendent." *Bulletin of the American College of Surgeons* 11 (January 1927): 12–13.

Driscoll, Veronica. *Legitimizing the Profession of Nursing: The Distinct Mission of the New York State Nurses Association*. Guilderland, NY: Foundation of the New York State Nurses Association, 1976.

Duncan, Merle. "Twelve-Hour Duty: Another View." *AJN* 24 (March 1924): 441.

Dunwiddie, Mary. *A History of the Illinois State Nurses' Association 1901–1935*. Chicago: Illinois State Nurses' Association, 1937.

"Editorially Speaking." *TNHR* 16 (February 1896): 101–103.

"The Educational Value of a Central Directory." *AJN* 13 (January 1913): 251–252.

"Education and Distribution of Nursing Services." *ISNA Bulletin* 29 (December 1932).

"The Eight-Hour Day." *AJN* 40 (December 1940): 1333.

"The Eight-Hour Day: A Progress Report." *AJN* 34 (February 1934): 163.

"The Eight-Hour Day for Special Nurses." *AJN* 37 (May 1937): 471.

"The Eight-Hour Plan Works." *TNHR* 91 (November 1933): 459–460.

Ericksen, Theresa. "A Graded Registry." *AJN* 8 (September 1908): 964–966.

Fairman, Julie. "New Hospitals, New Nurses, New Spaces: The Development of Intensive Care Units, 1950–1965." PhD diss., University of Pennsylvania, 1992.

Fairman, Julie, and Joan E. Lynaugh. *Critical Care Nursing: A History*. Philadelphia: University of Pennsylvania Press, 1998.

Federal Security Agency Public Health Service. *The United States Cadet Nurse Corps and Other Federal Nurse Training Programs*, PHS publication no. 38. Washington, DC: Government Printing Office, 1950.

Feeny, Sister Ignatius. "How May a Nurse Charge below Her Price without Lowering Her Standard." *AJN* 6 (August 1906): 766–767.

Fenwick, Ethel Gordon. "The Organization and Registration of Nurses." In *The Transactions of the Third International Congress of Nurses Held in Buffalo 18–21 September 1901*, edited by Committee on Publication, 337. Cleveland: J. B. Savage, 1901.

"Few Nurses Plan to Return to Prewar Positions." *Hospitals* 20 (February 1946): 125.

"Fifth Annual Convention of the Nurses' Associated Alumnae of the United States: Minutes of Proceedings, May 1–3, 1902." *AJN* 10 (July 1902): 766.

Fischer, Martin. "Nursing Education." *Modern Hospital* 17 (December 1921): 503–504.

Fiske, Annette. "Twelve-Hour Day for Specials? Individual Adaptation." *TNHR* 70 (June 1923): 519.

Flanagan, Lyndia. *One Strong Voice: The Story of the American Nurses Association*. Kansas City: American Nurses Association, 1976.

Flood, Marilyn. "The Troubling Expedient: General Staff Nursing in United States Hospitals in the 1930s—A Means to Institutional, Educational and Personal Ends." PhD diss., University of California, Berkeley, 1981.

Fondiller, Shirley. "Licensing and Titling in Nursing and Society: An Historical Perspective." In *Looking beyond the Entry Issue: Implications for Education and Service*, edited by National League for Nursing, 3–9. New York: National League for Nursing, 1986.

Foster, Reba Thelin. "The Organization of Nurses Clubs and Directories under State Association." *AJN* 9 (January 1909): 247–252.

Freidinger, Stella M. "Nursing Shortage or Unprecedented Demand?" *PCJN* 38 (June 1942): 350.

Friss, Lois. "Nursing Studies Laid End to End Form a Circle." *Journal of Health Politics, Policy and Law* 19 (1994): 597–631.

Gamble, Vanessa Northington. *Making a Place for Ourselves: The Black Hospital Movement, 1920–1945*. New York: Oxford University Press, 1995.

Geister, Janet. "Hearsay and Facts in Private Duty." *AJN* 26 (July 1926): 515–528.

———. "Plain Talk." *TNHR* 112 (March 1944): 202–205.

———. "Private Duty Nursing Then—and Now." *TNHR* 100 (April 1938): 386.

Gelinas, Agnes. "Professional Nursing; A Look into the Future." *AJN* 46 (January 1946): 129.

Giles, Dorothy. *A Candle in Her Hand: A Story of the Nursing Schools of Bellevue Hospital*. New York: G. P. Putnam's Sons, 1949.

Gilman, Alice. "The Twelve Hour Day for Graduate Nurses on Special Duty in the Hospital." *AJN* 21 (June 1921): 639–641.

Goldin, Claudia. *Understanding the Gender Gap: An Economic History of American Women*. New York: Oxford University Press, 1990.

Goldmark, Josephine. *Nursing and Nursing Education in the United States.* New York: Macmillan, 1923.

Goldsmith, Josephine. "New York's Practical Nurse Program." *AJN* 42 (September 1942): 1027.

Goldwater, S. S. "The Nursing Crisis: Efforts to Satisfy the Nursing Requirements of the War: A Way Out of the Difficulty." *AJN* 18 (August 1918): 1032.

Goode, Mary Anne. "Working Hours for Nurses." *TNHR* 51 (August 1913): 77–79.

"Grading Committee Adopts Official Program." *Modern Hospital* 28 (January 1927): 103–104.

"The Grading of Nurses." *AJN* 14 (April 1914): 503.

"Grading Schools of Nursing." *AJN* 26 (May 1926): 401.

"The Graduate Nurses' Association." *TNHR* 16 (January 1896): 41.

Grafstrom, Olivia A. "Letter to Editor." *TNHR* 20 (January 1898): 43–44.

Grey, Carolyn. "What Are the Aims of Nursing Education." *AJN* 21 (February 1921): 308–313.

Gross, S. D. "Report of the Committee on the Training of Nurses." *Transactions of the American Medical Association* 20 (1869): 172–173.

Grumbach, Kevin, et al. "Measuring Shortages of Hospital Nurses: How Do You Know a Hospital with a Nursing Shortage When You See One?" *Medical Care Research and Review* 58 (2001): 387–403.

Hall, Carrie. "Effect of the Grading Committee Report on Schools of Nursing." *AJN* 29 (February 1929): 133.

Hanson, Helen. "The Private Duty Nurse." *AJN* 23 (March 1923): 448–450.

Haupt, Alma C. "The Government's Subcommittee on Nursing." *AJN* 42 (March 1942): 257–263.

———. "National War Nursing Program." *Hospitals* 17 (April 1943): 26.

———. "Our War Nursing Program." *Southern Hospitals* 11 (January 1943): 13.

Hegyvary, Sue. *The Change to Primary Nursing: A Cross-Cultural View of Professional Nursing Practice.* St. Louis: C. V. Mosby, 1982.

Heller, Celia R. "Letter to Editor." *TNHR* 18 (June 1897): 337–340.

———. "A Word to Graduates." *TNHR* 24 (January 1900): 310–334.

Hicks, Emily. "A Crusade for Safer Nursing," *AJN* 38 (May 1938): 563–566.

———. "Hospital Personnel Shortage New Social Philosophy Is Needed." *TNHR* 116 (March 1946): 179–182.

Hine, Darlene Clark. *Black Women in White: Racial Conflict and Cooperation in the Nursing Profession 1890–1950.* Bloomington: Indiana University Press, 1989.

Hobson, Elizabeth Christophers. *Recollections of a Happy Life.* New York: G. P. Putnam's Sons, 1916.

Hollister, C. May. "How Can Skilled Nursing Service Be Procured by the Family of Moderate Means." *AJN* 6 (August 1906): 763–766.

Holmes, Grace. "An Ideal Central Directory." *AJN* 6 (June 1906): 606–608.

Hooks, Janet N. "Women's Occupations through Seven Decades." *Women's Bureau Bulletin*, no. 218. Washington, DC: Government Printing Office, 1947.

Horner, Harlan Hoyt. *Nursing Education and Practice in New York State with Suggested Remedial Measure.* Albany: University of the State of New York, 1934.

Hospitals, Dispensaries and Nursing, Papers and Discussions in the International Congress of Charities, Correction and Philanthropy Section III, Chicago, June 12th to 17th, 1893. New York: Garland Publishing, 1984.

"Hospital Service in the United States." *JAMA* 82 (12 January 1924): 124–125.

"Hospital Service in the United States." *JAMA* 92 (30 March 1929): 1054.

"Hospital Service in the United States." *JAMA* 96 (28 March 1931): 1012.

"Hospital Service in the United States." *JAMA* 106 (March 1936): 784.

"Hospital Service in the United States." *JAMA* 118 (March 1941): 1056.

Howland, Joseph. "How Can the Shortage of Nurses Be Met?" *Boston Medical and Surgical Journal* 183 (25 November 1920): 628–632.

"How the Toronto Nurses Are Meeting It." *AJN* 6 (April 1906): 415–416.

Hudgens, Robert. "When Higher Pays Fails." *Hospitals* 20 (November 1946): 37–39.

Hugolina, Sr. M. "Eight-Hour Day for Private Duty Nurses." *Hospital Progress* 19 (March 1938): 95.

Hunter, Barbara. "An All-Graduate Staff and an Eight-Hour Day." *AJN* 37 (May 1937): 473.

Hyde, Katherine. "Business Women as Registrar." *AJN* 15 (August 1915): 943.

Illinois Nurses Association. Papers. Illinois State Historical Library, Springfield, IL.

"Illinois State Nurses' Association." *AJN* 1 (1901): 925–927.

Inke, Lillian V. *The Outlook for Women as Practical Nurses and Auxiliary Workers on the Nursing Team*, Medical Services Ser., bulletin no. 203–5. Washington, DC: U.S. Department of Labor, Women's Bureau, 1953.

Institute of Medicine. *The Future of Nursing: Leading Change, Advancing Health*. Washington, DC: National Academies Press, 2011.

"In the Nursing World." *TNHR* 31 (October 1903): 241.

"In the Nursing World: Bellevue Graduates Association." *TNHR* 15 (May 1897): 275–276.

"In the Nursing World: Protective Association." *TNHR* 18 (May 1897): 274–275.

Johns, Ethel, and Blanche Pfefferkorn. *An Activity Analysis of Nursing*. New York: Committee on the Grading of Nursing Schools, 1934.

———. *The Johns Hopkins Hospital School of Nursing, 1889–1949*. Baltimore: Johns Hopkins Press, 1954.

Johnson, Sally. "How Are the Sick to Be Provided with Nursing Care." *AJN* 22 (February 1922): 353–356.

———. "A Trial of the Eight-Hour for Hospital Special Nurses." *Bulletin of the American Hospital Association* 9 (January 1935): 123–130.

Johnson, Susan Bard. "The Boston Nurses Club." *AJN* 9 (June 1909): 662–663.

"Joint Committee for the Coordination of Medical Activities." *Bulletin of the American College of Surgeons* 32 (September 1947): 280.

Joint Committee (ANA, NLNE, and NOPHN) to Outline Principles and Policies for the Control of Subsidiary Workers in the Care of the Sick. *Subsidiary Workers in the Care of the Sick*. New York: Joint Committee, 1940.

"Just a Word with You." *TNHR* 98 (May 1937): 455.

"Just a Word with You." *TNHR* 106 (February 1940): 93.

Kalisch, Philip, and Beatrice Kalisch. *The Advance of American Nursing*. Boston: Little, Brown, 1978.

———. *The Federal Influence and Impact on Nursing*. Hyattsville, MD: U.S. Department of Health and Human Services, Public Health Service, Health Resources Administration, Bureau of Health Professions, Division of Nursing, 1980.

Kanely, Lily. "A Successful Central Registry." *AJN* 9 (April 1909): 496–498.

Kavanagh, A. S. "Report of the Sub-committee on the Training of Nurses." In *Transactions of the 10th Annual Conference of the American Hospital Association Held in Detroit 1908*, edited by American Hospital Association, 155–176. Chicago: American Hospital Association, 1908.

Keeling, Arlene. "'Alert to the Necessities of the Emergency': U.S. Nursing during the 1918 Influenza Pandemic." *Public Health Reports* 125, suppl. 3 (2010): 105.

Kefauver, Christine. "What Is the Matter with the Training Schools." *TNHR* 59 (August 1920): 113–114.

Kelley, M. Kingston. "Nurses vs. Twelve-Hour Duty." *PCJN* 16 (February 1920): 81–82.

Kershaw, Hazel Grant. "Eight-Hour Duty for Specials: It Can Be Done." *AJN* 32 (March 1932): 259–261.

Kessler-Harris, Alice. *Out to Work: A History of Wage-Earning Women in the United States*, 20th anniversary edition. New York: Oxford University Press, 2003.

Klem, Margaret. "Who Purchase Private Duty Nursing Services?" *AJN* 39 (October 1939): 1069–1077.

Krieg, Richard M., and Judith A. Cooksey. *Provident Hospital: A Living Legacy*. Chicago: Provident Foundation, 1998.

Larrabee, Eric. *The Benevolent and Necessary Institution*. Garden City, NY: Doubleday, 1971.

"Legislation." *AJN* 40 (March 1940): 332.

"Letter to Editor." *AJN* 26 (November 1926): 888.

"Letter to the Editor: The Nurse's Salary." *New York Times*, 5 March 1912.

"Letter to the Editor: The Nurses' Trust." *New York Times*, 24 February 1912.

Lewinski-Corwin, E. H. *The Hospital Situation in Greater New York*. New York: G. P. Putnam's Sons, 1924.

"Licensed Attendants and Practical Nurses." *AJN* 46 (June 1946): 391–393.

Lightbourn, Lina. "How Can We Provide Skilled Nursing for People of Moderate Means." *AJN* 9 (September 1909): 977–983.

Littlefield, Chloe Cudsworth, Papers. Barbara Bates Center for the Study of the History of Nursing, University of Pennsylvania, School of Nursing.

Lockwood, Charles. "The Doctor Gives His Opinion." *PCJN* 24 (October 1928): 505–506.

Logan, Laura. "Conference on the Grading of Nursing Schools." *AJN* 25 (April 1925): 306.

———. "A Program for the Grading of Schools of Nursing." *AJN* 25 (December 1925): 1005–1012.

Lynaugh, Joan E. Papers. Barbara Bates Center for the Study of the History of Nursing, University of Pennsylvania, School of Nursing.

Lynaugh, Joan E. "Nursing the Great Society: The Impact of the Nurse Training Act of 1964." *Nursing History Review* 16 (2008): 17–18.

———. "Riding the Yo-Yo: The Worth and Work of Nursing in the 20th Century." *Transactions & Studies of the College of Physicians of Philadelphia* 11, no. 3 (1989): 201–217.

Lynaugh, Joan, and Barbara Brush. *American Nursing: From Hospitals to Health Systems*. Cambridge: Blackwell, 1996.

MacEachern, Malcolm. "Outlook Brightens for Relief of Nursing Situation." *Bulletin of the American College of Surgeons* 32 (June 1947): 150–154.

Macmillan, Helen. "Central Registration." *AJN* 4 (July 1904): 793.

"'Manhattan and Bronx' Dissolves." *AJN* 42 (December 1942): 1460.

Manley, Mary Ellen. "The Subsidiary Worker in the Nursing Care of the Sick." *Hospitals* 14 (February 1940): 61–64.

Manthey, Marie. "Primary Nursing Is Alive and Well in the Hospital." *AJN* (January 1973): 83–87.

Marshall, Helen. *Mary Adelaide Nutting: Pioneer of Modern Nursing*. Baltimore: Johns Hopkins University Press, 1972.

Martin, Sarah F. "Central Directories." *AJN* 10 (December 1909): 162–167.

"Massachusetts General Hospital Nurses' Alumnae, Boston." *AJN* 1 (September 1901): 890.

Maxwell, Anna. "The Private Nurse and Twenty-Four Hour Hospital Duty." *AJN* 17 (December 1916): 191–194.

McCormack, John. "The Practical Nurse." *TNHR* 117 (August 1946): 101–104.

McGee, Anita Newcomb. "The Growth of the Nursing Profession in the United States." *TNHR* 24 (June 1900): 441–445.

McIsaac, Isabel. "Discussion." *AJN* 6 (August 1906): 768.

McIver, Pearl. "Federal Aid for Nursing Education and Student War Nursing Reserve." *Hospitals* 17 (May 1943): 21.

———. "Our Nursing Resources." *Public Health Nursing* 34 (January 1942): 32–33.

———. "Registered Nurses in the USA." *AJN* 42 (July 1942): 769.

Mead, Marian. "Registry System of the Hennepin County Graduate Nurses' Association, Minneapolis, Minn." *AJN* 10 (August 1910): 819–824.

Mellichampe, Julia. "The Development and Value of a Nurses Registry." *AJN* 16 (October 1916): 24–28.

Melosh, Barbara. *"The Physician's Hand": Work Culture and Conflict in American Nursing.* Philadelphia: Temple University Press, 1982.

Mitchell, Mary Lee. "The Eight-Hour Day for the Private Duty Nurse." *AJN* 34 (May 1934): 443–445.

Moir, Helen. "Another Successful Eight-Hour Plan." *AJN* 33 (August 1933): 775–776.

Moore, Geoffrey, and Janice Hedges. "Trends in Labor and Leisure." *Monthly Labor Review* 94 (February 1971): 5.

"More Data on Private Duty." *AJN* 34 (May 1934): 458.

Mottus, Jane E. *New York Nightingales: The Emergence of the Nursing Profession at Bellevue and New York Hospital 1850–1920.* Ann Arbor, MI: UMI Research Press, 1980.

Mountin, Joseph W. "Nursing—A Critical Analysis." *AJN* 43 (January 1943): 31.

Munson, Helen W. *The Story of the National League of Nursing Education.* Philadelphia: W. B. Saunders, 1934.

My Oath: Fiftieth Anniversary of the Mills School of Nursing. New York: Mills School of Nursing, Bellevue Hospital, 1937.

National Association of Colored Graduate Nurses. Records. Manuscripts, Archives and Rare Books Division, Schomburg Center for Research in Black Culture, New York Public Library.

National League for Nursing Records. U.S. National Library of Medicine, Bethesda, MD.

National Nursing Council for War Service. *Distribution of Nursing Service during War.* New York: National Nursing Council for Service, 1942.

"Need for Co-ordinated Planning." *AJN* 48 (August 1948): 481–482.

Newell, Hope. *The History of the National Nursing Council.* New York: National Organization for Public Health Nursing, 1951.

New York Counties Registered Nurses Association. Papers. Foundation of NYS Nurses, Bellevue Alumnae Center for Nursing History, Guilderland, NY.

New York Hospital School of Nursing. Collection. New York Hospital Archives, Medical Center Archives, Samuel J. Wood Library, Weill Cornell Medicine, New York, NY.

New York Hospital School of Nursing Alumni Association. Records. Medical Center Archives, Samuel J. Wood Library, Weill Cornell Medicine, New York, NY.

"New York's Legislative Struggle." *AJN* 37 (May 1937): 516.

New York State Nurses Association. Papers. Foundation of NYS Nurses, Bellevue Alumni Center for Nursing History, Guilderland, NY.

"New York State Nurses Discusses New Legislation." *TNHR* 97 (January 1935): 74–76.

Nifer, Cora. "The Universal Shortage of Nurses and What Is Possible for the Training School to Do to Help the Situation." *Hospital Progress* 3 (April 1922): 155–157.

"Nonprofit Hospital Staff Now Covered by Social Security." *AJN* 83 (May 1983): 697–714.

Noyes, Clara. "Response, and President's Address." *AJN* 20 (July 1920): 782.

"Nurses and Nursing on the Pacific Coast." *TNHR* 13 (October 1894): 207.

Nurses Association of the Counties of Long Island. Papers. Foundation of the NYS Nurse, Bellevue Alumni Center for Nursing History, Guilderland, NY.

"Nurses Balance 1946 Supply against Needs." *Public Health Nursing* 36 (November 1944): 595.

"Nurses' Club Houses and Central Directories." *AJN* 8 (March 1908): 423–424.

"Nurses' Club of Brooklyn." *TNHR* 9 (May 1893): 236–237.

"Nurses' Clubs." *TNHR* 13 (February 1894): 90.

"Nurses' Clubs." *TNHR* 16 (December 1896): 675.

"Nurses Clubs and Associations." *TNHR* 19 (August 1897): 104.

"Nurses Contribution." *Hospitals* 17 (May 1943): 69.

"Nurses Form Trust to Get Higher Pay." *New York Times*, 22 February 1912.

"Nurses, Patients, and Pocketbooks—A Symposium," *Modern Hospital* 31 (December 1928): 73–78.

"Nurses, Patients, and Pocketbooks, Some Highlights from Dr. Burgess' Presentation of the Book to the National Nursing Association at Louisville." *AJN* 28 (July 1928): 674.

"Nurses' Protective Association." *TNHR* 22 (January 1899): 36–37.

"Nurses Seek Protection." *TNHR* 16 (April 1896): 186–200.

"Nursing at Recent Hospital Conventions." AJN 36 (1936): 1156–1162.

Nursing Bureau of Manhattan and Bronx. Papers. Archives of the Foundation of the New York State Nurses Association, Bellevue Alumni Center for Nursing History, Guilderland, NY.

"Nursing Needs and Nursing Resources." *AJN* 44 (May 1944): 431.

"Nursing Problems Receive Special Emphasis at Hospital Meetings." *TNHR* 97 (November 1936): 478.

"The Nursing Situation in New York State." *TNHR* 96 (1935): 253.

Nutting, M. Adelaide. *Educational Status of Nursing*. Washington, DC: Government Printing Office, 1912.

———. "How Can We Care for Our Patients and Educate the Nurse?" *Modern Hospital* 21 (September 1923): 305–310.

———. *A Sound Economic Basis for Schools of Nursing and Other Addresses*. New York: G. P. Putnam's Sons, 1926.

Nye, Sylveen V. "The Organization and Registration of Nurses." In *The Transactions of the Third International Congress of Nurses Held in Buffalo 18–21 September 1901*, edited by Committee on Publication, 346–347. Cleveland: J. B. Savage, 1901.

———. "The Proposed New York State Nurses Association." *TNHR* 25 (December 1900): 397.

"NY's Attendant Schools." *TNHR* 105 (November 1940): 413.

O'Brien, Patricia. "All a Woman's Life Can Bring: The Domestic Roots of Nursing in Philadelphia, 1830–1885." *Nursing Research* 36, no. 1 (1987): 12–19.

Oderkirk, Wendell W. "Setting the Record Straight: A Recount of Late Nineteenth-Century Training Schools." *Journal of Nursing History* 1, no.1 (November 1985): 30–37.

O'Dowd, Esther. "Twenty-Four Hour Duty from the Standpoint of the Nurse." *AJN* 24 (March 1924): 442.

"Organization of Nursing in Defense." *AJN* 41 (December 1941): 1415.

Palmer, Sophia. "Alumnae Associations." *TNHR* 14 (April 1895): 203–204.

Parsons, Sara E. *History of the Massachusetts General Hospital Training School for Nurses.* Boston: Whitcomb & Barrows, 1922.

———. "The Sliding Scale of Charges for Private Nurses." *AJN* 11 (June 1911): 694–696.

———. "Why Private Nurses Should Organize." *AJN* 16 (January 1916): 297–300.

Pennock, Meta Rutter, ed. *Makers of Nursing History: Portraits and Pen Sketches of Fifty-Nine Prominent Women.* New York: Lakeside Publishing, 1928.

"Personnel Shortage Closes Thousands of Hospital Beds." *Southern Hospitals* 15 (May 1947): 44.

Petry, Lucile. "The Adaption of Nursing Education to the Nursing Needs of the Nation." *Hospital Progress* 27 (August 1946): 257–259.

Petry, Lucile, Margaret Arnstein, and Ruth Gillan. "Survey Measures Nursing Resources." *AJN* 49 (December 1949): 770–772.

"The Philadelphia Biennial." *AJN* 40 (June 1940): 681.

Philadelphia Lying-In Charity Hospital. Papers. Pennsylvania Hospital Historic Collections, Pennsylvania Hospital, Philadelphia.

Philadelphia Medicine. Papers. Historical Society of Pennsylvania, Philadelphia.

Phillpotts, [Mrs.] "A Central Directory for Nurses and How Best to Manage It." *AJN* 4 (July 1904): 794–796.

"Physician Says Higher Salaries Give the Nurses Lofty Notions." *New York Times*, 2 March 1912.

Pritchard, Edith M. F. "National Nursing Now." *TNHR* 117 (December 1946): 417–420.

"Progress Notes on Eight-Hour Duty from the Jersey City Medical Center." *AJN* 34 (May 1934): 456.

"Protective Association." *TNHR* 18 (June 1897): 332–333.

"Protective Association." *TNHR* 18 (December 1897): 275.

"Protective Association." *TNHR* 19 (November 1898): 273–274.

Public Health Committee. Papers. New York Academy of Medicine, New York.

"The Quack Nurse." *TNHR* 10 (November 1893): 226–227.

"The Question of Compensation." *AJN* 5 (November 1904): 76.

Quintard, L. W. "Provisions Already Existing for the Care of the Sick of Moderate Means." *AJN* 7 (July 1907): 780.

"Recent Hospital Meetings." *AJN* 39 (November 1939): 1261–1264.

"Recent Hospital Meetings." *AJN* 40 (November 1940): 1272–1273.

Records of the Committee on the Directory for Nurses. Historical Medical Library of the College of Physicians of Philadelphia.

Reed, Julia. "Are Nurses Refusing Contagious Cases?" *AJN* 6 (June 1906): 773–775.

"Registry." *ISNA Bulletin* 30 (April 1933).

"Report of Committee on Nursing Problems." *JAMA* 137 (July 1948): 878–879.

"Report of Special Committee on Grading and Classification of Nurses," in *Transactions of the 16th Annual Conference of the American Hospital Association in Kingston 1914*, edited by American Hospital Association, 163–188. Chicago: American Hospital Association, 1914.

"Report of the Secretary of the Board of Nurse Examiners, July 1, 1941." *New York State Nurse* 13 (October 1941): 182. Reverby, Susan. *Ordered to Care: The Dilemma of American Nursing, 1850–1945.* Cambridge: Cambridge University Press, 1987.

Rhodes, Cora Belle. "Eight-Hour Duty." *PCJN* 28 (September 1931): 583–584.

Riddle, Mary. "The Grading of Nurses." In *Transactions of the 15th Annual Conference of the American Hospital Association in Ontario 1913*, edited by American Hospital Association, 130–140. Chicago: American Hospital Association, 1913.

———. "The President's Address." *AJN* 3 (August 1903): 841.

Robb, Isabel Hampton. "The Aims, Methods and Spirit of the Associated Alumnae of Trained Nurses of the United States and Canada." *TNHR* 21 (June 1898): 307.

Roberts, Mary. "Private Duty Nurses." *AJN* 34 (July 1934): 664–665.

Roberts, Mary M. *American Nursing: History and Interpretation*. New York: Macmillan, 1954.

Robinson, Victor. *White Caps: The Story of Nursing*. Philadelphia: J. B. Lippincott, 1946.

Rockefeller Foundation. Papers. Rockefeller Archive Center, Sleep Hollow, NY.

Rose, I. C. "The Necessity for Low Standards in the Beginning." *AJN* 4 (July 1904): 778.

Rosenberg, Charles. *The Care of Strangers: The Rise of America's Hospital System*. New York: Basic Books, 1987.

Russell, Martha. "Clubhouses, Hostelries, and Directories for Nurses." *AJN* 5 (August 1905): 803.

Rutley, Sophia. "Private Duty Nurses and Their Relationship to the Directory." *AJN* 15 (August 1915): 939–943.

Schryver, Grace Fay. *A History of the Illinois Training School for Nurses, 1880–1929*. Chicago: Board of Directors of the Illinois Training School, 1930.

Scott, William C., and Donald W. Smith. "The New Social Security Law and the Nurse." *AJN* 50 (November 1950): 686.

"See Shortage of Graduate Nurses by 1946 Even If War Is Over." *Hospital Management* 58 (November 1944): 64–65.

"Seventh Annual Convention of the Nurses' Associated Alumnae of the United States, Minutes of the Proceedings, May 12–14, 1904." *AJN* 4 (July 1904): 752.

Sharritt, Edna. "Where Are the Ex-service Nurses?" *AJN* 46 (December 1946): 849–850.

Sheahan, Sr. Dorothy. "The Social Origins of American Nursing and Its Movement into the University: A Microscopic Approach." PhD diss., New York University, 1980.

Sherman, Ruth Brewster. "Some Aspects of Private Nursing." *AJN* 10 (August 1910): 829–830.

Shorey, Zula. "Private Duty Nurses, We Challenge You!" *AJN* 42 (August 1942): 945–946.

"The Shortage of Nurses." *New England Journal of Medicine* 240, no. 25 (June 1949): 1029–1030.

Simmons, Laura. "When Is Private Duty Nursing a Luxury." *AJN* 43 (February 1943): 211.

"Sixth Annual Convention of the Nurses' Associated Alumnae of the United States, Minutes of the Proceedings." *AJN* 3, no. 11 (July 1903): 848–881.

"Skilled Nursing Care for the Great Middle Class." *AJN* 6 (April 1906): 414.

Sloan, Frank A. *The Geographic Distribution of Nurses and Public Policy*. Bethesda, MD: U.S. Department of Health, Education and Welfare, 1975.

"Small Hospitals Round Table." *Transactions of the American Hospital Association, 38th Annual Convention*, 535–539. Chicago: American Hospital Association, 1937.

Sochalski, Julie. "Nursing Shortage Redux: Turning the Corner on an Enduring Problem." *Health Affairs* 21 (2002): 157–164.

"Some Administrative Aspects of Special Nursing." *AJN* 31 (October 1931): 1166.

"Status of Twelve-Hour Duty." *AJN* 25 (August 1925): 660–661.

Staupers, Mabel Keaton. *No Time for Prejudice: A Story of the Integration of Negroes in Nursing in the United States*. New York: Macmillan, 1961.

Stevens, Rosemary. *In Sickness and in Wealth: American Hospitals in the Twentieth Century.* New York: Basic Books, 1989.

Stone, Frances. "The Management of a Registry for Nurses." *AJN* 3 (August 1903): 885–886.

Stover, Charles. "The Relation of the Nurse to the Total Sickness of the Community." *TNHR* 59 (December 1917): 327."The Subsidiary Worker." *AJN* 37 (March 1937): 284.

"A Suggested Way to Overcome 'Nurse Shortage' Problem." *TNHR* 100 (January 1938): 70.

Sullivan, Paul. "Dealing with Doctors Who Take Only Cash." *New York Times*, 23 November 2012.

Sumner, Helen L. *Report on the Condition of Women and Child Wage-Earners in the United States.* Washington, DC: Government Printing Office, 1910.

"The Superintendents' Convention: The Superintendents in Council." *TNHR* 13 (February 1894): 95–96.

"Supply and Demand for Professional and Practical Nurses." *AJN* 46 (February 1946): 77–78.

"The Supply of Nurses." *JAMA* 72 (25 January 1919): 276–277.

Swope, Ethel. "The Eight-Hour Day Makes Progress." *AJN* 33 (December 1933): 1151.

Tattershall, Louise M., and Marion E. Alternderfer. "Private Duty Nursing in General Hospitals." *AJN* 44 (July 1944): 651–654.

Taylor, Effie. "Trends in Nursing Today." *Bulletin of the American Hospital Association* 8 (April 1934): 75.

"Third Annual Convention of the Associated Alumnae of Trained Nurses of the United States: Minutes of the Proceedings." *AJN* 1, no. 1 (Oct. 1900): 67–95.

Thoms, Adah. *Pathfinders: A History of the Progress of Colored Graduate Nurses.* New York: Kay Printing House, 1929.

Thorton, Mary. "Commercial Directories." *AJN* 3 (December 1903): 243–244.

Threat, Charissa. *Nursing Civil Rights: Gender and Race in the Army Nurse Corps.* Urbana: University of Illinois Press, 2015.

"A Three-Point Program for '43." *AJN* 43 (January 1943): 2.

"Ties That Bind." *TNHR* 99 (October 1937): 404.

Titus, Shirley. "Meeting the Cost of Nursing Service." *AJN* 27 (March 1927): 166.

Tomes, Nancy. "The Silent Battle: Nurse Registration in New York State, 1903–1920." In *Nursing History, New Perspectives, New Possibilities*, edited by Ellen Condliffe Lagermann, 110. New York: Teachers College Press, 1983.

Toner, J. M. "Statistics of Regular Medical Associations and Hospitals of the United States: Section II, Statistics of the Hospitals in the United States, 1872–1873." *Transactions of the American Medical Association* 24 (1873): 314.

Tracy, Margaret. "The Eight-Hour Day for Special Nurses: At the University of California Hospital." *AJN* 35 (January 1935): 31.

"Twelve-Hour Day for Specials?" *TNHR* 70 (June 1923): 516–518.

"Twelve-Hour Special Duty in Hospitals." *AJN* 26 (August 1926): 623–624.

The United States Cadet Nurse Corps and Other Federal Training Programs. Washington, DC: Government Printing Office, 1950.

U.S. Bureau of Education. *The Report of the Commissioner of Education for 1902.* Washington, DC: Government Printing Office, 1903.

U.S. Bureau of Labor Statistics. *The Economic Status of Registered Professional Nurses 1946–47*, bulletin no. 931. Washington, DC: Government Printing Office, 1947.

U.S. Department of Commerce. *Current Population Reports Consumer Income*, ser. P-60, no. 7 (February 1951): 36.

———. *Fifteenth Census of the United States: 1930, Population*, vol. 4. Washington, DC: Government Printing Office, 1933.

———. *Fourteenth Census of the United States*, vol. 4, *Population*. Washington, DC: Government Printing Office, 1923.

———. *Thirteenth Census of the United States*, vol. 1, *Population*. Washington, DC: Government Printing Office, 1913.

U.S. Department of Commerce and Labor. *Special Reports: Occupations the Twelfth Census*. Washington, DC: Government Printing Office, 1904.

U.S. Department of Commerce and Labor, Bureau of the Census. *Special Report: Benevolent Institutions 1904*. Washington, DC: Government Printing Office, 1904.

U.S. Department of Health, Education, and Welfare. *Source Book: Nursing Personnel*. Bethesda, MD: U.S. Department of Health, Education, and Welfare, Public Health Service, Division of Nursing, 1974.

———. *Toward Quality in Nursing*, PHS publication no. 992. Washington, DC: Public Health Service, 1963.

U.S. Department of Labor, Bureau of Labor Statistics. *The Economic Status of Registered Professional Nurses 1946–47*. Washington, DC: Government Printing Office, 1947.

U.S. Department of the Interior. *Eleventh Census of the United States: 1890, Statistics of the Population of the United States, Part II*. Washington, DC: Government Printing Office, 1890.

———. *Ninth Census of the United States: 1870*, vol. 1, *The Statistics of the Population of the United States*. Washington, DC: Government Printing Office, 1870.

———. *Population of the United States in 1860; Compiled from the Original Returns of the Eighth Census under the Direction of the Secretary of the Interior*. Washington, DC: Government Printing Office, 1864.

———. *Tenth Census of the United States: 1880, Statistics of the Population of the United States*. Washington, DC: Government Printing Office, 1880.

U.S. Department of the Interior, Bureau of Education. *The Inception, Organization, and Management of Training Schools of Nursing*. Washington, DC: Government Printing Office, 1882.

Vandergon, Josephine. "Should the Private Duty Nurse Work Longer than Twelve Hours?" *PCJN* 16 (August 1920): 494–496.

Van Frank, Lucy. "Problems of the Registry." *AJN* 27 (December 1927): 1013–1014.

"The Viewpoint of the Nurse." *TNHR* 67 (November 1921): 427–432.

Wall, Barbra Mann. *Unlikely Entrepreneurs: Catholic Sisters and the Hospital Marketplace, 1865–1925*. Columbus: Ohio State University Press, 2005.

Walters, Jennie. "A Plan Suggested for Providing Skilled Nursing for Those of Moderate Means." *AJN* 8 (April 1908): 527–529.

"War Demand for Nurses Is Bound to Be Felt Most by Hospitals." *Hospital Management* 54 (October 1942): 51–52.

Ward, Peter. "The Eight-Hour Day for Graduate Nurses." *Hospitals* 10 (November 1936): 134.

Washbourne, F. A. "Discussion on 'How Can the Shortage of Nurses Be Met.'" *Boston Medical and Surgical Journal* 183 (25 November 1920): 631–632.

Weinberg, Dana. *Code Green: Money-Driven Hospitals and the Dismantling of Nursing*. Ithaca, NY: Cornell University Press, 2003.

Weller, Wilma. "How Shall We Provide for Families with Moderate Incomes." *AJN* 13 (September 1913): 1009–1010.

"We May Even Run Short of Nurses." *Modern Hospital* 45 (December 1945): 47–48.

"What about the Nursing Shortage." *Hospital Topics and Buyer* 25 (February 1947): 18–20.

"What Patients Think of the Eight-Hour Schedule." *AJN* 33 (December 1933): 1153.

"What Registries Are Doing," *AJN* 41 (August 1941): 902–908.

"What Registries Did: A Summary 1934–1935," *AJN* 35 (August 1935): 779–785.

"What Registries Did: A Summary 1935–1936," *AJN* 37 (July 1937): 729–736.

"What Registries Did in 1937," *AJN* 38 (October 1938): 1115–1123.

"What Registries Did in 1938," *AJN* 39 (September 1939): 998–1006.

"What Registries Did in 1941," *AJN* 42 (August 1942): 911–914.

"What Registries Did in 1942," *AJN* 43 (June 1943): 563–564.

"What Registries Did in 1944," *AJN* 45 (September 1945): 697.

White, William. "The Introduction of Professional Regulation and Labor Market Conditions; Occupational Licensure of Registered Nurses." *Policy Science* 20, no. 1 (April 1987): 34.

"Why Nurses Refuse Tuberculosis Cases." *AJN* 6 (June 1906): 772–773.

Wickenden, Elmira. "Peace Brings Its Own Serious Problems as Nurses Face Tomorrow." *Hospitals* 20 (February 1946): 42–44.

Wickenden, Elmira B. "National Nursing Council for War Services Sums Up Its Efforts to Meet the Need for Nurses." *Modern Hospital* 30 (March 1943): 76–78.Wickwire, Rhoda. "Forecast for Private Duty Nursing." *AJN* 37 (March 1937): 244–247.

Winslow, C.-E.A. "Program and Preliminary Results of the Committee on the Grading of Nursing Schools." *American Journal of Public Health* 18 (April 1928): 449.

Woman's Hospital of Philadelphia. Papers. Barbara Bates Center for the Study of the History of Nursing, University of Pennsylvania, School of Nursing.

Wright, Thew. "The Nurses' Official Registry of Buffalo." AJN 28 (April 1928): 321."A Year of Grace for Nurses in New York State." TNHR 104 (February 1940): 168.

Yett, Donald E. "The Chronic 'Shortage' of Nurses: A Public Policy Dilemma." In *Empirical Studies in Health Economics*, edited by H. E. Klarman, 375–376. Baltimore: Johns Hopkins Press, 1970.

———. *An Economic Analysis of the Nurse Shortage.* Lexington, MA: D. C. Heath, 1975.

"Your Money and Your Life for One Week of Private Duty Nursing." *AJN* 25 (December 1925): 992.

Zuber, Rebecca Friedman, and Terry Cichon. "Adding Private Duty Services: Organizational and Regulatory Issues to Consider." *Home Healthcare Nurse* 21 (2003): 461–465.

Index

Page numbers in *italics* represent figures and tables.

Nursing Council on National Defense (NCND), 124: Health and Medical Committee, 124; Subcommittee on Nursing, 124. *See also* National Nursing Council

nursing education: Cadet Nurse Corps as federal program for education, 127–129 (see United States Cadet Nurse Corps); conditions and standards, 39, 43, 46; continuing education, 100, 110; history of, 12–13; national standards, 20–21; reform, 67. *See also* schools of nursing

Nursing for the Future (Brown Report), 135–136, 138

nursing profession: American nursing roots, 4–5; attrition rates, 4; emerging labor market, 20–21, 78–79; gendered nature of, 2–3, 31, 125 (*see also* gender and nursing); nursing care prices, 60–61, 67, 71–72 (*see also* fees/fee setting); patient demand for nurses, 81, 123–142; as professional occupation, 12–31; racial composition, 1–2 (*see also* African American nurses); three-tiered hierarchy, 123; trained versus untrained nurses, 28–30; training, 21–27; woman's occupation, 2–3, 22–23. *See also* nursing care models; nursing education; nursing shortage; nursing working conditions; untrained nurses; *specific healthcare workers*

nursing shortages: first great shortage, 136–141; need for schools of nursing, 37; reports of, 7; roots, 3; significant periods, 8; sporadic episodes, 117, 120–121; strategies to resolve, 3–4, 127, 135–136, 138–139; working conditions as cause of, 140; World War I, 65, 70–72; World War II, 7, 123–127, 146

nursing working conditions: as cause of shortages, 140; hours, 27, 93–95, 103, 108, 110–121, 133, 137, 144, 145–146; meal charges, 38, 59, 94–96, 112–114; wages, 6, 18–19, 33–34, 103, 114, 115–121, 138–139 (*see also* fees/fee setting)

Nutting, M. Adelaide, 23, 67, 78

NYCR. *See* New York Central Registry

NYCRNA. *See* New York Counties Registered Nurses' Association

Nye, Sylveen, 43–44

NYSNA. *See* New York State Nurses Association

Official Registry (Chicago, Illinois), 176n1

Official Registry of the Nurses Association of Counties of Long Island (New York), 177n44

orderlies, 80, 127

PAGN. *See* Protective Association of Graduate Nurses of New York State

Parren, Thomas, 123

patients, middle-income, 59–62

per diem nurses, 119, 126, 137, 145

Perkins, Eliza, 37

Philadelphia General Hospital, training school, 36, 43, 147

Philadelphia Hospital. *See* Philadelphia General Hospital

practical nurses. *See* untrained nurses

Practical Nurses of New York, Inc., 135

primary nursing, 160n14

private duty nursing/nurses: African Americans, 2 (*see also* African American nurses); case assignment, 16, 74, 91–93, 95–96, 133; commercial employment agencies, 32–33; days per week worked, 73–75, *74*, 79; entrepreneurial approach, 5–6, 18, 149; episodic example of nursing, 117; as example for student nurses, 91; fees/fee setting, 56–59, 76, 79, 93, 99; golden age, 88–104; hospital-based service, 69, 75, 83, 118–119, 129, 144–145, 171–172n11; impact of Great Depression, 6, 105–122; male nurses for male patients, 3; military service, 126; mirror of familial traditions, 6, 13; origins of, 12–13; placement service (*see* central registries); portrait of, 14–20; relationship with LPNs, 133–136, 146; template for nurse employment, 6–7; wages, 6, 18–19, 140; working conditions, 6, 91–95, 130; workweek, 73, *74*. *See also* nursing profession; trained nurses

private duty registries. *See* nurse registries; *specific registries*

Procurement and Assignment Services for Physicians, Dentists, Veterinarians & Nurses, 125
professional nurse associations: affiliation with central registries, 49, 79–80, 80, 148; comparison to trade unions, 40–41, 58, 66, 103; formation of, 39–47; negotiation of employment matters, 148; segregated, 26
professional nurse registries. See central registries
Program for the Nursing Profession, A (Ginzberg), 135
protective, use of term in association names, 40
protective association, use of term in association names, 40–41
Protective Association of Graduate Nurses of New York State (PAGN), 44
Provident Hospital and Training School (Chicago, Illinois), 26, 163n48: School of Nursing, 46
public health field, 2, 83

race: barriers to ANA membership, 46; breakdown of nurses by race, 25, 25; professional nurse associations, 39; segregation in nursing workforce, 1–2, 25–26, 126–127, 135, 163n48. See also African American nurses
reform method (pricing approach), 71
registered nurses. See nurse registration acts
registries. See nurse registries; specific registries
Registry (Chicago, Illinois), 176n1
Reilly, Anne, 134
Reverby, Susan, 13, 47
Robb, Isabel Hampton, 41–42
Roberts, Mary, 77
Rockefeller, John, 84
Rockefeller Foundation, 23, 77, 83, 84–85: Hospital Library and Service Bureau, 85
Rose, I. C., 44

schools of nursing: alumnae associations, 34–35, 39–40, 42–44, 50, 55, 57, 79–80, 80, 90, 96; apprentice-based pedagogy, 5; components of good programs, 70–71; declining enrollment, 137–138;

educational requirements for admission, 23–24; federal aid, 127–128; growth of, 21–22, 37, 55, 63, 78–79; hospital-based, 5; increase in graduates, 123, 128; location of, 50; method of grading/classifying, 78; racial bias and segregated conditions, 25–26, 163n48; upgraded standards, 47. See also nursing education; student nurses; specific schools of nursing
scrubwomen, 33
Seaman, Valentine, 12
segregation in nursing workforce, 1–2, 25–26, 46, 163n48. See also African American nurses
short-course workers. See subsidiary workers
sliding scales (nursing care prices), 60–61. See also fees/fee setting
Social Security Act, 139
Spanish American War, 20
special nurses, 95, 171–172n11. See also private duty nurses
Spellman Seminary (Atlanta, Georgia), 25
Spokane Protective Nurse Association, 40
Springfield, Massachusetts, 15–16
staff nurses. See hospitals
Standard Curriculum for Schools of Nursing, 70–71
St. Luke's Hospital School of Nursing (New York City, New York), 52
student nurses: increasing—as shortage solution, 127; included in trained nurse category, 20; private duty nurses as example for, 91; use of student labor, 3, 5, 69–71, 88, 94–95, 128; wages, 33–34
Study of Incomes, Salaries and Employment Conditions Affecting Nurses, 115–116
subsidiary workers, 28, 38, 55, 62, 71, 80, 86, 129, 130. See also attendants; assistive personnel; untrained nurses
Subsidiary Workers in the Care of the Sick, 130
supply-side pricing approach, 71–72
Sydenham Hospital School of Nursing (New York City, New York), 55

temporary general duty nurses, 119
temporary staff nurses, 119, 120
temporary workers, 2
Thoms, Adah, 84
Threat, Charissa, 126–127
Todd-Fell Act. *See* New York State
Tomes, Nancy, 54
Toronto Method, 60
Toward Quality in Nursing, 151–152
trained nurses: ages of, 24, *25*, 29; application of term, 20; demographics, 24; gendered nature of workforce, 26–27, 29; geographic distribution, 24, *24*, 29; growth of, 21–27, 31; length of career, 24; marital status, 27, *27*; race of, 25, *25*; untrained nurses versus—, *22*, 28–30, 40. *See also* nursing profession; private duty nursing/nurses
Trained Nurse and Hospital Review, 21, 40, 45, 57, 132

unions, trade, 40–41, 58, 66, 103
United States Cadet Nurse Corps, 7, 8, 127–127, 142. *See also* nursing education
University of Pennsylvania, 147
untrained nurses: ages of, 29, *29*; elimination of practical nurses, 82; gendered nature of workforce, 29–30, *30*; geographic distribution, 29; hospital care, 70; labels, 28, 80; marital status, 30, *31*; race of, 30, *30*; trained nurses versus, *22*, 28–30, 40, 130–131
U.S. Bureau of Education, 21, 23, 50
U.S. Bureau of Labor Statistics, 139

U.S. Census: 1860, 20; 1870, 13; 1900, 20–21; 1904, 22; 1910, 50; 1920, 68; occupational category of "nurses," 20
U.S. Department of Health, Education, and Welfare (HEW), 20
U.S. Indian Service, 129
U.S. Public Health Service, 124–125, 129: Division of Nurse Education, 128
U.S. Veterans Administration, 129, 137, 152

Van Frank, Lucy, 89, 90–91, 95, 108
Vincent, George, 77
visiting nurse. *See* private duty nursing/nurses
voluntary laws, 54

wages. *See* fees/fee setting; nursing working conditions
ward helpers hospital care, 70
War Manpower Commission, 125: Procurement and Assignment Service, 126
Warrington, Joseph, 12
Winslow, C. E. A., 67
Woman's Hospital (Philadelphia, Pennsylvania), 12, 14, 35, 36
women in nursing, 2–3, 22–23, 30. *See also* gender and nursing
World War I, impact on nurse labor market, 65, 68–70
World War II, impact on nurse labor market, 7, 123–127, 146

Yale University School of Public Health, 67

About the Author

Jean C. Whelan, PhD, RN, was an adjunct associate professor at the University of Pennsylvania School of Nursing and the assistant director at the School of Nursing's Barbara Bates Center for the Study of the History of Nursing. Ms. Whelan served as president of the American Association for the History of Nursing from 2012 to 2016. Jean and her husband, Mark Gilbert, lived with their son, Paul, in Narberth, Pennsylvania.

Available titles in the Critical Issues in Health and Medicine series:

Laura L. Heinemann, *Transplanting Care: Shifting Commitments in Health and Care in the United States*

Laura D. Hirshbein, *American Melancholy: Constructions of Depression in the Twentieth Century*

Laura D. Hirshbein, *Smoking Privileges: Psychiatry, the Mentally Ill, and the Tobacco Industry in America*

Timothy Hoff, *Practice under Pressure: Primary Care Physicians and Their Medicine in the Twenty-first Century*

Beatrix Hoffman, Nancy Tomes, Rachel N. Grob, and Mark Schlesinger, eds., *Patients as Policy Actors*

Ruth Horowitz, *Deciding the Public Interest: Medical Licensing and Discipline*

Powel Kazanjian, *Frederick Novy and the Development of Bacteriology in American Medicine*

Claas Kirchhelle, *Pyrrhic Progress: The History of Antibiotics in Anglo-American Food Production*

Rebecca M. Kluchin, *Fit to Be Tied: Sterilization and Reproductive Rights in America, 1950–1980*

Jennifer Lisa Koslow, *Cultivating Health: Los Angeles Women and Public Health Reform*

Jennifer Lisa Koslow, *Exhibiting Health: Public Health Displays in the Progressive Era*

Susan C. Lawrence, *Privacy and the Past: Research, Law, Archives, Ethics*

Bonnie Lefkowitz, *Community Health Centers: A Movement and the People Who Made It Happen*

Ellen Leopold, *Under the Radar: Cancer and the Cold War*

Barbara L. Ley, *From Pink to Green: Disease Prevention and the Environmental Breast Cancer Movement*

Sonja Mackenzie, *Structural Intimacies: Sexual Stories in the Black AIDS Epidemic*

Stephen E. Mawdsley, *Selling Science: Polio and the Promise of Gamma Globulin*

Frank M. McClellan, *Healthcare and Human Dignity: Law Matters*

Michelle McClellan, *Lady Lushes: Gender, Alcohol, and Medicine in Modern America*

David Mechanic, *The Truth about Health Care: Why Reform Is Not Working in America*

Richard A. Meckel, *Classrooms and Clinics: Urban Schools and the Protection and Promotion of Child Health, 1870–1930*

Terry Mizrahi, *From Residency to Retirement: Physicians' Careers over a Professional Lifetime*

Manon Parry, *Broadcasting Birth Control: Mass Media and Family Planning*

Alyssa Picard, *Making the American Mouth: Dentists and Public Health in the Twentieth Century*

Heather Munro Prescott, *The Morning After: A History of Emergency Contraception in the United States*

Sarah B. Rodriguez, *The Love Surgeon: A Story of Trust, Harm, and the Limits of Medical Regulation*

David J. Rothman and David Blumenthal, eds., *Medical Professionalism in the New Information Age*

Andrew R. Ruis, *Eating to Learn, Learning to Eat: School Lunches and Nutrition Policy in the United States*

James A. Schafer Jr., *The Business of Private Medical Practice: Doctors, Specialization, and Urban Change in Philadelphia, 1900–1940*

David G. Schuster, *Neurasthenic Nation: America's Search for Health, Happiness, and Comfort, 1869–1920*

Karen Seccombe and Kim A. Hoffman, *Just Don't Get Sick: Access to Health Care in the Aftermath of Welfare Reform*

Leo B. Slater, *War and Disease: Biomedical Research on Malaria in the Twentieth Century*

Piper Sledge, *Bodies Unbound: Gender-Specific Cancer and Biolegitimacy*

Dena T. Smith, *Medicine over Mind: Mental Health Practice in the Biomedical Era*

Kylie M. Smith, *Talking Therapy: Knowledge and Power in American Psychiatric Nursing*

Matthew Smith, *An Alternative History of Hyperactivity: Food Additives and the Feingold Diet*

Paige Hall Smith, Bernice L. Hausman, and Miriam Labbok, *Beyond Health, Beyond Choice: Breastfeeding Constraints and Realities*

Susan L. Smith, *Toxic Exposures: Mustard Gas and the Health Consequences of World War II in the United States*

Rosemary A. Stevens, Charles E. Rosenberg, and Lawton R. Burns, eds., *History and Health Policy in the United States: Putting the Past Back In*

Marianne Sullivan, *Tainted Earth: Smelters, Public Health, and the Environment*

Courtney E. Thompson, *An Organ of Murder: Crime, Violence, and Phrenology in Nineteenth-Century America*

Barbra Mann Wall, *American Catholic Hospitals: A Century of Changing Markets and Missions*

Frances Ward, *The Door of Last Resort: Memoirs of a Nurse Practitioner*

Jean C. Whelan, *Nursing the Nation: Building the Nurse Labor Force*

Shannon Withycombe, *Lost: Miscarriage in Nineteenth-Century America*

Printed in the United States
By Bookmasters